Troubleshooting

Basic Writing Skills for Canadian Students

SECOND
CANADIAN
EDITION

John A. Roberts
MOHAWK COLLEGE

William Herman
THE CITY COLLEGE OF THE CITY UNIVERSITY OF NEW YORK

Jeffrey M. Young

Harcourt Brace & Company, Canada

Toronto Montreal Fort Worth New York Orlando
Philadelphia San Diego London Sydney Tokyo

Canadian Cataloguing in Publication Data

Roberts, John A., 1944–
Troubleshooting: basic writing skills for Canadian students

2nd Canadian ed.
Includes index.
ISBN 0-7747-3544-9

1. English language – Rhetoric. 2. English language – Rhetoric – Problems, exercises, etc. 3. English language – Grammar. 4. English language – Grammar – Problems, exercises, etc. I. Herman, William, 1926– . II. Young, Jeffrey M. III. Title.

PE1408.R624 1996 808'.042 C96-930129-4

Director of Product Development: *Heather McWhinney*
Acquisitions Editor: *Kelly V. Cochrane*
Projects Manager: *Liz Radojkovic*
Developmental Editor: *Su Mei Ku*
Director of Publishing Services: *Jean Davies*
Editorial Manager: *Marcel Chiera*
Editorial Services Assistant: *Stacey Roderick*
Production Manager: *Sue-Ann Becker*
Production Co-ordinator: *Sheila Barry*
Cover Design: *Sonya V. Thursby/Opus House*
Typesetting and Assembly: *Matthew Beck*
Printing and Binding: *Webcom Limited*

This book was printed in Canada.

1 2 3 4 5 01 00 99 98 97

Preface

Troubleshooting: Basic Writing Skills for Canadian Students is based on the third American edition of *Troubleshooting,* and has been revised to include nearly four hundred references to Canadian history, culture, politics, and geography. In addition, Canadian spellings have been incorporated into both the text and the exercises. This edition also contains a brief index that both students and instructors alike will find handy for quick and easy reference to the more important grammatical constructions covered in the book.

The rules of English composition are often troublesome to students. This book is designed to help students spot their problems and improve their skills. Using the book will not turn the work into fun, but it will make it possible to do the work efficiently and effectively.

As in the previous editions, only the most basic material is covered in grammar, usage, and mechanics; formal terminology is kept to a minumum. Each chapter begins with a brief section which explains the practical importance of the material to be dealt with. The material itself is then broken down into a number of points, each of which is presented separately in simple language and followed by illustrations and practice exercises. Cumulative review exercises are interspersed throughout the chapter, giving the student frequent opportunity to bring together the rules and principles learned in several points. Whenever possible, the student is shown *why* a rule is needed, rather than asked merely to take it on faith. At the end of the chapter, the most essential "how to" concepts are covered in a short boxed section just before an extensive and comprehensive set of chapter review exercises. The important points are restated in summary form at the back of the book, to serve as a study aid.

Exercises of varied types have been included: choose the correct answer, fill in the blanks, write your own sentences. The final exercise of each chapter review provides another twist. Two or three paragraphs of material similar to typical student writing are presented, and the student is asked to rewrite them, correcting the errors.

This edition contains new, clearer explanations of subjects, verbs, and possessives. Many exercises throughout the book have been revised, expecially where the answers were ambiguous in previous editions. The Answers to Exercises section has been thoroughly checked. In general, the relaxed pace of the book has been retained. The book makes no assumptions about students' knowledge and provides students with numerous varied opportunities for success. We hope that students who use this book will not only learn to write correct sentences but also develop a *feel* for sentences.

Preface to the Second Canadian Edition

The makeup of college populations has diversified considerably since the first edition of *Troubleshooting* was published. More students from a wide range of backgrounds are attending college than ever before. To meet the needs of these students, a number of changes have been made to the new edition which will make the material more relevant to Canada's multicultural environment, and will also reflect developments in popular music, literature, and culture in this country.

Revisions have been made to many of the nearly four hundred references to Canadian history, culture, politics, and geography, to reflect current trends in these areas. At the same time, the basic structure and the relaxed pace of the earlier edition has been retained. Examples, exercises, and answers have been thoroughly checked and revised where necessary, and any ambiguities which existed in the previous edition have been eliminated.

I hope that you enjoy using *Troubleshooting* as much as I have enjoyed writing the second edition.

J.R.

A Note from the Publisher

Thank you for selecting *Troubleshooting: Basic Writing Skills for Canadian Students*, Second Canadian Edition, by John Roberts, William Herman, and Jeffrey M. Young. The authors and publisher have devoted considerable time and care to the development of this book. We appreciate your recognition of this effort and accomplishment.

We want to hear what you think about *Troubleshooting*. Please take a few minutes to fill in the stamped reply card at the back of the book. Your comments and suggestions will be valuable to us as we prepare new editions and other books.

To the Student

In addition to the exercises in this book, there is also an answer key that will enable you to check your answers to the exercises. The key, which is at the back of the book, will be most helpful if you use it to check your work *as soon as you finish* each exercise. In this way you will find out right away whether you have understood the material and learned how to apply the rules correctly. If you discover that you have made mistakes, you may be able to figure out for yourself what is wrong — or at least you will be alerted to ask your instructor for help.

Contents

PART I

Grammar Review

PRETEST

Note: This test is designed to identify any problems you may have with basic grammar (subjects and verbs). All the material tested here will be fully explained in Chapters 1 and 2, which follow.

I. Write *S* if the sentence is missing a subject, *V* if the sentence is missing a verb, or *C* if the sentence is correct as it stands.

_______ 1. Carolyn cooking a gourmet dinner tonight.

_______ 2. Doris and her friends to the planetarium every Thursday.

_______ 3. Used his father's credit card at the gas station.

_______ 4. He is an amateur boxer.

_______ 5. Was ready for action.

_______ 6. A kiss is still a kiss.

_______ 7. Whenever it rains, we stay inside and television.

_______ 8. There were swimming in Lake Erie.

_______ 9. Babies cry.

_______ 10. He plannning to join the club.

_______ 11. We walking around the city.

_______ 12. We have been enumerated in order to vote.

_______ 13. Are plannning a surprise party.

_______ 14. That is no way to treat a person.

_______ 15. Is building his own house in Winkler.

_______ 16. My notes need to be retyped.

_______ 17. Two types of flowers growing in the garden.

_______ 18. Joey in a good mood today.

_______ 19. Toto, Tiki, and Jenny meow a lot.

_______ 20. The kids ate their dinner and ran upstairs.

II. Underline the complete subject.

1. Jamie is going out for the track team.
2. The Expos and the Mets play tonight.
3. Correct grammar is an important aspect of good writing.
4. In the cabana is the rowboat.
5. Jazz is my favourite kind of music.
6. Hans and Lisa bought that car.
7. Organic food is healthful but expensive.
8. Exercising is part of my morning routine.
9. Around the corner fled the stray dog.
10. That hibachi near the garage is broken.

III. Underline the complete verb.

1. My father is retiring from business.
2. We have never been to Europe.
3. She grew more and more tired.
4. I never promised you a rose garden.
5. You should be sure to check the oil.

6. Holding down a job is never easy for Luke.
7. I have tried my hardest to succeed.
8. Woodworking requires skill and patience.
9. We spent our paycheques yesterday.
10. I always visit my parents on the civic holiday.

CHAPTER 1

Subjects

IMPORTANT TERMS INTRODUCED IN THIS CHAPTER

subject the person or thing about which the rest of the sentence makes an assertion.

simple subject the noun or pronoun that the sentence is primarily about.

complete subject the simple subject PLUS any words that modify or describe it.

noun a word that names a person, place, thing, or idea.

pronoun a word that takes the place of a noun.

compound subject the combination (with *and* or or) of two or more subjects that share the same verb.

A sentence is a group of words that expresses a complete thought. The thought may tell something, ask a question, express a request or command, or express a strong emotion or feeling. *Every sentence must contain a subject*—except requests or commands, where the subject is not in the sentence but is only understood (in the request, "Turn off the lights," the subject is really *you*—the person addressed; but the word *you* is not *in* the sentence). The subject is the person or thing about which the rest of the sentence makes an assertion. In other words, any sentence must *be about* someone or something, and therefore *every sentence must have a subject.*

POINT 1 Identify the subject of the sentence by asking who or what is doing something (or being something).

Rain falls.

In this sentence, the subject is *rain.* We find the subject by asking, "Who or what falls?" The answer to that question, *rain, is* the subject.

Mario works hard.

Who or what is doing something? Or who or what works? *Mario* works. *Mario* is the subject of the sentence.

The girl sings in the choir.

Who or what sings? The *girl* sings. What, then, is the subject of this sentence?

- Subjects may be either *singular* or *plural. A* singular subject refers to *one* person or thing; a plural subject refers to *more than one.* Plural subjects usually end in *-s.* Some exceptions include *men, women,* and *children.*

Singular		Plural	
one	boy girl car dog pencil	*more than one*	boys girls cars dogs pencils

In the previous sentences, the subjects were singular *(rain, Mario, girl). You* can find plural subjects in a sentence by asking the same "who or what" question.

The sandwiches were delicious.

Who or what were delicious? The answer to that question, *sandwiches,* is the subject, and it is plural.

My sisters are named Lynn and Karen.

Who or what are named? *Sisters* is the plural subject of this sentence.

Buses run every hour on the hour.

Who or what run? *Buses* is the plural subject of this sentence

Exercise: Point 1

Determine the subject in each of the following sentences by answering the "who or what" question.

1. The plumber works.

   Who or what works? The subject is ______ plumber ______

2. Doug acts in the play.

   Who or what acts? The subject is ____________________

3. The tree fell in the storm.

   Who or what fell? The subject is ____________________

4. The motorcycle roared.

   Who or what roared? The subject is ____________________

5. Lucy eats an apple a day.

   Who or what eats? The subject is ____________________

6. Our family celebrates Christmas.

   Who or what celebrates? The subject is ____________________

7. Those speakers sound great.

   Who or what sounds? The subject is ____________________

8. My sister plays basketball on the weekends.

   Who or what plays? The subject is ____________________

9. Fans cheer in the stands.

   Who or what cheers? The subject is ____________________

10. The store was robbed last night.

   Who or what was robbed? The subject is ____________________

Another Exercise: Point 1

For each of the following sentences, write *S* if the subject is singular or *P* if it is plural. Underline the simple subject.

___S___ 1. Sally ran after the bus.

_______ 2. My friend built a new beach house.

_______ 3. Ducks swim in that pond.

_______ 4. The airplane needs to take on fuel at Mirabel.

_______ 5. Our daughter gave us a surprise party.

_______ 6. Sam writes extremely well.

_______ 7. The clouds obscured the sun.

_______ 8. Jason sings in the choir.

_______ 9. Ms. Peterson bought a snowmobile.

_______ 10. The snowstorm lasted for hours.

POINT 2 A subject may be a noun.

A *noun* is a word used to name a *person, place,* or *thing.*

Persons	Places	Things
Ruth	Saskatchewan	cat
Louis	Main Street	tooth
Mrs. Maxwell	Belgium	house
man	Russia	car
teacher	Lake Erie	love

Most of the subjects we have seen are nouns. However, not every noun in a sentence is a subject. Remember, we determine a subject by asking who or what performs the action. Each of the following sentences contains more than one noun, but each sentence has only one subject.

Jim works in a store.

First determine the subject. Who or what works? Jim works. So *Jim* is the subject. Are there any other nouns in this sentence? That is, are any words used to name a person, place, or thing? *Store* is a thing; therefore it is a noun.

Janet mailed the letter.

Which words are nouns? How can you determine the subject of this sentence?

Exercise: Point 2

Underline all the nouns in each of the following sentences. Then circle the subject of the sentence.

1. (Alberta) joined Confederation in 1905.
2. Henry runs a mile every day.
3. Flowers grow best in sunlight.
4. Exercise strengthens the body.
5. That boy joined our club.
6. My watch comes from Japan.
7. The MPs voted on the bill.

8. Hata wrote a letter to her member of Parliament.
9. Starvation worries people all over the world.
10. Bills are a part of life.

Review Exercise: Points 1 and 2

Fill in the blank with an appropriate subject.

1. ____Nova Scotia____ is a province in Atlantic Canada.
2. ________________ taught me everything I know.
3. ________________ are delicate instruments.
4. ________________ deliberated for ten hours.
5. ________________ are vehicles.
6. ________________ takes a great deal of skill.
7. ________________ appeared on television.
8. My ________________ is my mother's brother.
9. ________________ make good pets.
10. ________________ was my favourite teacher.

POINT 3 A subject may be a pronoun.

A pronoun is a word that takes the place of a noun. It takes the position that a noun can take in a sentence. For example, the sentence

The detective solves the case.

can be changed to

She solves the case.

Detective is a noun; *she* is a pronoun. Like nouns, pronouns **may be** singular or plural. The following pronouns may be used as subjects:

Singular Pronouns

I — when the subject is the speaker himself or herself

I ride the bus daily.

you — when the subject is the person spoken to

You owe me ten dollars.

he — when the subject is masculine and singular

He drives a Ford.

she — when the subject is feminine and singular

She wants to buy a stereo.

it — when the subject is a thing or an action, neither masculine nor feminine, and singular

It is a good way to exercise.

Plural Pronouns

we — when the subject is a group which includes the speaker

We sang in the choir.

you — when the subject is the persons spoken to

You all **finished** the assignment.

they — when the subject is a group of persons or things not including the speaker

They voted in the last election.

Exercise: Point 3

Rewrite the following sentences, changing the noun subjects to pronoun subjects.

1. Nunzio is a shrewd businessman.

   He is a shrewd businessman.

2. My wife has just graduated from Mount Royal College.

   ____

3. Nude sunbathing does not bother me.

   ____

4. John and I are going to write a song.

   ____

5. Large corporations make a lot of money.

   ____

6. Queen Elizabeth has visited Canada.

   ____

7. Learning to write well takes time.

____

8. Normand surely knows how to water-ski.

____

9. All my relatives sent me birthday cards.

____

10. Jorge and his dog understood each other.

____

POINT 4 A subject may be an *-ing* word.

Fishing is my hobby.

To determine the subject of this sentence, ask who or what is my hobby. The answer to that question, *fishing, is* the subject.

Do not be confused by a sentence such as

I enjoy fishing.

To determine the subject of this sentence, ask who or what enjoys. The answer, *I*, is the subject.

Parachuting may be dangerous.

Who or what may be dangerous? *Parachuting* is the subject of the sentence.

Tim likes to go parachuting.

Who or what likes? Tim is the subject.

Exercise: Point 4

Underline the subject in each of the following sentences.

1. Singing is her chief talent.
2. Driving drives me crazy.
3. Jogging is good exercise.
4. I am losing my patience.
5. I don't like cleaning my apartment.
6. You are finding it difficult to concentrate.

7. Sewing was never her favourite activity.
8. Advertising is a good way to get votes.
9. They always go skiing in January.
10. Cooking is his favourite hobby.

POINT 5 A subject may consist of more than one word.

So far, most of the subjects have been just one word: *rain, Mario, plumber, cars, I, we, jogging, biking,* and so on. This noun or pronoun that the sentence is primarily about is called the *simple subject.* When the subject of a sentence contains more than one word, all those words make up the *complete subject.* The simple subject is part of the complete subject.

In the following examples, the simple subject is underlined, and the complete subject is circled.

(The man sitting in the bleachers) is eating a hot dog.

(The fresh vegetables from my garden) are tasty.

Note that the *complete subject* contains (1) the simple subject and (2) any words that modify or describe the simple subject.

A *compound subject* consists of two or more subjects that share the same verb.

Pat and Louise work together.

Pat and Louise is the compound subject.

Mowing the lawn and raking the leaves are two of my least favourite activities.

Mowing the lawn and raking the leaves is the compound subject.

Exercise: Point 5

Underline the complete subject in each of the following sentences.

1. Collecting stamps is my hobby.
2. His sister is an expert pianist.
3. Looking for an apartment is hard work.
4. Herb and Everett are starting a dynamic new business.
5. Choosing a spouse can be confusing.
6. Using common sense is important.
7. Bowling on Wednesdays keeps me sane.
8. Clara's radio needs to be repaired.

9. Jack and Jill went up the hill.
10. A green light means that we may go.

Review Exercise: Points 1–5

Fill in the blank with an appropriate subject.

1. ______Jogging______ is a good way to get exercise.
2. ____________________ go great with a barbeque.
3. ____________________ use a lot of gasoline.
4. ____________________ is more fun than watching television.
5. ____________________ is a great singer.
6. ____________________ is exciting but dangerous.
7. ____________________ comes once a year.
8. ____________________ makes me remember the good old days.
9. ____________________ always beat us in tennis.
10. ____________________ fought against the Allies.

Another Review Exercise: Points 1–5

Choose a subject from Column A and match it with a group of words from Column B. Write the complete sentence in the space provided. Make sure the subject answers the "who or what" question.

Column A	Column B
Practical jokes	are twin brothers.
Ms. Murphy	can get you into trouble.
Collecting coins	can give you tired feet.
Robert and Richard	is running for mayor.
Shopping for shoes	is my hobby.

1. ______Practical jokes can get you into trouble.______
2. ____________________
3. ____________________
4. ____________________
5. ____________________

POINT 6 A subject may appear anywhere in the sentence.

So far, all the subjects have been at the beginning of the sentence. However, subjects sometimes appear elsewhere. They are still easy to find if you ask the same "who or what" question.

There were alligators in the swamp.

Who or what were in the swamp? *Alligators* were in the swamp. *Alligators* is the subject of this sentence.

Here are two different problems.

Problems is the subject.

All night long, James listened to records.

Who or what listened? *James* listened; therefore *James* is the subject.
Note: There and *here* are never subjects.

Exercise: Point 6

Underline the simple subject in each of the following sentences.

1. Around the corner went the motorcycle.
2. In the box seats was the commissioner of the CFL.
3. There was a long line at the ticket booth.
4. Here is one way to solve the problem.
5. There is work to be done.
6. Down the ladder came a fire fighter with a baby in his arms.
7. There was no way out.
8. Through the train walked the conductor.
9. In town this week is a great new show.
10. There was a sale in the department store today.

POINT 7 The simple subject is never within a phrase that begins with such words as *on, in, of, before, behind, near.*

A phrase of this sort can be *part of* a complete subject, but it cannot be the whole subject.

The man on the corner is playing a clarinet.

Who or what is playing? The answer to that question reveals the subject; clearly, it is the *man* who is playing the clarinet. The corner is not doing the playing.

The jar on the shelf is filled with Japanese black soybeans.

Who or what is filled? The *jar,* not the shelf.

The book in the library was written by Mordecai Richler.

Book, not library, is the subject.

Once you spot and eliminate any confusing phrases of this sort, it is easy to recognize the subject.

The roof ~~of the house~~ collapsed.
Three members ~~of the group~~ were arrested.

The words listed in Point 7 are called *prepositions.* Other common prepositions include the following:

about	below	from	past	upon
above	beside	inside	through	with
across	between	into	to	within
after	beyond	off	toward	without
around	by	out	under	
at	during	over	until	

Exercise: Point 7

Determine the simple subject in each of the following sentences by asking the "who or what" question.

1. A program of popular music was scheduled.

   Who or what was scheduled? The subject is ___program___

2. The woman on the bus wore a jacket and tie.

   Who or what wore? The subject is________________

3. That man with a gun is dangerous.

   Who or what is dangerous? The subject is________________

4. Those weeds in the garden should be pulled.

   Who or what should be pulled? The subject is________________

5. That problem on the blackboard is difficult.

   Who or what is difficult? The subject is ________________

6. Dreaming of days gone by is hopeless.

   Who or what is hopeless? The subject is ________________

7. The people on the wharf are talking.

   Who or what are talking? The subject is________________________________

8. Teachers in nursery schools must be patient.

   Who or what must be patient? The subject is____________________________

9. The calm before the storm is threatening.

   Who or what is threatening? The subject is______________________________

10. Those beers in the cooler are ready.

    Who or what are ready? The subject is __________________________________

Review Exercise: Points 1–7

Underline the complete subject in each of the following sentences.

1. Melvin wants to study law.
2. Obeying the speed limit helps conserve fuel.
3. He and I will do it together.
4. The switch in the glove compartment opens the trunk.
5. Eating low-calorie foods is one way to lose weight.
6. On the beach is a lighthouse.
7. The stores on Duckworth Street are closed today.
8. There must be something wrong with you.
9. The man in the bullpen will soon come in to pitch.
10. Around the corner is the new super mailbox.

HOW TO USE SUBJECTS CORRECTLY

1. To identify the subject ask yourself *who* or *what* performs the action.
2. Remember that a subject may be a noun a pronoun an *-ing* word or a group of words.
3. A subject may appear anywhere in the sentence.

Chapter Review

I. Write *S* if the example has a subject or *X* if it does not. Underline the simple subjects that you find.

_______ 1. Was writing letters to me daily.

_______ 2. Listening to my stereo relaxes me in the evening.

_______ 3. That dog with the floppy ears is mine.

_______ 4. Fighting with his sister.

_______ 5. A collection of rare books is a real treasure.

_______ 6. Ms. Strauss is coming to visit me.

_______ 7. Were doing their best.

_______ 8. In the closet is a pillow.

_______ 9. Leonard Cohen was a cultural hero of the the 1960s.

_______ 10. Spring cleaning is a necessary chore.

II. Underline the complete subject in each of the following sentences.

1. A fear of dogs is common to many people.
2. Phyllis travels to Japan with her husband.
3. Going on a picnic is a great way to spend an afternoon.
4. One part of my idea involves you.
5. Home repair might become a lost art.
6. Juggling requires good eyesight and co-ordination.
7. There are three gas stations at that corner.
8. Of all my friends, Chris is the nicest.
9. Blowing my nose unclogs my ears.
10. That leak in the radiator should be fixed.
11. Choosing courses wisely is a student's responsibility.
12. She is the one for me.
13. The filter of an air conditioner should be cleaned regularly.
14. Going to the dentist was a painful experience for me.
15. We all believe his explanation.
16. Repaving the road takes time.
17. Who wrote the textbook?

18. Lost in space, the astronaut tried to radio Earth.

19. He got a job in the new shopping mall.

20. Over the river, the exploding fireworks shed light.

III. Fill in the blank with an appropriate subject.

1. Her ______________________ was parked illegally.

2. In the cupboard is a ______________________ .

3. ______________________ helps keep the bugs away.

4. ______________________ is the country just south of Canada.

5. ______________________ are coming to see us.

6. My ______________________ is learning how to play tennis.

7. The rearview ______________________ has to be adjusted.

8. ______________________ is one way to stay in shape.

9. Rainy ______________________ keeps people indoors.

10. ______________________ taste great when they are barbequed.

11. The ______________________ were shattered during the storm.

12. Three ______________________ were arrested for drunken driving.

13. ______________________ come out only at night.

14. ______________________ is prime minister of Canada.

15. In the sink was a ______________________ of dirty dishes.

16. ______________________ can give me a headache.

17. ______________________ never want to see you again.

18. ______________________ is my idea of fun.

19. ______________________ are beautiful house plants.

20. Through the city marched ______________________ .

CHAPTER 2

Verbs

IMPORTANT TERMS INTRODUCED IN THIS CHAPTER

verb a word that expresses action or a state of being.

main verb the word that expresses the primary action in a sentence.

linking verb a verb that expresses a condition or state of being (rather than an action).

helping (auxiliary) verb a verb that helps the main verb make its statement.

complete verb the main verb PLUS any helping or linking verbs that appear in a sentence.

tense shows the time when the action of the verb happened (past, present, future).

irregular verb a verb that does not form its past tense in the regular way (*-ed* is **not** added to the end of the verb).

In any sentence, something must happen; that is, something must be done or felt by the subject of the sentence. A verb is a word that is used to express action; it tells us what is happening. In order to be complete, every sentence must contain a verb. Effective use of the various types and forms of verbs leads to effective communication.

POINT I A *verb* is a word (or group of words) used to express action.

Arthur fixed the flat tire.

What action is taking place in this sentence? What happened? The subject of this sentence, *Arthur,* took part in the action of fixing a flat tire. What did the subject do? He *fixed. Fixed* is the verb in this sentence.

I work in a public school.

What action is taking place? What does the subject, *I,* do? I *work.* Therefore *work* is the verb in this sentence.

The girl ate her dinner.

What did the subject, *girl,* do? She *ate. Ate,* therefore, is the verb in this sentence.

Ted will do the job quickly.

What is the action? The subject, *Ted, will do. Will do* is the verb.

Exercise: Point 1

In each of the following sentences, draw one line under the simple subject and two lines under the verb.

1. Paul mailed the letter.
2. The police officer directs the traffic.
3. I took that exam yesterday.
4. The dog chased the cat around the yard.
5. Roberto operated the ice cream maker.
6. The cow slept in the shade.
7. A good investment pays for itself.
8. A good fan cools a hot room.
9. The firefighter rescued the child from the burning building.
10. The spider crawled across my stomach.

POINT 2 **The *tense* of a verb shows the time when the action happened — past, present, or future. Many verbs can be changed from the present tense to the past tense by adding *-d* or *-ed* to the end.**

1. *Present tense*—the action takes place now.

   I walk.
   I vote.
   I scream.
   I jump.

2. *Past tense*—the action expressed by the verb has already taken place (at some time in the past).

   I walked.
   I voted.
   I screamed.
   I jumped.

Note that each of these verbs was changed into the past tense by adding *-d* (when the word already ends in *e*, such as *vote)* or *-ed* to its end. Verbs of this kind are called *regular verbs.*

There are, however, many verbs in English which do not follow the same pattern. These are called *irregular verbs* and will be dealt with in Point 5.

3. Either the present or the past tense can be used to express continuous or frequently repeated action, as well as a single action.

   I walk to class every morning.
   Kathy worked here for six months.

Exercise: Point 2

Change the following verbs from the present tense into the past tense by adding *-d* or *-ed* to the end.

1. smile ______ smiled ______
2. laugh ____________
3. agree ____________
4. fix ____________
5. bounce ____________
6. love ____________
7. explode ____________
8. adopt ____________

9. rent ______________________________

10. call ______________________________

Review Exercise: Points 1 and 2

Write *Pr* if the verb is in the present tense or *Pa* if the verb is in the past tense. Underline the verb in each section.

__Pr__ 1. Russ smokes a pack of cigarettes a day.

______ 2. The poet imagined a better world.

______ 3. He confessed his part in the Riel Rebellion.

______ 4. The candle sheds a soft light.

______ 5. The neighbours play bridge every Thursday.

______ 6. I wandered through the public garden.

______ 7. I joined the fraternity as a sophomore.

______ 8. I cook her breakfast every morning.

______ 9. Carlos watered his bonsai.

______ 10. Our doctor treats his patients kindly.

Another Review Exercise: Points 1 and 2

Fill in the blank with an appropriate verb. In some of the sentences, only one tense (past or present) makes sense. In other sentences, either tense will work. Make sure the verb you choose shows action.

1. Yesterday Normand ____called____ his mother on the telephone.
2. I ______________ or the candidate from the Yukon.
3. She ______________ if she would ever return.
4. We ______________ to the mall twice a week.
5. Theresa ______________ tomatoes in her garden.
6. To avoid an accident, the driver ______________ to one side.
7. I ______________ to send her a card on her birthday.
8. In a thunderstorm lightning often ______________ a tree.

9. Peanuts and beer _________________ well together.
10. The baby _________________ all night long.

POINT 3 A *linking verb* is used to link the subject to a descriptive word in the sentence or to another noun.

All the verbs we have seen so far in this chapter have been action words. Such verbs as *jump, call, scream,* and *walk* express a specific action. Another kind of verb, the linking verb, functions differently.

Wendy is very beautiful.

The linking verb *is* links the subject, *Wendy,* to a word that describes her. The descriptive word in this case is *beautiful.* Note that the verb is does not show a particular *action.* It simply serves a "linking" or "connecting" purpose.

Ayama is a skydiver.

Here the linking verb *is* links the subject to another noun, *skydiver.*

I grew weary of the journey.

The linking verb *grew* links the subject, *I,* with a descriptive word, *weary.* These words that describe the subjects are called *adjectives.*

Note: A linking verb is often some form of the verb *to be (am, is, are, was, were).* Other verbs such as *seem, look, sound, grow, appear,* and *become* may also sometimes be linking verbs.

Exercise: Point 3

Underline the linking verb in each of the following sentences.

1. Wan <u>is</u> going.
2. You seem to read my mind.
3. This cigarette tastes stale.
4. The union members are ready to strike.
5. They were standing and applauding the famous athlete.
6. The actor appeared to have forgotten his lines.
7. She looked angry as she spoke.
8. The steak was rare and juicy.
9. The sky grew dark before the thunderstorm.
10. He sounded furious.

POINT 4 Verbs ending in *-ing* require another verb (often some form of the verb *to be*) before them.

I going to the store.

The verb in this sentence, *going*, is incomplete because it does not tell us when the action takes place. In order to make it complete, another verb must precede it. We may add a verb in either the present or the past tense. The sentence should read

I am going to the store.

(*am going* is the complete verb) or

I was going to the store.

(*was going* is the complete verb).

The little boy jumping and laughing.

Once again, the sentence has no complete verb. We need to add another verb before the *-ing* word.

The little boy kept jumping and laughing.

Notice that it is not necessary to add another verb before every *-ing* word in the sentence. The verb *kept* before the *-ing* word *jumping* is sufficient to complete the verb form *laughing*.

The following chart shows the present and past tenses of the verb *to be*. It is important to memorize these tenses, as it is impossible to use *-ing* words without a working knowledge of this verb.

Present Tense		Past Tense	
I	am	I	was
you	are	you	were
he, she, it	is	he, she, it	was
we you they	are	we you they	were

Note: You have probably noticed that these *-ing* words are of the same sort as the *-ing* words that we used as subjects in Chapter 1. Many kinds of words have more than one use in a sentence. The trick lies in learning the right way to handle them for each use.

More information on how verbs *help* other verbs in sentences will be provided in Point 7.

Exercise: Point 4

In each of the following sentences, underline the *-ing* word and circle the helping verb.

1. Brian (is) washing his car.
2. The player began circling the bases.
3. Canadian soldiers were fighting at Vimy Ridge.
4. Kevin is weeding the garden.
5. I am preparing for the worst.
6. Mr. Potts is running for a post on the city council.
7. They keep trying to resolve their problems.
8. Canadians are choosing a new prime minister.
9. Lucy was singing in the nightclub.
10. We are attempting to improve our performance.

Another Exercise: Point 4

Fill in the blank with the proper form of the verb *to be*.

1. We _____are_____ going on a camping trip. (present tense)
2. I ______________ waiting for that bus for an hour. (past tense)
3. You ______________ trying too hard. (present tense)
4. Janice ______________ balancing her chequebook. (past tense)
5. We ______________ vacationing in the United States. (past tense)
6. They ______________ remodelling theirbasement. (present tense)
7. The children ______________ making all kinds of noise. (past tense)
8. I ______________ studying for an English exam. (present tense)
9. Bobby ______________ swatting flies. (present tense)
10. The mayor ______________ shaking everybody's hand. (past tense)

Review Exercise: Points 1–4

Underline the complete verb in each of the following sentences.

1. Ted was cleaning his room.
2. She seemed elated about the news.

3. He drives like a maniac.
4. I am vacuuming the carpet.
5. The baby grows more interesting every day.
6. Debra cut slices of her birthday cake.
7. We are developing new habits.
8. The day turned cold and bleak.
9. They started issuing free passes to Canada's Wonderland.
10. He remembered his father's advice.

POINT 5 Some verbs are *irregular.* They do not follow a set pattern when they change tenses.

In Point 4 of this chapter, we saw how the verb *to be* changed its form in unusual ways. *To be* is an irregular verb.

All verbs have principal parts. That is, a verb has different forms to suit its different uses. See how the principal parts of the verb *to begin* work:

Present	Past	Past Participle
begin	began	have begun

Present—begin: It is happening now.

I begin my homework.

Past—began: It happened already.

I began it an hour ago.

Past Participle—have begun: Note that this form of the verb always has a helping verb (some form of the verb *to have)* before it.

I have begun it already.

Become familiar with the way the verb *to have* works, as it will be important when you need to use the past participle.

Irregular Verb (to have)

Present Tense		*Past Tense*	
I you we you they	have	I you we you they he , she, it	had
he, she, it	has		

Study the following examples:

Present	**Past**	**Past Participle**
give	*gave*	*have given*
I give.	I gave.	I have given.
You give.	You gave.	You have given
He gives.	He gave.	He has given.
She gives.	She gave.	She has given.
It gives.	It gave.	It has given.
We give.	We gave.	We have given.
They give.	They gave.	They have given.

Here is a list of the most common irregular verbs with their principal parts:

Present	**Past**	**Past Participle**
be	was	have been
blow	blew	have blown
break	broke	have broken
bring	brought	have brought
catch	caught	have caught
choose	chose	have chosen
come	came	have come
deal	dealt	have dealt
dive	dived (dove)	have dived
do	did	have done
draw	drew	have drawn
drink	drank	have drunk
drive	drove	have driven
eat	ate	have eaten
fall	fell	have fallen
fly	flew	have flown
forget	forgot	have forgotten
freeze	froze	have frozen
give	gave	have given
go	went	have gone
grow	grew	have grown
know	knew	have known
lay	laid	have laid
lead	led	have led
lie	lay	have lain
lose	lost	have lost
raise	raised	have raised
ring	rang	have rung
rise	rose	have risen
see	saw	have seen
send	sent	have sent

Present	Past	Past Participle
set	set	have set
shake	shook	have shaken
sing	sang	have sung
sink	sank	have sunk
sit	sat	have sat
speak	spoke	have spoken
steal	stole	have stolen
swim	swam	have swum
take	took	have taken
wear	wore	have worn
write	wrote	have written

Note: You will be able to recognize when most of these are correct just from the way they sound. But you should review this list carefully and learn any principal parts you do not know.

Give special attention to the following pair of verbs. These are commonly confused.

lie (to recline)

Now I will **lie** down and take a nap. (present tense)
About an hour ago I **lay** down to take a nap. (past tense)
I am **lying** down to take a nap.
I **have lain** down in that bed before.

lay (to put, to place)

I **lay** the book on the table. (present tense)
Yesterday I **laid** the book on the table. (past tense)
I am **laying** my gun down forever.
I **have laid** my gun down forever.

A Quick Exercise: Right or Wrong?

1. I have laid my music down on the harpsichord.
2. The five-dollar bill was just lying there.
3. I like to just lay around in bed.
4. My driver's licence lay under the table all day.
5. Lying in the sun on the beach is my favourite activity.

Exercise: Point 5

Fill in each blank with the correct form of the verb that appears in parentheses below the blank.

1. There must have ___been___ full moon out tonight.
(be)

2. I thought I had ________________ that clock when I dropped it.
(break)

3. Yesterday, for the third time, I ________________ the Daily Double.
(lose)

4. I could have ________________ another kilometre if you had not stopped me.
(swim)

5. My, how you children have ________________ !
(grow)

6. The treasure from the ship must have ________________ to the bottom of the ocean floor.
(sink)

7. Have you ________________ your shares in the stock market?
(deal)

8. I would never have ________________ there if I knew it was your spot.
(lie)

9. Did you hear about the goose who ________________ the golden egg?
(lay)

10. The band must have ________________ a dozen different songs.
(sing)

Another Exercise: Point 5

Write your own sentences, using the verb forms given in parentheses.

1. (have brought) ________________________________

2. (have flown) ________________________________

3. (lay) ________________________________

4. (have led) ________________________________

5. (lie) ________________________________

6. (have eaten) ________________________________

7. (ate) ______________________________

8. (sank) ______________________________

9. (lying) ______________________________

10. (have laid) ______________________________

11. (have lain) ______________________________

12. (laid) ______________________________

13. (swam) ______________________________

14. (have drunk) ______________________________

15. (did) ______________________________

POINT 6 The *to* form of a verb (known as an infinitive) is incomplete and needs another verb before it.

He **to run** in the race. (incomplete)
He **hopes to run** in the race. (complete)
She **to start** yesterday. (incomplete)
She **was expecting to start** yesterday. (complete)

Exercise: Point 6

Underline all the verbs in each sentence. Mark *C* if the sentence contains verb forms that are complete, *I* if it contains forms that are incomplete.

__C__ 1. The boys plan to come tomorrow.

____ 2. The boy to shake the apples from the tree.

____ 3. She meant to take a tour of Montreal.

____ 4. My younger sister is longing to have a horse of her own.

____ 5. The leaves to fall in September.

____ 6. They are hoping to go on a picnic tomorrow.

____ 7. My mother to go back to college next year.

____ 8. The lake to freeze if the temperature drops.

____ 9. Larry's brother tried to join the Royal Canadian Air Force at sixteen.

____ 10. Do you expect to see Dolores on your vacation?

POINT 7 Be sure to identify the *complete* verb in a sentence.

In Point 4, we saw that *-ing* words need a form of the verb to *be* to help them, or make them complete. In addition to that combination, there are many other forms verbs may take. For example, the verb *walk:*

walk	had been walking	would walk
walks	has walked	should walk
am walking	have walked	could walk
is walking	had walked	must walk
was walking	shall walk	can walk
have been walking	will walk	might have walked

I **am walking** to school.
She **has walked** to school.
They **have walked** to school.
We **had walked** to school.
You **should walk** to school.
He **might have walked** to school.

These are only a few of the forms in which the verb *walk* may appear. *Helping (auxiliary)* verbs help the main verb make its statement. When a helping verb and a main verb act together to express a single action or state of being, that group of verbs is called a *verb phrase* (or *complete verb).* In each of the preceding examples, the *complete verb* appears in darker type. Sometimes words such as *only, just, not ever, never, always,* and *not* may appear in the middle of a complete verb. They are *not,* however, part of the complete verb.

They **have** never **walked** to school.
You **should** always **walk** to school.

Exercise: Point 7

Underline the complete verb in each of the following sentences.

1. She <u>should have been elected</u> class treasurer.

2. He has always wanted an outfit like that one.

3. They should never have lost that game.

4. Louise was appointed chairperson of the committee.

5. You should have learned from your mistakes.

6. Monica is learning to build cabinets.

7. He has just purchased a condominium in Sackville.

8. Gretchen had never experienced that before.

9. We had been hoping for better news.

10. It would not have alarmed me.

Review Exercise: Points 1–7

In each of the following sentences, draw one line under the complete subject and two lines under the complete verb.

1. Joe would have been the perfect candidate for the job.
2. Alice Munro and W.O. Mitchell are writing in Canada.
3. The pollution seems to be getting worse.
4. The caterpillars have eaten the leaves.
5. We are prepared to do anything necessary.
6. I am looking for true love.
7. The professor should not have assigned so much homework.
8. You will have to plug it in.
9. Joining the club will be good for your spirits.
10. She was recalling her childhood.

POINT 8 A sentence may contain two or more verbs.

The sentences we have seen so far have contained one verb. It is true that some of the verbs have consisted of more than one word *(have walked, am preparing,* and so on), but we have not seen sentences which contain two or more complete verbs. Consider this sentence:

Joan **ran** for public office and **won**.

In this sentence, *ran* is a verb, and so is *won*. This sentence contains two verbs.

I **have applied** to three colleges and **have been accepted** by two of them.

Again we see a sentence with two complete verbs.

The boys **were pitching, hitting,** and **running** in the competition.

Here is a sentence with three verbs. Note that it is not necessary to repeat the word *were* before each *-ing* word.

Exercise: Point 8

Underline all the verbs in the following sentences.

1. Randy washed the dishes and then dried them.
2. Tourists were swimming in the ocean and tanning themselves on the beach.
3. We stripped the wallpaper and painted the walls.
4. The fans were cheering and waving banners.
5. Renata took She course and learned to speak French.
6. He was moaning and groaning all night long.
7. In the summer, I sneeze a lot and get itchy eyes.
8. I called her and told her the news.
9. They were angry and did not hesitate to tell us so.
10. We have always worked hard, and now it is paying off.

HOW TO USE VERBS CORRECTLY

1. Find the verb by asking what action takes place in the sentence.
2. Make sure the tense — past present or future — is accurate.
3. Remember that incomplete verbs need another verb before them.

Chapter Review

I. Write *C* if the example has a *complete verb* or *I* if it has an *incomplete verb*.

_______ 1. We expecting a snowstorm tonight.

_______ 2. You should ask your boss for a raise.

_______ 3. I was watching television when the lights went out.

_______ 4. He apparently going to win the contest.

_______ 5. I driven across the country twice.

_______ 6. You must have heard the news bulletin.

_______ 7. Alan and Della laughing in the library.

_______ 8. We used to own a lava lamp.

_______ 9. He eager to buy an Instant Win lottery ticket.

_______ 10. The earth revolves around the sun.

II. Underline the complete verb in each of the following sentences.

1. I should never have brought that dog home.
2. Toni was talking with her professor.
3. I was raising the flag.
4. The criminals hid in the warehouse.
5. Raoul was spreading the good news.
6. Golf had never been so enjoyable.
7. We preserve our own vegetables every year.
8. The children want to play.
9. Ghislain has been named valedictorian.
10. We have always spent our summers in Summerside.
11. Phoebe had never before cooked spaghetti.
12. Avdo going to the dump tomorrow.
13. Miguel appears to be making progress.
14. Hata is worrying.
15. He was whining like a baby.
16. Toshiko is an editor at a big publishing company.
17. He arrived late too often and lost his job.
18. She looked in the mirror and saw that her hair was turning gray.
19. The city lights look beautiful tonight.
20. We have begun saving money and planning for the future.

III. Fill in the blanks with appropriate verbs.

1. She ________________ installing the storm windows.
2. I should ________________ bought it when it was on sale.
3. Leslie ________________ lovely in that dress.
4. Yesterday, I ________________ and had a great time.
5. We ________________ and ________________ until class was over.

6. My mother ____________________ when I ____________________

7. I ____________________ that magazine and ____________________ it every month.

8. She is ____________________ until midnight tonight.

9. You should ____________________ and ____________________ whenever you get the chance.

10. I ____________________ ready, willing, and able.

11. The job ____________________ interesting, but I ____________________ not to take it.

12. I ____________________ ____________________ taken you there if you ____________________ asked me.

13. Aniffa is ____________________ and ____________________ in the drama.

14. Stuart ____________________ hard, but he is ____________________ the course.

15. The teacher ____________________ the entire class session ______________ the poem "The Lonely Land."

16. We ____________________ around, looking for a theatre.

17. The fireworks display ____________________ a sight to behold.

18. I have ____________________ the best possible job.

19. Marija is ____________________ scales on the piano.

20. You ____________________ never ____________________ to get away with this.

Mastery Test

Note: This test is designed to tell you how well you have mastered the information presented in Chapters 1 and 2. It would be useful to compare your success on this test with your success on the Pretest to see how much you have improved.

I. Write *S* if the sentence is missing a subject, *V* if the sentence is missing a verb, or *C* if the sentence is complete and correct as it stands.

_______ 1. My employer at the staff meeting.

_______ 2. Were rehearsing for opening night.

_______ 3. We arranging to pick up the piano.

_______ 4. I see you.

_______ 5. Must be ready to explode.

_______ 6. He very dapper in that three-piece suit.

_______ 7. Was undecided about my future.

_______ 8. Choosing a career is a big decision.

_______ 9. Oil and coal energy sources.

_______ 10. President of the Flagpole Sitters Club.

_______ 11. Extreme heat seems to drive people crazy.

_______ 12. Always hopes for the best.

_______ 13. It is true.

_______ 14. I should never have invited you.

_______ 15. Thinking aloud often quite productive.

_______ 16. Will we never find a solution?

_______ 17. He shaken the dust from the mop.

_______ 18. Looking for bargains is my grandfather's hobby.

_______ 19. There are singing in the woods.

_______ 20. She was nominated, but she declined.

II. Underline the complete subject.

1. With the aid of a telescope, the class saw Jupiter.
2. Jasna and her friend arrived late.
3. Many detergents get clothes clean.
4. The piano and the drums are my specialties.
5. Into the stratosphere shot the Anik satellite.

6. The murmur of the ocean is music to my ears.
7. By changing your mind, you ruined our plans.
8. My dog is better than your dog.
9. A volcano is a mountain that expels ashes and lava.
10. Every sentence must have a subject.

III. Underline the complete verb.

1. Our plans include a trip to Niagara Falls.
2. I might have known better than to trust him.
3. Citronella candles keep the bugs away.
4. Last night they told us of their plans.
5. You are home!
6. This case smells of foul play.
7. He went out and had a good time.
8. Sculpture has always been my hobby.
9. We have been wondering where you were.
10. I have just spent my week's salary.

PART II

Writing Better Sentences

CHAPTER 3

Subject-Verb Agreement

In any sentence, the subject and the verb must agree. If the subject is singular, the verb must be singular. If the subject is plural, the verb must be plural.

Singular refers to *one.*

The rooster crows.
The train stops.

In each of these sentences, the subject is singular. Only one rooster is involved: only one train is mentioned.

Plural refers to *more than one.*

The roosters crow.
The trains stop.

Here the number of roosters or trains is indefinite. That is, we may be talking about two roosters or fifty roosters. In any case, it is clear that more than one rooster is involved. The subject, *roosters*, therefore, is plural.

POINT 1 Use singular verbs with singular subjects and plural verbs with plural subjects.

Singular

The **man jumps** over the fence.
The **detective solves** the case.

In each of these examples, the subject is *singular* (*one* man; *one* detective). The verb must therefore be singular (*jumps; solves*). The subject and the verb *agree.*

Plural

The **men jump** over the fence.
The **detectives solve** the case.

Now the subjects are plural (there is *more than one* man and *more than one* detective). The verb must therefore be plural (*jump; solve*). The subject and the verb *agree.*

Exercise: Point 1

Write *S* for a singular subject or *P* for a plural subject. Then finish the sentence. Finally, underline the verb in your sentence.

S 1. The detective solves the case.

____ 2. Trees ____

____ 3. The professor ____

____ 4. A book ____

____ 5. Children ____

____ 6. Motorcycles ____

____ 7. My nephew ____

____ 8. Accidents ____

____ 9. Karen ____

____ 10. The apartments ____

POINT 2 When it is used as a subject, a pronoun must agree with the verb.

Remember: The following subject pronouns are singular:

1, you, he, she, it

The following subject pronouns are plural:

We, you, they

Be certain to use a singular verb with a singular subject pronoun and a plural verb with a plural subject pronoun.

Note that except in the case of *was*, the pronoun *I* always takes a plural verb.

I *was* happy to hear from you.
I *jump* that fence every day.

Exercise: Point 2

Change each subject given in the parentheses into a pronoun and complete the sentence. Then underline the verb in your sentence.

1. (Mr. Chan) He is a businessman
2. (My sister) __________
3. (All of us) __________
4. (Cats) __________
5. (The desk) __________
6. (Jacques and I) __________
7. (The police officer) __________
8. (Jogging) __________
9. (Windsor) __________
10. (The two women) __________

POINT 3 When a subject is compound (includes two or more elements), make sure it agrees with the verb.

Compound subjects joined by *and* take plural verbs.

> Saskatoon and Yorkton **are** in Saskatchewan.

The subject includes the names of two cities and is therefore plural. For this reason the plural verb, *are*, is used.

> My parents, my brother, and my sister **send** me birthday cards every year.
> Lucy and I **are** going to the show.

Note: One way to see whether a plural verb should be used is to try substituting the pronouns *we* or *they* (which are plural) for the subject.

> **They** send me birthday cards every year.
> **We** are going to the show.

However, when a compound subject expresses a singular idea, it takes a singular verb.

> My friend and colleague **is** a good person.

Here the two parts of the subject, (1) *friend,* and (2) *colleague,* both refer to the same person. Since only *one person* is being described, a singular verb, *is,* is used.

Bacon and eggs **is** my favourite breakfast.,

Bacon and *eggs* refer to the same meal.

▸ *Note:* Compound subjects sometimes include the word *and*. Always determine whether the subject is singular or plural before choosing a verb.

Compound subjects joined by *or* or *nor* take singular verbs when both subjects are singular. The use of *or* or *nor* suggests that only *one* of the singular subjects is involved at a time in the action; therefore, use a singular verb.

Either Doug or Abby **cooks** lasagna every weekend.

Cooks is a singular verb.

Neither the Toyota nor the Nissan **is** running properly.

Is is singular.

When a singular subject is joined to a plural subject by *or* or *nor*, the verb agrees with the subject closer to the verb.

Either the players or the coach **is** responsible for the team's shoddy performance.
Neither my brother nor my three sisters **care** what I do.

Coach is singular, and so is *is*.

Sisters and *care* are plural.

Exercise: Point 3

Each sentence begins with a compound subject. Add a verb and complete the sentence.

1. The players and coaches sign autographs before the game.
2. My father or his friends ______________________________
3. Iva and Lu ______________________________
4. A gentleman and a scholar ______________________________
5. Either my aunt or my uncle ______________________________
6. Cars, boats, and trains ______________________________
7. Spring and summer ______________________________
8. Salary and benefits ______________________________
9. The owner and manager ______________________________
10. Pieces of wood and glue ______________________________

Review Exercise: Points 1–3

Write *S* for a singular subject, *P* for a plural subject, *CS* for a compound subject with a singular meaning, or *CP* for a compound subject with a plural meaning. Add a verb and complete the sentence.

CP 1. Jim and I are best friends.

_______ 2. Professor Bukari _______________

_______ 3. Neither my dog nor my cats _______________

_______ 4. Traffic jams _______________

_______ 5. Rudi and his gerbil _______________

_______ 6. Either staples or paper clips _______________

_______ 7. Violins and cellos _______________

_______ 8. The owner and captain _______________

_______ 9. Millionaires _______________

_______ 10. Stu, Nicola, and I _______________

POINT 4 Some indefinite pronouns are singular and take singular verbs.

The following indefinite pronouns are singular:

> Words ending in *-one* or *-body* (*anyone, anybody, everyone, everybody, someone, no one*)
> *either, neither*
> *another, anything, each, everything, much, nothing, one, other, something*

When one of these pronouns is the subject of a sentence, use a singular verb.

> **One** of us **owns** a car.

One is the subject. Don't be confused by the use of *of us*. What you are really saying is, "I own a car," or "She owns a car," or "He owns a car." Only *one person* owns a car; therefore the subject is singular and must take a singular verb, *owns*.

> **Nobody wants** to go to the party.

Not one single person wants to go.

> **Everyone** who was invited **is** here.

Every single person is here.

> **No one helps** prepare the dinner, but **everyone wants** to eat.
> Either colour **is** fine.

There are two colours, but the speaker is going to choose only one of them.

Either one **suits** me perfectly.
Neither of us **is** ready to go.
Neither player **wants** to bat.

Like *either* and *neither,* the word *each* concerns one thing or person at a time. *Both* concerns two things or persons together.

Each of us **has** a daughter.
Each of the employees **is** responsible for the upkeep of the area.

Exercise: Point 4

Complete the sentences and circle the verb. Use the present tense.

1. One of them carries a large suitcase.
2. Anyone ______
3. Everyone ______
4. Nothing ______
5. Anybody ______
6. Everything ______
7. Somebody ______
8. Nobody ______
9. No one ______
10. Neither ______

Another Exercise: Point 4

Circle the correct verb given in the parentheses.

1. Neither of us (care, cares) to attend.
2. Either of you (get, gets) the starring role.
3. Anything (serves, serve) the purpose.
4. Neither one of them (deserve, deserves) the award.
5. Neither pair of pants (fit, fits) correctly.
6. Either flavour (taste, tastes) delicious.
7. Either seat (are, is) fine with me.

8. Each of the tools (work, works).

9. Neither of those candles (has, have) a wick.

10. No one (do, does) the work properly.

Review Exercise: Points 1–4

Circle the correct word given in the parentheses.

1. The green car (race, races) through the street.

2. Neither of my friends (call, calls) me anymore.

3. No one (bother, bothers) me anymore.

4. Neither of those batteries (work, works).

5. Sears (are, is) a big mail-order house.

6. Sunbathers and children (is, are) on the beach.

7. Phil and Margaret (buy, buys) A-Plus lottery tickets every month.

8. One of you (die, dies)!

9. Never again will they (hitchhike, hitchhikes).

10. The boxer and his manager (knows, know) their business.

Another Review Exercise: Points 1–4

Write *S* for a singular subject, *P* for a plural subject, *CS* for a compound subject with a singular meaning, or *CP* for a compound subject with a plural meaning. Complete the sentence, using the present tense, and underline the verb.

S 1. Anyone is welcome in my house.

_______ 2. Fishing ____

_______ 3. Everyone ____

_______ 4. Buildings and grounds ____

_______ 5. You and I ____

_______ 6. Either of those recipes ____

_______ 7. Somebody ____

_______ 8. Neither of those responses_______________________________

_______ 9. They ____

_______ 10. Anne, Susan, and I_______________________________________

POINT 5 Some indefinite pronouns are plural and take plural verbs.

The indefinite pronouns *both, few, many, others*, and *several* are plural. When these pronouns act as subjects, use a plural verb.

Many of us **enjoy** watching the tennis matches.

Enjoy is a plural verb.

Others **find** them boring.

Find is plural.

Both of us **want** to see the show.
Both you and I **are** going to vote in the next election.

Note: Some indefinite pronouns (*all, any, more, most,* and *some*) can be either singular or plural, depending on the meaning of the sentence.

Singular – Most of our time **is** spent here.
Plural – Most of the fans **are** gone.

Exercise: Point 5

Circle the correct word in the parentheses.

1. (Each, Both) of us are packed and ready to go.
2. Many of us (need, needs) a vacation.
3. Several phones (is, are) ringing.
4. (Each, Both) of the canisters is empty.
5. Each of the citizens (vote, votes) once.
6. Few people (wish, wishes) upon stars.
7. Others (want, wants) to change jobs.
8. Both of them (visit, visits) often.
9. (Each, Both) of us minds his own business.
10. Both Alex and Marty (work, works) for Bell Canada.

POINT 6 Singular subjects followed by phrases that describe the subject take singular verbs: plural subjects take plural verbs.

The car with the two flat tires **is** mine.

Car is the singular subject of the sentence. The phrase *with the two flat tires*, which describes the subject, does not influence the choice of a singular or plural verb form. Do not write this sentence as

The car with the two flat tires **are** mine.

Flat tires, although plural, is not the subject of this sentence.

The education of adults **is** important.

Education, the subject of the sentence, is singular and takes the singular verb form, *is*.

Note: The verb must agree with the subject stripped of its modifiers. Subjects are sometimes followed by phrases beginning with *with, as well as, together with, including*, and so on. These phrases are not part of the subject and do not influence the choice of a singular or plural verb form.

The cabdriver as well as his passengers **was** startled by the sight of the horse in the street.

Here the subject, *cabdriver*, is singular, and therefore takes the singular verb *was*.

The actors, including the star of the show, **were** appreciative of the applause.

Actors is plural.

Exercise: Point 6

Circle the correct verb in the parentheses.

1. The bus as well as the car (was, were) damaged in the accident.
2. The presentation of the trophies (follow, follows) the game.
3. The books of Farley Mowat (is, are) interesting.
4. John, along with thirty friends, (was, were) in attendance.
5. The moon as well as some stars (is, are) visible tonight.
6. The children together with their father (watch, watches) the movie.
7. The seasons of the year (is, are) all distinct in Canada.
8. The street singer with a crowd around him (perform, performs) beautifully.
9. A pile of rocks (have, has) to be moved.

10. Sadie, in addition to her friends, (is, are) protesting the school board's decision.

Review Exercise: Points 5 and 6

Complete the following sentences.

1. Both food and drink ___are necessities of life.___
2. Each time ______
3. Both notebooks and rulers ______
4. Both coaches as well as their teams ______
5. The ballerina, along with other dancers, ______
6. Everyone ______
7. Both shoes and sneakers ______
8. Each member of the band ______
9. Part I together with Part II ______
10. The musicians, including the drummer, ______

Review Exercise: Points 1–6

Circle the correct word in the parentheses.

1. Both you and I together Ahmed (want, wants) ice cream.
2. Neither of the sandwiches (have, has) onions.
3. Rakes and mowers (is, are) used by gardeners.
4. Each of the boys (need, needs) a haircut.
5. I will be glad to see anyone who (wish, wishes) to come.
6. Neither of the boys (was, were) allowed to enter the race at Mosport.
7. Chris, Gina, and all their children (visit, visits) us weekly.
8. Those cars, including the white Ford, (is, are) parked illegally.
9. Both women (was, were) hired.
10. A wild and woolly dog (run, runs) around our apartment.

Another Review Exercise: Points 1–6

Complete these sentences.

1. Neither of the appointments ___was convenient for me.___
2. Coffee, as well as tea, ________________
3. Both coffee and tea ________________
4. Either one of the movies ________________
5. You and I ________________
6. Each daughter of mine ________________
7. Nobody who is anybody ________________
8. Strolling through the park ________________
9. My girlfriend ________________
10. The area including First and Second Streets ________________

POINT 7 **A *collective noun* (group word) takes a singular verb when the group is being referred to as a single unit: it takes a plural verb when the members of the group are being considered as a set of individuals.**

The jury **is** deliberating in the back room.

The subject, *jury*, refers to the group as a whole.

The jury **are** arguing among themselves.

Here *jury* refers to the individual members of the group, all of whom are arguing.

Edmonton Northlands **is** the site of a sports complex.
The rolling meadowlands **were** green in the springtime.

Some collective nouns are *group, crowd, team, band, family, audience, number, dozen, lot,* and *kind.* You can think of other words that are used to describe groups of persons or things.

Exercise: Point 7

Circle the correct verb in the parentheses.

1. A lot (was, (were)) trying out for the team.
2. My family (is, are) the most important thing in the world to me.

3. The band (was, were) louder than we expected.
4. A lot (was, were) accomplished at the last meeting.
5. The audience (was, were) booing and throwing tomatoes.
6. A number of items (is, are) missing.
7. A class (is, are) cancelled almost every week.
8. One team (is, are) Monique and Andra.
9. Today our committee (reach, reaches) a decision.
10. A dozen (are, is) prepared to strike.

POINT 8 When the verb comes before the subject of the sentence, it is especially important to identify the subject and make the verb agree with it.

Common sentences of this sort are those which begin with *there is* or *there are*.

> There **is** a better way to get there from here.

The subject of this sentence, *way*, is singular; therefore we use the singular verb form, *is*.

> There **are** times when your dog seems to be the best friend you have.

Times, the subject, is plural, calling for a plural verb, *are*.

> Beyond that field **sits** an abandoned house.

House is singular and so is *sits*.

> Just ahead **waits** the enemy.

Enemy, which can be a group word, is singular in this case. The verb, **waits,** must also be singular.

> Here **is** what I mean.

What I mean, the subject, is singular and requires a singular verb, *is*.

Exercise: Point 8

Circle the correct verb in the parentheses, and underline the simple subject.

1. There (is, are) a way to stop the leaking tap.
2. There (is, are) veterans of the war here tonight.
3. Inside the shack (is, are) a stray dog.

4. Over there (is, are) the premier of our province.

5. Behind that door (wait, waits) danger.

6. There (is, are) more than one way to skin a cat.

7. Under that rock (is, are) over a hundred ants.

8. In our system, there (is, are) one lieutenant governor for each province.

9. Right behind me (is, are) everyone who supports me.

10. Beside the table (was, were) a high chair.

POINT 9 Words or names that are plural in form but singular in meaning take a singular verb.

Be careful: A word ending in *-s* or *-es* is not necessarily plural!

Social studies **is** one course I will take this semester.

Social studies is the name of one course, and therefore singular.

The Nets York Times **has** a large circulation.
The sports news **is** on television at 6:15.

Exercise: Point 9

All of the subjects in these sentences end in s or es, but only some of them are plural. Mark S for a singular subject or *P* for a plural subject. Then complete the sentence.

__P__ 1. The Red Wings __lead the league.__

____ 2. The *Daily News* ____

____ 3. Animals ____

____ 4. Shakespeare's *Hamlet* ____

____ 5. The five senses ____

____ 6. Mathematics ____

____ 7. Shouts ____

____ 8. Games ____

____ 9. Economics ____

____ 10. Business ____

Review Exercise: Points 7–9

Fill in the blank with the correct form of the verb given in the parentheses. Look again at the chart on pages 27–28 if necessary.

1. There ____are____ twenty students in this class.
   (to be)
2. The *London Times* ________ an excellent newspaper.
   (to be)
3. Up the hill ________ Jack and Jill.
   (to run)
4. There ________ danger involved in that plan.
   (to be)
5. ________ you any spare change?
   (to have)
6. L.M. Montgomery ________ written many children's books.
   (to have)
7. Yesterday there ________ a terrible snowstorm.
   (to be)
8. *The Pickwick Papers* ________ a novel by Charles Dickens.
   (to be)
9. The Expos ________ a baseball team.
   (to be)
10. There ________ a good audience tonight.
    (to be)

Another Review Exercise: Points 7–9

Complete these sentences.

1. The House of Commons ____is part of the government.____
2. My family ________
3. Many ________
4. There is ________
5. Here are ________
6. Liberal arts ________
7. Beside the field ________

8. Our English class ________________________________

9. The members of our class ________________________________

10. A heap of trash ________________________________

HOW TO MAKE SURE THAT SUBJECTS AND THEIR VERBS AGREE

1. Remember that it is the singular or plural *meaning* of a subject, not its form, which determines whether it takes a singular or a plural verb.
2. When the verb comes before the subject, be especially careful to identify the subject before deciding on the form of the verb.

Chapter Review

I. Circle the correct verb in the parentheses.

1. Almost everybody (has, have) some difficulty with writing.
2. Neither the chipmunk nor the squirrels (is, are) bothering us.
3. Both of us (is, are) voting in the next election.
4. Milo, Aharon, and I (was, were) offering our help.
5. Neither of you (jump, jumps) to conclusions.
6. Some say the Native people (have, has) been treated unfairly.
7. There (was, were) only two choices on the menu.
8. Rudy as well as his cat (like, likes) milk.
9. She (are, is) my boss and friend.
10. Sunbathing (is, are) my favourite form of exercise.
11. Either of us (have, has) to pay the fine.
12. The twins and their parents (travel, travels) together.
13. Nobody (believe, believes) your alibi.
14. The United States and Canada (is, are) neighbours.
15. "Safe" and "out" (is, are) two calls in baseball.
16. Neither of them (dance, dances) to rock music.
17. Each (serve, serves) a different purpose.

18. The hammer as well as the saw (make, makes) work easier.
19. Jacques (was, were) working for his uncle last year.
20. Our team (play, plays) hard every night.
21. Neither of the boys (has, have) to shave.
22. The Johnsons, including their son Mike, (ski, skis).
23. The Seven Wonders of the World (is, are) extraordinary.
24. Mount Royal and Olympic Stadium (is, are) in Montreal.
25. Time (fly, flies) when you're enjoying yourself.
26. Either Cathy or the Chans (cook, cooks) dinner on Fridays.
27. Each of the brothers (has, have) been on television.
28. My husband and I (was, were) late for the movie.
29. There (was, were) no way out of the tunnel.
30. You (is, are) nobody until somebody (love, loves) you.

II. Fill in the blank with an appropriate form of the verb.

1. The enemy ________________ captured late last night.
(to be)
2. I ________________ the workers are safe now.
(to suppose)
3. Nothing ________________ those two.
(to excite)
4. It ________________ as testimony to a great person.
(to stand)
5. One of us always ________________ the right answer.
(to guess)
6. The Dhimans ________________ in the next apartment.
(to live)
7. Violins and cellos ________________ musical instruments.
(to be)
8. Someone ________________ to take me to the station.
(to have)

9. I ________________ disappointed with their performance.
(to be)

10. They ________________ the best of times.
(to be)

III. Fill in the blank with the appropriate form (singular or plural) of a subject.

1. The ________________ is not working today.
2. ________________ are expecting their first child.
3. ________________ signed up for the marathon.
4. ________________ of us cares much for caviar.
5. ______________ and ______________ are examples of foul weather.
6. ________________, together with Mr. Buryta, are going sailing.
7. ________________, ________________, and ________________ want more food.
8. ________________ went shopping for a used car.
9. There are never enough ________________ in the day.
10. ________________ is a good way to pass the time.

IV. Write *C* if the sentence is correct or *X* if it contains an error in agreement. Correct each incorrect sentence on the line below it.

_______ 1. Sylvie, as well as Amy, do not wish to register.

____

_______ 2. Alex Colville are a famous Canadian painter.

____

_______ 3. One of you have to sit on my lap.

____

_______ 4. Babies are innocent and adults is not.

____

_______ 5. Neither of us are in the mood.

____

_______ 6. Weddings is fun.

____

_______ 7. Alfonso buy records and listens to them in his room.

____

_______ 8. Both of them wishes they were going.

____

_______ 9. Grammar and spelling is being tested.

____

_______ 10. Anyone who winks at me embarrass me.

____

V. Complete these sentences.

1. Each of the teams in the CFL ____________________
2. Either of those latex paints ____________________
3. Swimming in salt water ____________________
4. The National Arts Centre ____________________
5. There are ____________________
6. Here is ____________________
7. Rain and sleet ____________________
8. The group, including fifty women, ____________________
9. The skater ____________________
10. Frederico and Luis ____________________

VI. Rewrite this entire passage in the following space, changing the subject from *a carpenter* to *carpenters*. Keep in mind that verbs and other words that refer to the subject will have to be changed from singular to plural.

A carpenter uses many different tools in his work. When he is faced with a job that is particularly difficult, he has to use his patience as well as his skill. Without patience, a hammer, a saw, or a screwdriver will do a carpenter no good. He has to be able to understand the problem, and find the best way to solve it. Sometimes, the quickest solution is not the best one. His customer, or client, has to be pleased with his work, or he loses his chance to be hired for another job. There is a great pressure on the carpenter to succeed. By no means is his job an easy one.

Carpenters use many different tools in their work.

VII. Rewrite this passage in the following space, changing the subject from *a person* to *people.*

A person who grows up in the tropics gets used to warm weather. There is never a major snowstorm there, although hurricanes are not unusual. A Canadian, on the other hand, has to learn to live with harsh weather for several months of each year. A person who travels from one continent to another is almost always surprised at the change of climate. Although a person from the tropics thinks that warm weather is nice all year round, a Canadian may enjoy the change of seasons.

VIII. Rewrite this passage in the following space, making subjects and verbs agree.

In Margaret Laurence's novel *The Stone Angel*, the main character are Hagar Shipley, a ninety-year-old woman who reflect upon her past. She remember her life as a young girl in a bleak prairie town, her being married to a farmer, and her relationship with her two sons, Marvin and John. Her widowhood and years alone are made her a short-tempered complainer, but her humour, pride, and self-reliance shows the virtues of a pioneer life that she learn as a young girl, qualities that makes her, in the eyes of Laurence's readers, a believable and lovable human being.

CHAPTER 4

Fragments

A *fragment* is something broken away from the whole. If you're not careful drying a dish and drop it, you're left with fragments, or broken pieces. In the same way, if you're not careful writing sentences, you might end up with a lot of fragments. And since a sentence is supposed to express a complete thought, it is important that you don't break it up into meaningless parts that leave your reader confused.

A complete sentence should include a subject and a verb. When one or the other is missing, we are left with a sentence fragment. In conversation, we use fragments all the time. Sometimes, for special emphasis, a writer may use a fragment. But for college writing, you should write complete sentences.

POINT I Make sure every sentence has a subject and a verb.

Joe works at a bank.

The verb, *works*, tells what kind of action the subject, *Joe*, takes. He *works*.

The **baton twirlers look** cold in this November weather.

Look is a linking verb. It connects the subject, *baton twirlers*, with the descriptive word *cold*.

Exercise: Point 1

In each of the following complete sentences, draw one line under the simple subject and two lines under the verb.

1. Heating costs are on the upswing.
2. Robert W. Service wrote poems about the Klondike.

3. There is a pickle in the refrigerator.
4. Many people read best-selling novels during the summer.
5. That train is late as always.
6. Babies require a great deal of attention.
7. A good meal improves my disposition.
8. You are a sight for sore eyes.
9. Gardening is therapeutic for some.
10. These are the best years of your life.

Another Exercise: Point 1

Mark *C* for a complete sentence. Mark *F* for a fragment. Make the fragments into complete sentences by adding a subject, a verb, or both, and a period at the end. Finally, draw one line under the simple subject and two lines under the verb.

__C__ 1. Doris is working late tonight.

____

_____ 2. Near the centre of town

____

_____ 3. Ate at a famous restaurant

____

_____ 4. He won The Canadian Grand Prix last year

____

_____ 5. I swept that floor already

____

_____ 6. At my grandparents' house

____

_____ 7. There is a phone call for you

____

_____ 8. With only fifty cents

____

_______ 9. The University of New Brunswick

____

_______ 10. She plans to hitchhike to British Columbia

____

Point 2 Watch out for *-ing* words. No word ending in *-ing* can ever be the complete verb of a sentence.

Don't mistake an *-ing* word for the complete verb of a sentence. Are these sentences or fragments?

Sitting on the bench feeding the pigeons.
Wondering about his future.
The woman running down the street.
Was calling his friends, rounding them up, and handing out the tickets for the game.

None of the preceding is a complete sentence. Each, however, can be made into a complete sentence by adding a subject or a verb, or *sometimes* both.

The man was sitting on the bench feeding the pigeons. (Add subject and verb.)
My father is wondering about his future. (Add subject and verb.)
The woman **was** running down the street. (Add verb.)
Harry was calling his friends, rounding them up, and handing out tickets for the game. (Add subject.)

Now each of these is a complete sentence because it has a subject and a complete verb.

Don't be fooled by length. A fragment need not be short. There is a lot of action in the last example – calling, rounding up, handing out – but the subject is missing. You need to say who is doing all that action.

Exercise: Point 2

Make each fragment into a complete sentence and rewrite the entire sentence in the space provided. Add a subject or a verb, or both if necessary. Put a period at the end of the complete sentence.

1. the customer asking a question

   The customer was asking a question.

2. birds singing in the trees

   ____

3. the man trying to escape

   ____

4. always working on her house

____

5. the woman beginning a new career

____

6. practising the piano

____

7. the attendant checking the tire pressure

____

8. the convict trying to evade the Ontario Provincial Police

____

9. smiling at me from across the room

____

10. Heng making his career plans

____

Review Exercise: Points 1 and 2

Place a *C* before a complete sentence or an *F* before a fragment. Make each fragment into a complete sentence, and put a period at the end.

F 1. Racing wildly through the park

The motorcyclist was racing wildly through the park.

_____ 2. Was falling in love

____

_____ 3. She called

____

_____ 4. Three businessmen

____

_____ 5. Rarely displayed any emotion

____

_______ 6. The hail dropping like stones from the sky

____

_______ 7. Are you shouting or am I deaf

____

_______ 8. The punishment that he deserved

____

_______ 9. The burglar left the apartment in a shambles

____

_______ 10. Choosing a new major

____

POINT 3 A group of words containing a subject and a verb is called a clause.

In the English language, there are two types of clauses:

1. *Independent:* has a subject and a verb
can stand alone as a complete sentence
2. *Dependent:* has a subject and a verb
cannot stand alone because it begins with a word or word group such as *because, since, though, although, if, as if, where, unless, as soon as, whereas, in order that, when, whenever, while, before, after, as, until, so that, as long as, such as, provided that, during.*

This is an independent clause:

He ran to the store.

But if we put any of the preceding words in front of it, it becomes a dependent clause:

Because he ran to the store
Since he ran to the store
Before he ran to the store
When he ran to the store
If he ran to the store
After he ran to the store

A dependent clause standing alone is a fragment. Turn it into a complete sentence by adding an independent clause.

He was late for work because he ran to the store.
He got there before it closed, since he ran to the store.
He put on his tennis shoes before he ran to the store.

He lost his keys when he ran to the store.
Why did he get there late, if he ran to the store?
He sat down to catch his breath after he ran to the store.

By itself, a dependent clause doesn't make sense because it is a fragment of a thought, even if you put a period at the end.

Until I joined the "Y."

Dependent clause alone = fragment.

Until I joined the "Y," I never exercised regularly.

Independent clause added to dependent clause = complete sentence.

Elements that can stand alone usually can be identified by reading them aloud.

Exercise: Point 3

Mark *I* for an independent clause and *D* for a dependent clause.

__D__ 1. Because Sam speaks French.

______ 2. Unless you change your attitude.

______ 3. She wants to go, too.

______ 4. If you must miss your appointment.

______ 5. Until we get to the beach.

______ 6. As long as you're here.

______ 7. When I arrive at your place.

______ 8. Such as lamps and drapes.

______ 9. Since we have to repay the loan.

______ 10. You know the answer.

Another Exercise: Point 3

Mark *I* for an independent clause and *D* for a dependent clause. If the clause is independent, and therefore a complete sentence, capitalize the first letter and put a period at the end. If the clause is dependent, and therefore a fragment, add an independent clause to make it a complete sentence and put a period at the end.

__I__ 1. We went to the movies.

______ 2. while we are waiting

______ 3. Abby and I are married

_______ 4. because some people prefer Labatts

_______ 5. although I promised otherwise

_______ 6. before the song begins

_______ 7. if it is a good place to shop

_______ 8. the Rockies are magnificent

_______ 9. unless you give me a raise

_______ 10. after he sprained his ankle

POINT 4 When a dependent clause comes at the beginning of a sentence, it is followed by a comma.

A dependent clause may come at the beginning of a sentence or at the end. When it comes at the beginning, always separate it from the independent clause with a comma.

When he spoke, the audience was silent.
Before they arrived, I set the table.
Since you asked, I will tell you.

However, if the independent clause comes first, you may or may not need a comma. It depends on whether or not the meaning is clear. Use a comma only if it is necessary to make the meaning clear.

The audience was silent when he spoke.
I set the table before they arrived.
I will tell you, since you asked.

Exercise: Point 4

Place a comma in each sentence if it is necessary.

1. Because it is raining, we cannot go outside.
2. While you wait you may read a magazine.
3. Stephen Leacock the Canadian humourist died in 1944.
4. If you want to go you will have to buy a ticket.
5. If you go swimming wear a swimcap.
6. Unless you change your ways you will lose your job.
7. When he left the room was dark.

8. After this inning the game will be over.
9. I want to try even if it is difficult.
10. After I swept the floor I dusted.

Review Exercise: Points 1–4

Turn each of these dependent clauses into a complete sentence by adding an independent clause before or after it. Be sure to place a comma where it is required and a period at the end of each sentence.

1. even though he is tired

   He hopes to go tonight even though he is tired.

2. since I fell for you

3. if I decide to go along with your wishes

4. although he has been teaching for twenty years

5. until they discover a cure for the common cold

6. while he was standing at the meat counter in the supermarket

7. unless he changes his vile ways

8. after the sun goes down

____

____

9. as the world turns

____

____

10. before we packed the car

____

____

POINT 5 Every sentence must have at least one independent clause.

Don't let a dependent clause stand alone. That's a fragment. Add an independent clause to make it into a complete sentence.

An independent clause is the main idea, a complete thought. It can be a complete sentence in itself. A dependent clause serves only to further the meaning.

> While we watched television, the stew burned.

The main idea is that the stew burned. The dependent clause merely gives additional information. In this case, it tells when.

Exercise: Point 5

Underline the independent clause in each of the following sentences.

1. Even though there is enough time, <u>I feel rushed</u>.
2. Unless you work harder, you will receive a poor grade.
3. As long as you use suntan lotion, you will not get burned.
4. The show begins when the curtain rises.
5. My paper was better after I revised it.
6. If I am nominated, I will not run.
7. I didn't like olives until I had them on pizza.
8. I am happy when I am reading.
9. As soon as the match ends, the winner will be crowned.
10. Lock the door before you leave.

Another Exercise: Point 5

Turn each of these fragments into a complete sentence by adding an independent clause before or after it. Be sure to place a comma where it is required and a period at the end of each sentence.

1. since we painted the house

   Since we painted the house, we've gotten lots of compliments.

2. as soon as I finish the assignment

3. before calling to say thank you

4. until the tide comes in

5. whenever you need a friend

6. even though we have known each other for years

7. while working the night shift

8. because there is no other choice

9. although there was little hope for recovery

10. whenever I'm feeling depressed

POINT 6 Avoid other common types of fragments, such as the "list" type.

> Our family loves celebrating holidays. For example, Victoria Day and Canada Day.

For example, Victoria Day and Canada Day is a fragment in that it does not express a complete thought. It is a piece of the previous sentence that has been broken apart from the original.

> Our family loves celebrating holidays such as Victoria Day and Canada Day.

Here the fragment has been pieced back together with the sentence to make one complete and correct sentence.

> I like sports. Like baseball, football, and golf.

Fragment.

> I like such sports as baseball, football, and golf.

Correct.

Review Exercise: Points 1–6

In the space provided, make the following fragments into complete and correct sentences.

1. including my friend Sonya

   Several people, including my friend Sonya, are going.

2. as soon as the mail arrives

3. to attempt to break the world record

4. for example, hockey and football

____

5. even though we used to be friends

____

6. after she finished the manuscript

____

7. including my parents and me

____

8. such as the dictionary and the thesaurus

____

9. while I was weeding the garden

____

10. to find his way home

____

POINT 7 Command sentences do not contain obvious subjects, but they are still complete and correct.

In the sentence "Come here," the subject is understood although it is not specifically mentioned. The subject of this sentence is *you.*

Note the following examples of command sentences which contain *understood subjects.*

> Hello.
> Watch out!
> Get out of here.

All these sentences are complete and correct.

Exercise: Point 7

In the space provided write *C* if the example is a complete and correct sentence or *F* if it is a fragment.

__C__ 1. Don't drink the water.

_____ 2. Go somewhere else, please.

_______ 3. Go.

_______ 4. Rossland, B.C., highest city in Canada.

_______ 5. Save your money.

_______ 6. Start boiling the potatoes.

_______ 7. Forget everything I told you.

_______ 8. Before it is too late.

_______ 9. As soon as she arrives.

_______ 10. Shout "Surprise!" as soon as she arrives.

HOW TO AVOID FRAGMENTS

1. Make sure every sentence has a subject and a verb.
2. Don't mistake an *-ing* word for the complete verb.
3. Make sure every sentence has at least one independent clause.

Chapter Review

I. Mark *C* for a complete sentence or *F* for a fragment. Add a period to each complete sentence.

_______ 1. After cleaning out the gutters

_______ 2. They lost the battle

_______ 3. The Canadian ambassador to the U.S.

_______ 4. As the candidate raised his fist

_______ 5. Come over for dinner

_______ 6. Never say die

_______ 7. Expecting to hear from you soon

_______ 8. Finishing the marathon

_______ 9. Dietmar and his beautiful wife

_______ 10. Even though it is early

II. Mark *C* for a complete sentence or *F* for a fragment. Add a period to each complete sentence.

_______ 1. Until the morning comes

_______ 2. Provided that you pass the exam

_______ 3. Sports cars are fun

_______ 4. Chasing its own tail

_______ 5. Last but not least

_______ 6. I was amazed at the performance

_______ 7. If they get their act together

_______ 8. Bring it tomorrow

_______ 9. Such as the Canucks and the Flames

_______ 10. My sister combing her hair

III. Underline the independent clause in each of these sentences.

1. We played lacrosse until it grew dark.
2. Even though it was foggy, we made a smooth landing at Gander.
3. Because he hurt himself, he could not play.
4. I should quit smoking because it's unhealthy.
5. Although she has a quick temper, Huda kept calm.
6. While I'm here, I should call my aunt.
7. After you run, take a shower.
8. We bought his album after we saw him in concert.
9. I brought my guitar since I knew you would be here.
10. When you come to the third stop light, turn left.

IV. Fill in the blank and complete the sentence with an appropriate independent clause. Add commas where necessary.

1. Because I want to know you better ________________________________
2. Even though I am broke ________________________________
3. Unless you change your mind ________________________________
4. When the time comes ________________________________
5. As long as you are away ________________________________
6. ________________________________ after we go for a swim.
7. ________________________________ while you chop the onions.
8. ________________________________ so that you can find your way.

9. ______________________________ whenever I visit my grandparents.

10. ______________________________ although he was shy.

V. Mark *C* for a complete sentence or *F* for a fragment. Add a period to each complete sentence.

_______ 1. Call me if you need me

_______ 2. If you desire a change of pace

_______ 3. Opening a charge account

_______ 4. When I heard the news

_______ 5. After everything has been said and done

_______ 6. For a good reason

_______ 7. As soon as the rain stops

_______ 8. I know

_______ 9. It's okay with me

_______ 10. Later on in the show

VI. Mark *C* for a complete sentence or *F* for a fragment. Rewrite the fragments to make them complete sentences. Capitalize each sentence and put a period at the end.

_______ 1. the traffic was heavy

____

_______ 2. a gorgeous autumn afternoon

____

_______ 3. to make the dean's list

____

_______ 4. to find a bigger apartment

____

_______ 5. after chasing my dog around the block

____

_______ 6. with all the noise and confusion of a busy airport

____

_______ 7. at the last possible moment

____

_______ 8. laughing and crying at the same time

____

_______ 9. before I change my mind

____

_______ 10. like root beer and ginger ale

____

VII. Each of the following examples contains one fragment and one independent clause. Combine the fragment with the independent clause to make one complete sentence. Remember to use commas where they are needed.

1. As long as you're not lazy. I won't complain.

____

2. We're celebrating tonight. Because I gave up cigarettes.

____

3. If you want to play. Change your clothes.

____

4. Having moved to the country. He leads a quieter life.

____

5. After all. We have known each other for a year.

____

6. We hated summer. Until we bought an air conditioner.

____

7. Since you left me. I am so lonely.

____

8. You have to fix the leak. Before you can go sailing.

____

9. As soon as we arrived in Cavendish. We ran out to the beach.

____

10. We are raising a family. Because we love children.

____

VIII. Each of the following examples contains at least one fragment. Combine the fragment (or fragments) with the independent clause to make one complete sentence.

1. I worked hard. So that I could get a promotion.

____

2. Although she enjoys painting. She doesn't take art courses.

____

3. We went to the circus. Saw lions. Saw clowns.

____

4. Tell me the truth. If you know it.

____

5. There may have been improvements. Since he was elected mayor.

____

6. I love facing danger. Wherever I can find it.

____

7. I am too tired. To go for a walk.

____

8. He was arrested. Because he was drinking and driving.

____

9. You will find the underwear. In the drawer. Where I keep my socks.

____

10. Judging the distance. Holding her breath. She jumped.

____

IX. The following passages contain many fragments. Rewrite each passage in complete sentences. Some of the fragments can be combined with independent clauses. For others you will need to add a subject, a verb, or a new independent clause.

Today, more and more people are becoming interested in discovering their roots. After the beginning of the American Revolution. Many people loyal to the British cause fled to Canada. And settled in various parts of the country. Especially Ontario and the Maritimes. Some of the larger settlements were at places such as the Niagara Peninsula, Cornwall, Kingston, the Fredericton area. Halifax and Charlottetown. If a person finds that his or her relatives were United Empire Loyalists. That person may be able to use the initials UE after his or her name. For this reason. Many Canadians are interested in tracing their ancestries.

Ten years ago there were not as many shopping malls. As there are today. In a mall, many stores are gathered together. Under one roof. Shoppers appreciate the convenience a mall can offer. Because they can make one stop and accomplish all their shopping. In one place. On Saturday, malls are usually very crowded. People walking, talking, eating, and buying all over the place. Malls are air-conditioned. So that shoppers can browse comfortably. You can buy a birthday card, a mattress, and a baseball mitt all under one roof. Or pizza. A great way to shop.

When we moved from an apartment to a house. We discovered that we had more belongings than we thought. So much stuff had to be packed. In boxes. In suitcases. And even in large garbage bags. We rented a truck. From the local gas station. So we could avoid spending the extra money to hire a mover. We certainly put in a full day's work. That day. Although the process was long and hard. It was worth it.

CHAPTER 5

Run-ons

A sentence expresses a complete thought. You saw in Chapter 4 how fragments can interfere with the meaning of a sentence. Run-on sentences can cause similar problems of unclear meaning.

Whereas a fragment occurs when a sentence is broken apart, a run-on develops when one sentence runs into another one. This happens in one of two ways:

1. You finish one independent clause and go on to write another without putting any punctuation between.

   The train stops here it is always late.

2. You put just a comma between the two independent clauses.

   The train stops here, it is always late.

▸ *Remember:* An independent clause has a subject and a complete verb, and it does not begin with any of the words that begin a dependent clause. You may want to look back at the list of such words in Chapter 4, Point 3.

In the preceding run-ons, each of the independent clauses can stand alone as a sentence:

The train stops here.
It is always late.

The three exercises that follow will give you practice in recognizing run-ons.

Exercise: Recognition

Each of the following is an example of a run-on sentence. Draw a line between the independent clauses. Cross out incorrect commas.

1. I like rock music/I don't like jazz.
2. The invitation was beautiful it was hand-lettered.
3. The tide is high it is a good time to swim.
4. Marcel is a trucker, he is from Saskatchewan.
5. I often take your advice you are usually right.
6. Babies are cute they cry a lot.
7. He is my friend he understands me.
8. The trip was postponed we had no sleeping bags.
9. The firefighters were called, they handled the blaze.
10. I raked the beach, there is no seaweed left.

Another Exercise: Recognition

Mark *C* for a complete sentence or *RO* for a run-on sentence.

RO 1. They were neighbours, they were good friends.

_______ 2. There is a leash law, no one obeys it.

_______ 3. Change that tire it is flat.

_______ 4. A bad grade bothers me, don't think it doesn't.

_______ 5. She is packing cartons, they will take them away.

_______ 6. Eleni has wanted to buy the ring since she saw it in the store window.

_______ 7. Alert is on Ellesmere Island it is Canada's most northern community.

_______ 8. I love to eat that's why I am fat.

_______ 9. There was a lovely sunset, we watched it.

_______ 10. Give me a chance I can do better.

A Third Exercise: Recognition

Mark *C* for a complete sentence or *RO* for a run-on sentence.

RO 1. What should we do, I don't know.

_______ 2. He was a star athlete he won trophies.

_______ 3. We walked around the block.

_______ 4. If you ask me, I will tell you.

_______ 5. The snowploughs came through, they cleared the street.

_______ 6. She entered the marathon she placed third.

_______ 7. The MP made a statement, it was surprising.

_______ 8. Ed drives too fast he will get in an accident.

_______ 9. She couldn't light the candle the wick was gone.

_______ 10. Brian made a mistake he corrected it later.

Now that you can recognize run-on sentences, it is important to know how to correct them. *There are four ways to correct a run-on sentence.* Each method is described in one of the following points.

POINT 1 Connect two independent clauses with a comma plus one of these connecting words: *and, but, for, or, nor, yet, so.*

▸ *Remember:* A comma by itself is not sufficient.

Students write papers, **and** teachers correct them.

This is now a complete and correct sentence. The two independent clauses are connected by a comma *and* the connecting word *and.*

The men cooked dinner, **so** the women mixed the drinks.
The train stops here, **but** it is always late.

Exercise: Point 1

Change each of the following run-on sentences into a complete and correct sentence by placing a comma plus a connecting word where necessary. Rewrite the new, correct sentence in the space provided.

1. It was my mother's birthday, I called her on the phone.

   It was my mother's birthday, so I called her on the phone.

2. Going out to dinner is fun it is expensive.

   ____

3. I won't do it, you can't make me.

   ____

4. We can usually see for miles, today it is too cloudy.

____

5. I want that job, I don't think I have enough experience.

____

6. We found some shells on the beach they were beautiful.

____

7. The temperature reached 45° C. It was in Saskatchewan in 1947.

____

8. Tell me your problem I can help you.

____

9. Our daughter is in the third grade, she is very bright.

____

10. I've never tried blueberry ice cream I bet I will like it.

____

Another Exercise: Point 1

What is one way to correct a run-on sentence? By connecting two independent clauses with a comma *plus* one of these connecting words (fill in the blanks):

______________, ______________, ______________,

______________, ______________, ______________,

______________.

POINT 2 **Separate two independent clauses with a semicolon.**

Students write papers; teachers correct them.

The semicolon separates the two independent clauses and makes the sentence complete and correct.

The men cooked dinner; the women mixed the drinks.
The train stops here; it is always late.

In addition, connecting words such as *however, therefore, consequently, nevertheless, likewise, besides, also, then,* and *furthermore* may be used after the semicolon.

These words are stronger and more emphatic than *and, but,* and the other other words listed in Point 1.

Because these are strong words, it is often a good idea to put a comma after them. The word *then* is an exception; it does not generally take a comma.

> Students write papers; **then** teachers correct them.
> The men cooked dinner; **therefore,** the women mixed the drinks.
> The train stops here; **however,** it is always late.

Exercise: Point 2

Correct each of the following run-on sentences by placing a semicolon between the independent clauses. Add commas where they are needed. Rewrite the complete and correct sentence in the space provided.

1. I received the most votes therefore I was elected.

   I received the most votes; therefore, I was elected.

2. The ship sails from Argentia it leaves at 2:00 p.m.

   ____

3. We lost however we still lead the league.

   ____

4. The play was a tragedy, we left the theatre weeping.

   ____

5. You want your freedom nevertheless you will have to get a job.

   ____

6. I am running for office, furthermore I intend to win.

   ____

7. She must be out of town otherwise she would be here.

   ____

8. First buy your ticket then get in line.

   ____

9. Those shoes are comfortable I'll take two pairs.

   ____

10. There was no heat consequently we froze all night.

    ____

Review Exercise: Points 1 and 2

Fill in the blank with either a comma and a connecting word or a semicolon and a connecting word, making the sentence complete and correct. Place a comma after the connecting word if it is needed. Use five of each type.

1. We rented a floor buffer, ________________ it did not work.
2. Joe ran all the way home ________________ he was tired.
3. I cooked a hamburger for dinner ________________ I forgot to buy a roll.
4. The horse I bet on came in second ________________ I lost money.
5. The window was shattered ________________ we had to get a new one.
6. The candle burned for hours ________________ we did not have to use the lamp.
7. Apple pie is delicious ________________ it is fattening.
8. The show came on too late ________________ she wasn't really interested in seeing it.
9. Summers are hot and humid ________________ winters are cold and dry.
10. He was wealthy ________________ he could buy anything he wanted.

Another Review Exercise: Points 1 and 2

Fill in the blanks. Tell two ways to correct a run-on sentence.

1. Connect two ________________ clauses with a ________________ plus one of these connecting words: ________________ , ________________ , ________________ , ________________ , ________________ , ________________ , ________________ .
2. Separate two________________ clauses with a ________________ .

POINT 3 **Make two independent clauses into two sentences by using a period, a question mark, or an exclamation mark.**

Students write papers. Teachers correct them.

Since an independent clause is already a sentence, we can easily make the two clauses into two sentences by placing a period between them.

The men cooked dinner. The women mixed the drinks.
The train stops here. However, it is always late.

The strong connecting word however becomes part of the second sentence.

Note how the following run-on sentence can be made into two sentences by inserting a question mark.

Did you go to the party I didn't.

can be changed into

Did you go to the party? I didn't.

Exercise: Point 3

Make each of the following run-on sentences into two separate sentences. Add correct punctuation and a capital letter.

1. She asked for a raise she got it.

   She asked for a raise. She got it.

2. That is a new hall the acoustics are fantastic.

   ____

3. He is a good father, he pays attention to his children.

   ____

4. The birds are chirping, they sound so happy.

   ____

5. The parade is beginning let's get a good spot.

   ____

6. Your paper is late, therefore it will lose a grade.

   ____

7. He failed the test, consequently he will have to take it again.

   ____

8. Why did you go partying you were tired.

9. That suit fits you should buy it.

10. Bowling is fun for the whole family, it is good exercise.

Review Exercise: Points 1–3

Rewrite these run-ons in each of the three ways you know how to correct them.

1. The sun went down, the mosquitoes came out.

   The sun went down, and the mosquitoes came out.

   The sun went down; the mosquitoes came out.

   The sun went down. The mosquitoes came out.

2. Ben ran a good race, he came in second.

3. We applauded the actress she came out for a second bow.

4. I like Chaucer, I like Shakespeare even better.

5. I am happy to be here, I'm glad you are with me.

6. Turn right here park where you can.

7. I quit smoking, I feel much better.

8. I love visiting you, you treat me so well.

9. I have hay fever I take allergy pills.

10. I'm in my second childhood I feel young again.

POINT 4 Change one of the independent clauses into a dependent clause.

Remember: When a dependent clause comes at the beginning of a sentence, it is followed by a comma. (See Chapter 4, Point 4.)

When students write papers, teachers correct them.

The addition of the word *when* makes *students write papers* a dependent clause. This sentence is now complete and correct.

Before the men cooked dinner, the women mixed drinks.
Though the train stops here, it is always late.

▶ *Note:* Look back at Chapter 4, Point 3, if you need to review how to make independent clauses dependent.

Exercise: Point 4

Each of the following run-on sentences contains two independent clauses. Correct the sentence by making one of them into a dependent clause.

1. We went to the museum, Bob went to the ball game.

   While we went to the museum, Bob went to the ball game.

2. You are my friend I trust you.

   ____

3. I don't like crowds, I enjoy going to the beach.

   ____

4. The temperature dropped it started to rain.

   ____

5. I answered the phone, the caller hung up.

   ____

6. The kids are building sand castles, the adults have a conversation.

   ____

7. Let's find our seats, the show begins.

   ____

8. I locked the door, they still broke in.

   ____

9. You were fired the place has not been the same.

   ____

10. You were gone the plumber came.

    ____

Review Exercise: Points 3 and 4

All the following sentences are run-ons. Correct each of them in two ways: (1) separate the independent clauses into two sentences with a period and a capital letter;

(2) make one of the clauses into a dependent clause and add any necessary punctuation.

1. We moved here we have been very happy.

   We moved here. We have been very happy.

   Since we moved here, we have been very happy.

2. Trash is collected on Mondays it is taken to the dump.

3. There is no easy remedy we must research the matter further.

4. I started taking violin lessons I improved my style.

5. That type of defence will never work the other team is too good.

6. We go swimming every night during the summer the pond is nearby.

7. We drove cross-country we had no idea how beautiful Canada is.

8. You don't look well, lie down for a while.

9. The professor raised his voice he was very angry.

10. He looks grubby, he has not shaved for weeks.

____

____

THE FOUR WAYS TO CORRECT A RUN-ON SENTENCE

1. Connect two independent clauses with a comma plus one of these connecting words: *and, but, for, or, nor, yet, so.*
2. Separate two independent clauses with a semicolon.
3. Make the two independent clauses into two sentences by using a period, a question mark, or an exclamation mark.
4. Change one of the independent clauses into a dependent clause.

Chapter Review

I. Mark *C* for a complete sentence or *RO* for a run-on. Draw a line between the independent clauses in run-ons. Cross out incorrect commas.

______ 1. Shirts sometimes come with cardboard in them it protects them from wrinkling.

______ 2. You need matches to start a fire.

______ 3. Fred wears madras shirts, they have gone out of style.

______ 4. Before you paint, you have to strip the surface.

______ 5. She was hired because she was the best one for the job.

______ 6. There is a late show tonight, what time does it start?

______ 7. Al called last night he is getting married.

______ 8. Rest is important vitamins will help.

______ 9. It is your turn, roll the dice.

______ 10. Max takes flying lessons, he is getting a licence.

II. Mark *C* for a complete sentence and *RO* for a run-on. Correct the run-ons by using one of the four points.

______ 1. Guns are dangerous, they can cause a lot of trouble.

____

_______ 2. After the guests left, we cleaned up.

____

_______ 3. Lilacs are fragrant, we should grow some.

____

_______ 4. Construction workers wear hard hats they need protection.

____

_______ 5. Come outside you want to see the stars.

____

_______ 6. Poker is a great game, it takes skill as well as luck.

____

_______ 7. I read a great novel you can borrow it.

____

_______ 8. Shakespeare wrote comedies, tragedies, and histories.

____

_______ 9. I chose a button-down shirt, I like that style.

____

_______ 10. I wrote a letter to the editor, it was printed.

____

III. Each of the following run-on sentences can be corrected by adding proper punctuation and sometimes a capital letter. Circle the correction that makes the run-on into a complete and correct sentence.

1. We want to buy a new car (, ;) but it is too expensive.
2. She is a teacher (, ;) therefore (,) she has her summers off.
3. I wrote my member of Parliament (, . H) he replied with a form letter.
4. He started slowly (, . T) then (,) he speeded up and won the race.
5. Al went to the ball game (, ;) he ate peanuts and drank beer.
6. Italy is a lovely country (, . A) and so is Spain.
7. We had a picnic (, ;) and Marie played the guitar.
8. Although we got lost (, . W) we arrived on time.

9. Young people are often energetic (, ;) furthermore (,) they have great ambition.

10. Since we bought the fan (, ;) it has been much cooler in here.

IV. Each of the following run-ons can be corrected by the addition of a connecting word. Fill in the blank with an appropriate word.

1. Bring me my slippers, ______________________ see if you can find my pipe.
2. I've never been there, ______________________ I don't want to go.
3. I would like to get a bird's-eye view of things, ______________________ I can't fly.
4. You must do your homework, ______________________ you'll get a poor grade.
5. I don't usually read that magazine, ______________________ I did see the article.
6. The movie was hilarious, ______________________ I saw it twice.
7. I like playing tennis, ______________________ I'm not very good at it.
8. I take lessons, ______________________ I practise every day.
9. She wears army boots, ______________________ she rides a motorcycle.
10. I have hay fever, ______________________ it only bothers me in August.

V. Make each of the following run-on sentences into a complete and correct sentence. Use each of the four ways at least once.

1. Farming is hard work, it is satisfying.

   ____

2. We listened to oldies on the radio, it was an evening of memories.

   ____

3. Some people say horse races are fixed they are fun to watch.

____

4. Avoid poison ivy, it can irritate your skin.

____

5. A fireplace is romantic it can keep you warm.

____

6. My teacher was close to me she was almost my best friend.

____

7. I arrived late, I missed the interview.

____

8. I can balance my chequebook, I cannot complete my income tax forms.

____

9. I ate three donuts today however I am still hungry.

____

10. Writing is an important skill it takes time to develop.

____

VI. Tell one way to correct a run-on sentence.

Connect two ____________ clauses with a comma *plus* one of these connecting words: ____________ , ____________ , ____________ , ____________ , ____________ , ____________ , ____________ .

VII. Correct these run-ons in each of the four ways you have learned.

1. Ming loves golf, he plays a round every day.

____

____

____

____

2. I built a desk I keep it in my bedroom.

3. We travelled to Europe we saw the Eiffel Tower.

4. English is my favourite subject I get good grades.

5. I mixed the ingredients I put the batter in the oven.

6. I love summer, I don't like the humidity.

7. The mail arrives late here, the letter carrier walks a long route.

8. I enjoyed the dinner I feel a bit bloated now.

9. I see moisture in the basement, there must be a leak somewhere.

10. The wine is imported from France it is very good.

VIII. As independent clauses, all the following thoughts are complete by themselves, but you can make more interesting sentences by combining pairs of them. Use a connecting word where appropriate. Write the new sentences on the lines provided. Be sure to use correct punctuation.

Ofra is a whiz at photography
he is a great athlete
cheeseburgers are absolutely scrumptious
Tom is lazy
he is going to school to get his degree
he knows how important exercise is
Sally is an excellent painter
Tansu wants to be a registered nurse
hamburgers are delicious
the sprinter won the world championship

1.

2.

3. ______

4. ______

5. ______

IX. Here is another set to work with:

a summer breeze is lovely
sometimes it seems he can communicate with us
she bought a Volkswagen
it requires a lot of stamina
he is my best friend
that dog is very smart
it cools the body and the mind
backpacking is a great way to spend the day
he has moved to Swift Current
she traded in her Ford

1. ______

2. ______

3. ______

4. ______

5. ______

X. Rewrite each of the following paragraphs. Change the run-ons into complete and correct sentences.

The cost of fossil fuels affects us all, the price of home-heating fuel keeps rising, it gets too expensive to stay warm. One way to solve the problem is to buy a wood-burning stove, in some cases you can heat a whole house with the stove. Wood is also costly, if you have access to a supply it can save you money. Also, a stove is a beautiful addition to a house or apartment, it comes in many different styles each kind suits a different purpose.

______

______

______

______

______

______

______

______

Cats make great pets, you have to be affectionate with them. They are rather independent animals they do not always come when you call them. Many people prefer dogs, you can train them to come, or sit, or fetch a bone. With cats, on the other hand you have to be willing to let them live their own lives if you attempt to train them you may become discouraged. If you put two cats in the same room you are in for quite a treat. They chase each other, usually all in fun and when one catches the other the real show begins. Oftentimes they will cuddle and clean each other sometimes they will fight. The wise pet owner will know when to break up a fight and when to let it go since it is only play for the cats. They can be great company if you understand them.

Tennis is a sport that has gained great popularity over the last ten years, both men and women enjoy it. Tennis courts are being built all over, they can be found in cities, in the country, and in the suburbs. People of all ages can play in fact some of the greatest players in the world are in their teens or early twenties. The most important and prestigious tournament is held every summer at Wimbledon, a suburb of London however Canada's most important tournaments are the Canadian Open Men's Championships and the Canadian Open Women's Championships. One does not have to be a star athlete to enjoy tennis, it is great fun for those who just want some fresh air and exercise.

CHAPTER 6

Misplaced Modifiers

Clear and logical word order is a very important aspect of effective sentence writing. Most of the time, you order the words in sentences without giving them much thought. For example, you would never write "Canada Day today is." You would just naturally write "Today is Canada Day." The words fall into the right order easily and make sense.

There are, however, certain times when your choice of word order is not so clear-cut. If you use the wrong order, your sentence may turn out to be confusing, if not downright silly.

> We were told at midnight the show would begin.
> The man dived into the pool with the moustache.

These sentences are confusing or silly because the modifiers are misplaced. In this chapter you'll learn how to avoid misplaced modifiers that result in confusing or silly sentences.

POINT 1 A *modifier* is a word (or group of words) that describes or explains another word (or group of words) in a sentence.

> He wore a **ragged** suit.

The word *ragged* modifies *suit.* That is, it describes the suit.

> The **short** woman wore **high-heeled** shoes.

This sentence contains two modifiers; *short* and *high-heeled. Short* tells us something about the woman, and *high-heeled* describes her shoes.

That man **on the corner** is playing the clarinet.

Here we see how a group of words, *on the corner*, describes the word *man*. The modifier distinguishes that man from any other man — he is *on the corner.*

All these modifiers describe a noun (a person, place, or thing). Modifiers can also describe verbs.

Hank ran **quickly** after the ball.

Quickly describes, or modifies, the verb *ran*. It tells us *how* Hank ran after the ball.

We left the party **early.**

Here the modifier, *early*, tells *when* we left.

She swam **alongside** the boat.

The modifier, *alongside the boat*, explains the verb, *swam*. It tells us *where* she swam.

Exercise: Point 1

Either a noun or a verb is underlined in each of the following sentences. Circle the word or words that modify the underlined word.

1. The (sunken) ship held many treasures.
2. The cat tiptoed silently through the room.
3. Ernie is repairing the picket fence.
4. She ran with all her strength to first base.
5. With some reluctance, Lucy moved away from her family.
6. Home-made ice cream is tastier than this stuff.
7. Baffin Island is the largest island in Canada.
8. Anthony plays lovingly with his niece.
9. The bike with three red stripes is mine.
10. That handsome man is my boyfriend.

POINT 2 Place a modifier as close as possible to the word it modifies.

I showed my tooth to the dentist with a crack in it.

As this sentence is written, the dentist him- or herself has a crack. It is obvious that the phrase *with a crack in it* modifies the noun *tooth.* As it stands, the modifier is misplaced. The word order should be changed to

I showed my tooth with a crack in it to the dentist.

Now the modifier has been placed as close as possible to the word it modifies, and the sentence is clear.

He told me he was going to the movie that night in the morning.

This sounds as if the night is in the morning. Actually the modifier, *in the morning*, explains when he *told* me. The sentence should read,

In the morning he told me he was going to the movie that night.

Notice that in this sentence, the modifier cannot be placed right next to the word it modifies. The subject, *he*, is in the way. This often happens with words that modify verbs.

Exercise: Point 2

Place the modifier given in the parentheses in an appropriate spot in the sentence. Rewrite the entire sentence in the space provided, and underline the word that is modified.

1. (in a sharkskin coat) A man sold us a lottery ticket.

   A man in a sharkskin coat sold us a lottery ticket.

2. (along the boardwalk) We strolled until the sun set.

3. (excitedly) The crowd cheered when Lindros came onto the ice.

4. (yellow) The banana comes in its own natural wrapper.

5. (climbing the steps) I saw my grandmother in her house.

6. (as usual) He spoke only about himself.

7. (approaching the finish line) We watched the horses.

8. (happily) Sergio smiled when he heard the news.

9. (in a whisper) She warned me never to do that again.

10. (elastic) The man in the circus is a sideshow attraction.

___

Review Exercise: Points 1 and 2

Write *C* if the modifier is correctly placed in the sentence or *MM* if it is misplaced. Where the modifier is misplaced, correct the sentence as shown in the first example.

MM 1. Rick got an A on the test. Amazingly,

____ 2. The monster waited in the ugly cave.

____ 3. There was a rat waiting for us behind the door.

____ 4. The quarterback made the decision to run, instantaneously.

____ 5. Heading for a crash we watched the motorcyclist.

____ 6. The city council voted to fund the project unanimously.

____ 7. Max was chasing the dog wearing only his underwear.

____ 8. The panhandler approached the millionaire without a cent to his name.

____ 9. The furnace exploded, but no one was hurt with a crash.

____ 10. My father bought a toupee who is bald.

POINT 3 When dealing with modifiers, ask yourself, *what goes with what?*

The flowers appealed to the woman displayed in the vase.

The modifier, *displayed in the vase*, certainly does not refer to the woman. It is important to determine that the modifier *goes with* the noun *flowers*. The sentence should read:

The flowers displayed in the vase appealed to the woman.

By determining that *displayed in the vase* goes with *flowers*, we can now place the modifier in its proper position — near the word it modifies.

The man dived into the pool with the moustache.

Again, the moustache surely does not belong to the pool. The sentence should read,

The man with the moustache dived into the pool.

Problems with misplaced modifiers often occur because you think faster than you can write. The key to this type of writing problem lies in proofreading – in checking what you have written. Reread what you write, asking yourself, "Is this what I mean to say?" Look at the modifiers and ask, "What goes with what?"

Exercise: Point 3

Determine what goes with the underlined word in each of the following sentences. Rewrite the modifer in the space provided.

1. Poetry appeals to many Canadians of the fifteenth century.

   of the fifteenth century goes with poetry.

2. Suddenly riding her bicycle he saw the child.

   ____________________ goes with child.

3. Dressed in many colours we saw the clown.

   ____________________ goes with clown.

4. The table belonged to his great-aunt in the basement.

   ____________________ goes with table.

5. That dog belongs to the woman with the floppy ears.

   ____________________ goes with dog.

6. The siren wailed and we covered our ears loudly.

   ____________________ goes with wailed.

7. Promising better times for all we listened to the politician.

   ____________________ goes with politician.

8. The cheque was cashed the next day for fifty dollars.

   ____________________ goes with cheque.

9. The girl fed the lions with the creamy complexion.

   ____________________ goes with girl.

10. Barking at the fire hydrant we watched the dog.

    ____________________ goes with dog.

POINT 4 **Be sure that words such as *almost, even, hardly, just, merely, only, nearly,* and *scarcely* refer clearly to the words they modify.**

Consider the difference in meaning between these two sentences:

I almost ate all the vegetables.
I ate almost all the vegetables.

In the first sentence, *almost* is a misplaced modifier. If you think about it, you can see that to almost eat something is not to eat it at all. The second sentence, however, is much clearer. In this case, the speaker ate *almost* all the vegetables: that is, the speaker ate many of them, but not all.

Johnny, we **hardly** knew you.

The modifier, *hardly,* is placed right next to the verb *knew.* Like all modifiers, it explains the word it modifies. We can tell *how well* the speaker knew Johnny.

In which of these sentences is the modifier properly placed?

I read the newspaper **nearly** every day.
I **nearly** read the newspaper every day.

The first sentence is correct. The second is wrong, because you cannot *nearly read* a newspaper. Either you read it or you don't.

Exercise: Point 4

For each sentence, a modifier is given in parentheses. Place it near the word it modifies.

1. (almost) After ^ an hour, he was ready to go.
2. (even) She does not know his name.
3. (hardly) You are the one I need for this job.
4. (just) She had finished painting when I touched the doorknob.
5. (just) There are three eggs left in the refrigerator.
6. (only) I received the passing grade on the exam.
7. (nearly) I put on a last burst of speed and won the race.
8. (scarcely) The host had provided enough food for all the guests.
9. (merely) The police officer informed us of our rights.
10. (nearly) This time we made it.

Review Exercise: Points 1–4

Each of the following sentences contains a misplaced modifier. Correct them by placing the modifier near the word it describes.

1. The birds are singing in the trees their songs of love.
2. I heard about the big music festival on the radio.
3. I fell over from almost laughing so hard.
4. She sighed when the good news came happily.
5. Everyone nearly loves a barbeque.
6. Pete turned away when he saw the girl of his dreams bashfully.
7. He sat watching his neighbours below on the roof.
8. We needed someone to work overtime badly.
9. I am talking and relaxing on the telephone.
10. You are the one for me only.

POINT 5 Avoid placing a modifier between two words when its explanation can apply to either word.

His teacher told him **frequently** to study.

Does *frequently* refer to *told him* or to *to study?* We cannot tell if the teacher told him many times or if the teacher told him to study often. This sentence may be rewritten as either

His teacher frequently told him to study.

or

His teacher told him to study frequently.
She said **before she left** she would visit him.

In this example, we cannot tell what part of the sentence the modifier refers to. Does *before she left* refer to when she was speaking or to when she would visit him? There is simply no way of knowing. This sentence may be rewritten as either

Before she left, she said she would visit him.

or

She said she would visit him before she left.

Once again, the rule to follow here is *make sure the modifier refers clearly to the words it modifies.*

Exercise: Point 5

Rewrite each of the following sentences in two different ways.

1. She told him every day to change his socks.

   Every day she told him to change his socks.

   She told him to change his socks every day.

2. Clara said after her operation she felt better.

3. He told me always to be practical.

4. We were told at midnight the show would begin.

5. Ruth promised on her way out to close the door.

HOW TO AVOID MISPLACED MODIFIERS

1. Keep the modifiers near the words they modify.
2. Ask yourself, "What goes with what?"
3. Be sure that words such as *almost, even, hardly, merely, only, nearly,* and *scarcely* refer clearly to the words they modify.
4. Don't place a modifier between two words when its explanation may apply to either word.

Chapter Review

I. Write *C* if the modifier is correctly placed. Write *MM* if it is misplaced. Then, in the MM sentences, circle the modifier and draw an arrow to show where it should go.

_______ 1. The man was stopped for speeding in the blue sweater.

_______ 2. I almost saw the whole movie, but I fell asleep around midnight.

_______ 3. Hanging on one hinge, Nguyen left the door.

_______ 4. The initials were those of the lovers carved on the tree.

_______ 5. There are only two parking spaces left in the lot.

_______ 6. Every four hours the doctor told him to take a pill.

_______ 7. Sitting on the porch, I smoked my last cigarette.

_______ 8. The woman walked into the elevator with high heels.

_______ 9. The jet landed at the airport with 200 passengers.

_______ 10. I can hardly remember my own name.

II. Do these examples the same way you did the last set. Write *C* or *MM* and show where the misplaced modifiers should be correctly placed.

_______ 1. I watched the mechanic fix the car with admiration.

_______ 2. He made it in time barely.

_______ 3. Reaching into the cupboard, I found the bag of cookies.

_______ 4. We borrowed a mower from a neighbour that was broken.

_______ 5. Climbing up a telephone pole we saw a squirrel.

_______ 6. Gilles, as usual, was lagging behind.

_______ 7. The cat was rescued after the building had been set on fire by a fire fighter.

_______ 8. We've almost found all the pieces to the puzzle.

_______ 9. Vandals from the corner stole the sign.

_______ 10. I need food badly.

III. Again, mark *C* for correct and *MM* for misplaced modifier. Then correct the *MM* sentences with an arrow.

_______ 1. Zita was driven to the party by her mother.

_______ 2. I've hardly seen any of those films.

_______ 3. The signal, which was flashing intermittently, turned red.

_______ 4. By my favourite author, I read a new book.

_______ 5. Rashid visited his family in Whitehorse.

_______ 6. The boy waved to the Queen with a crew cut.

_______ 7. Nearly everyone we invited showed up.

_______ 8. She said in an interview she was happy.

_______ 9. We flew in a plane through a terrible storm with a faulty engine.

_______ 10. Midori was skiing when she broke her ankle down the slope.

IV. Place the modifier given in the parentheses in an appropriate spot in the sentence. Use an arrow.

1. (after the game) The coach treated the team to beers.
2. (wearing a ten-gallon hat) We saw a cowboy in the street.
3. (vigorously) The crowd cheered when the speaker stood.
4. (in the supermarket) We buy vegetables five kilometres from here.
5. (running down the hall) The principal stopped the students.
6. (in the crib) She gave the baby a bottle.
7. (red) I bought a shirt to go with my yellow slacks.
8. (that had been painted) We bought a picture by an artist from British Columbia.
9. (that she bought yesterday) She used a shampoo and then her usual conditioner.
10. (when they reach town) They promised to visit her.

V. Do this exercise the same way you did the last one.

1. (almost) The criminal laughed when he was arrested.
2. (with brass buttons) He bought a suit and treated himself to a fancy dinner.
3. (around town) Hamed loves to ride his scooter.
4. (barely) The cat escaped before the blaze spread.
5. (in the attic) We put insulation down, and now we are cool.
6. (friendly) There is a teller in that bank.
7. (noisy) There is a dog in our neighborhood.
8. (occasionally) He surprised his wife with a rose.
9. (made of brass) She bought a bookend for her husband.

10. (just) We are about ready to leave.

VI. Each of the following sentences contains a misplaced modifier. In the space provided, rewrite the sentence in its correct form.

1. Sam fixed the pocket with a needle and thread which had a hole in it.

____

2. I said when I got home I would tell you about my trip.

____

3. The tire went flat with the puncture.

____

4. The hunter escaped from the bear's claws barely.

____

5. In the latest designer fashions the buyers watched the models parade on stage.

____

6. Robin brought her dog to the veterinarian with an injured tail.

____

7. He vowed to love, honour, and cherish her on his wedding day.

____

8. My father-in-law snores when he sleeps loudly.

____

9. She bought a ring from the jeweller that was made of gold and enamel.

____

10. We first baked a cake for our friends in the new oven.

____

11. I ran into the barefooted street.

____

12. We sent invitations to all our friends in blue envelopes.

____

13. He left the clothing store and bought a newspaper with a new pair of socks.

____

14. That salesperson sold me a Pontiac with a bow tie.

____

15. Jumping rope I watched my sister from the car.

____

16. Chakriya said before she was twenty she would be a millionaire.

____

17. I would like a banana and a glass of water in my sundae.

____

18. The suit is at the cleaners with the brass buttons.

____

19. The hospital has been torn down where I was born.

____

20. I banged up a car in an accident that did not belong to me.

____

VII. Rewrite each passage, correcting any sentences that contain misplaced modifers.

I forgot to nearly send holiday greetings this year. All my relatives would have been disappointed in other parts of the country. It really is not that much of a strain since I need to send about ten cards only. It is as easy as writing, "Hi, how are you?" and mailing it on a note in an envelope. I usually work from a list that I keep in my desk of my friends' and relatives' names. I luckily remembered about the cards three days before the holiday; I just hope that too late I did not mail them.

____

____

____

____

____

____

Raising a family really is an easy task. Everyone thinks he knows the best way; anyone scarcely does it perfectly. Many people read Dr. Spock's book which presents clearly one accepted method. Everyone nearly has heard of that book at least.

No matter what method they follow, parents are advised constantly to be kind and affectionate toward their children. Some parents say after the baby is born their lives are changed completely for the better. They don't mind if the baby cries even. They rock the baby pacing the floor back to sleep. They accept the trouble calmly, knowing the baby will outgrow soon that stage. If they have prepared themselves for the new arrival as they could early and completely, they are never really upset almost by the little problems that come up.

These days, many people are trying health foods in all parts of the country. The "back to nature" movement has nearly affected everyone in one way or another. Producers of health foods use no perservatives in their products which they claim are bad for the system. Cereals such as granola a totally natural food are especially popular. People are also eating unstarched rice which is supposed to be good for the digestive system particularly. Ice cream even comes in new, natural flavours such as banana and coconut which is made with fresh bananas. Certainly health food companies are trying hard to attract customers interested in better nutrition.

CHAPTER 7

Dangling Modifiers

In Chapter 6, we saw the problems that can come from a misplaced modifier. If we read, "Running at 70 km per hour, I saw a cheetah," we may get a mental picture of an amazingly fast human. Still, with a bit of thought, we realize that it is the cheetah that is the speedy one. But what about this: "Running at 70 km per hour, it was time to take a picture." Who or what was running? We don't know; there is absolutely nothing in the sentence to tell us. What we have here is a *dangling modifier.* It is a modifier with nothing to refer to. But, as you will see, the problem is easy to recognize and easy to correct.

POINT 1 A modifier is said to be *dangling* when there is no word in the sentence for it to modify.

Waiting for the bus, it started to rain.

The modifier, *waiting for the bus,* does not modify anything. It seems to modify *it,* but there is no logical connection between the words. *Who* was waiting for the bus? We cannnot tell from this sentence.

Listening to records, my stereo blew a fuse.

Was the *stereo* listening to the records? Of course not. The modifier, *listening to records*, is dangling because there is no word in the sentence for it to modify. We simply do not know who was taking part in the action of listening.

At the age of three, my mother told me bedtime stories.

In this sentence, it seems as if *my mother* was three years old when she was telling bedtime stories to her child. This, of course, is impossible. Who or what was three years old? Clearly, it is the speaker. Thus, the sentence should be rewritten as

When I was three, my mother told me bedtime stories.
Running in the race, sweat formed on my brow.

What word does *running in the race* modify? Unless the *sweat* was running in the race – which is highly unlikely – we again have a dangling modifier. There is no word in the sentence for *running in the race* to modify.

Exercise: Point 1

Draw one line under the dangling modifier in each of the following sentences.

1. Driving in heavy traffic, my head started to ache.
2. Seasoning meat, pepper is often used.
3. Crossing the border, my bags were searched.
4. Choosing a career, my counsellor helped.
5. An iron was used, preparing my costume.
6. Mowing the lawn, lemonade is refreshing.
7. Examining philosophy, a text was helpful.
8. Thinking aloud, ideas came to me.
9. Suntan lotion helps, getting a tan.
10. Practising the piano, a metronome is useful.

Can you see why the modifier in each of these sentences is dangling?

POINT 2 **When a sentence begins with a group of words introduced by an *-ing* word, the person or thing performing the action (the subject) should be identified right after the *-ing* phrase.**

Pondering my future, a decision was reached.

The modifier, *pondering my future*, is dangling, since there is no word for it to modify. Clearly, *a decision* is not pondering my future. We must determine who or what is performing the action (who or what is pondering my future). It would make perfect sense for the subject to be *I*. Therefore, this sentence should be revised to read:

Pondering my future, I reached a decision.

The subject, *I*, is placed directly after the *-ing* phrase.

Expecting trouble, our plans were changed.

Again we have a dangling modifier in *expecting trouble.* Who or what was expecting trouble? We need a subject, and since the sentence refers to *our* plans, the subject should be *we*. The sentence should read:

Expecting trouble, *we* changed our plans.

Walking down the aisle, tickets were collected.

should be changed to

Walking down the aisle, the *conductor* collected tickets.

or

Walking down the aisle, *he* collected tickets.

- Notice that after the modifier, the subject introduces an *independent clause.* Notice also that a comma is placed between the modifier and the independent clause.

- *Remember:* Always ask *who* or *what* performs the action indicated by the modifier.

Exercise: Point 2

Write *DM* if the modifier is dangling or *C* if it has a subject to refer to and the sentence is, therefore, correct. Underline the subject.

__C__ 1. Chasing his sister, Billy fell and bruised his knee.

_____ 2. Feeling happy, cheers were given.

_____ 3. Running scared, the cat climbed up the tree.

_____ 4. Being alone, I spent the evening reading.

_____ 5. Laughing hysterically, the joke was repeated.

_____ 6. Following the recipe, Patty cooked a great meal.

_____ 7. Slipping on the ice, her leg was broken.

_____ 8. Rollerskating, knee pads are useful.

_____ 9. Appreciating the performance, the audience applauded.

_____ 10. Throwing curveballs, a young pitcher must be careful not to hurt his arm.

Review Exercise: Points 1 and 2

Complete these sentences by adding an independent clause with an appropriate subject.

1. Preparing to land, ____the pilot radioed the tower.____
2. Making a decision, ____________________

3. Training for the marathon, ____________________
4. Staring out the window, ____________________
5. Adjusting her rear-view mirror, ____________________
6. Checking my shoe size, ____________________
7. Following close behind, ____________________
8. Growing prematurely bald, ____________________
9. Crying in the crib, ____________________
10. Finally breaking through the clouds, ____________________

Another Review Exercise: Points 1 and 2

Complete these sentences in the same way you did those in the preceding exercise.

1. When ready, the dinner will be served.
2. Although a stranger, ____________________
3. At my high school graduation, ____________________
4. While shopping for a home computer, ____________________
5. From under the table, ____________________
6. In her younger days, ____________________
7. By the way you dress, ____________________
8. On my stereo television, ____________________
9. If damaged in shipment, ____________________
10. When used properly, ____________________

Sometimes the sentence has a word for the dangling phrase to modify, but it is in the wrong place. Therefore:

POINT 3 Put the modifier as close as possible to the word it explains.

This is the same rule we encountered in Chapter 6, when we were dealing with misplaced modifiers.

> Charging at the matador, the bull snorted and kicked.

Who or what was charging at the matador? The bull, of course. In this sentence, the modifier, *charging at the matador's* applies clearly to the word it modifies – *the bull.*

Attending college, four courses are taken by Ethel each semester.

Who or what is attending college? *Four courses* certainly are not. *Ethel* is attending college. In this sentence, it is not clear which noun the modifier applies to. The best way to correct this sentence is to rewrite the independent clause:

Attending college, Ethel takes four courses each semester.

Notice that in both corrected examples, the (former) dangling modifier modifies the subject of the main clause.

Exercise: Point 3

In all the following sentences, there are modifiers that do not apply clearly to the word they modify. Underline the subject and rewrite the sentence, making the modifier apply clearly to the word it modifies. If there is no subject, supply an appropriate one.

1. Reaching the finals, the game was won by the Tigers.

   Reaching the finals, the Tigers won the game.

2. Playing skillfully, a touchdown was made by the home team.

   ____

3. Shouting, an opinion was offered by Joe.

   ____

4. Painting the ceiling, her hair turned white.

   ____

5. Speaking for the community, the issue was raised by Mrs. Santos.

   ____

6. Losing his temper, shouts came from his father.

   ____

7. Running frantically, a loose shoelace tripped the ball carrier.

   ____

8. Being fond of romance, late-night movies appeal to Julie.

   ____

9. Endorsing the cheque and handing it to the teller, twenty dollars was paid to Alex.

   ____

10. Lighting the candle, hot wax got all over me.

___

POINT 4 Sometimes you can turn a dangling modifier into a dependent clause.

Refer back to Chapter 4, Point 3, if you need to refresh your memory about dependent clauses.

> Walking to school, a dog bit my ankle.

Here it seems as if the dog was walking to school, which is doubtful. The dangling modifier can be made into a dependent clause, and the sentence made into a correct one, by rewriting the sentence as follows:

> While I was walking to school, a dog bit my ankle.

The dependent clause *while I was walking to school* is placed next to *dog.* Obviously, it does not describe or modify the dog. Yet this is a correct sentence. Why? The answer is that a dependent clause is no longer a modifier, so it does not need to come at a precise place in the sentence. This sentence could just as well have been written:

> A dog bit my ankle while I was walking to school.
> Charging extra for delivery, the pizza is still reasonably priced.

may be changed to

> Although the restaurant charges extra for delivery, the pizza is still reasonably priced.

or

> The pizza is still reasonably priced, although the restaurant charges extra for delivery.
> When in high school, my grandmother gave me a fountain pen.

It is highly unlikely that the fountain pen was presented when the grandmother was in high school. This sentence should be changed to:

> When I was in high school, my grandmother gave me a fountain pen.

or

> When in high school, I was given a fountain pen by my grandmother.

Exercise: Point 4

Correct the following sentences by making the dangling modifier into a dependent clause. Rewrite the entire sentence in the space provided.

1. Fooling around, the lamps got broken.

While we were fooling around, the lamps got broken.

2. Dashing through the snow, a stone upset the sleigh.

____

3. Pedalling fiercely, my bicycle moved faster.

____

4. Eating dinner, the dishes got dirty.

____

5. Leaving the stadium, a section of the bleachers collapsed.

____

6. Taking out the garbage, snow started to fall.

____

7. Calling her on the phone for the first time, my throat was dry.

____

8. Watching a horror movie, her palms started to sweat.

____

9. Going into the sixth grade, my father's company transferred him to a different town.

____

10. Spending a lot of time partying, her grades slipped.

____

Review Exercise: Points 1–4

Revise the following sentences to eliminate the dangling modifiers.

1. Scoring in the final seconds, the game was won.

   Scoring in the final seconds, our team won the game.

2. Going to the grocery store, food for dinner was purchased.

____

3. Travelling alone, Air Canada took Ashoona from Fredericton to Halifax.

____

4. Running for mayor, handshakes were given to everyone by Ms. Lee.

____

5. Flexing his muscles, his biceps bulged.

____

6. Escaping from prison, the warden captured the convict.

____

7. Smiling broadly, her hair blew in the wind.

____

8. Recalling the past, a memory of her friend came to mind.

____

9. Crying and kicking, the parents sent the child to his room.

____

10. Smoking a cigar, the room started to stink.

____

In addition to groups of words beginning with an *-ing* word, there are other types of modifiers which dangle if the writer is not careful. Each of these types is described in one of the following points.

POINT 5 **A group of words that has an *-ing* word *somewhere* in it must refer clearly to the subject of the sentence.**

After **sneezing,** my handkerchief was used.

The modifier, *sneezing,* seems to apply to *handkerchief.* Handkerchiefs, however, do not sneeze all by themselves. As was the case with the other dangling modifiers, we need a subject. This sentence may be revised to read,

After sneezing, **I** used my handkerchief.

The addition of the subject, *I,* makes the sentence complete and correct. *I* was the one who did the sneezing.

Before eating, her hands are washed.

should be changed to

Before eating, she washes her hands.

Remember: The *-ing* word tells us that there is some action taking place; it is important to identify *who* or *what* takes part in this action.

Exercise: Point 5

Complete these sentences.

1. Since moving to Manitoba, *I have learned to appreciate open land.*
2. Before selecting a business partner, ______
3. While waiting for the Eatons service technician. ______
4. After getting a credit card, ______
5. By having the oil filter changed, ______
6. On hearing about your divorce, ______
7. While installing a skylight in my house, ______
8. While riding my bicycle, ______
9. Since moving to the country, ______
10. By choosing to live in Dawson Creek, ______

POINT 6 **Modifiers beginning with a *to* form of a verb must refer clearly to the word they modify. That is, like other modifiers, they should be placed as close as possible to the word they modify.**

To see Jupiter, a telescope is necessary.

The modifier, *to see Jupiter,* cannot logically apply to *telescope.* A telescope does not see Jupiter. The sentence may be rewritten as follows:

To see Jupiter, one must use a telescope.

Now we have a subject — *one.* Who or what is seeing Jupiter? One — that is, someone — is.

To play tennis, a racquet is necessary.

The racquet itself certainly doesn't play tennis. Only people can play. Thus, we need a subject for the modifier, *to play tennis,* to apply to. The sentence might read,

To play tennis, **you** need a racquet.

To answer the question, Chapter Six should have been read.

should be changed to

To answer the question, students should have read Chapter Six.

Exercise: Point 6

Complete these sentences.

1. To appreciate the music, you should turn up the volume.
2. To clean the roof gutters, ______
3. To be a good friend, ______
4. To stay healthy, ______
5. To understand poetry, ______
6. To find the secret of life, ______
7. To avoid trouble, ______
8. To play professional baseball, ______
9. To prepare lasagna, ______
10. To finish a cabinet, ______

Review Exercise: Points 1–6

Rewrite the following sentences, eliminating any dangling modifiers.

1. Skating on the frozen pond, his ankles buckled.
   While he was skating on the frozen pond, his ankles buckled.
2. To run for public office, certain requirements must be met.
   ______
3. After putting up a scarecrow, the birds tore it apart.
   ______
4. While marching in the parade, the drum Carl was playing broke.
   ______
5. Jumping rope, Andrea's ankle was sprained.
   ______
6. To make a decision, convictions must be firm.
   ______
7. To go camping, a tent and a flashlight are necessary.
   ______

8. When reading the book, the character reminded me of you.

____

9. Driving in Winnipeg, a cat was hit by Mr. Al-Raschid.

____

10. To pass this course, one paper each week is required.

____

HOW TO AVOID DANGLING MODIFIERS

1. Ask yourself if there is a word in the sentence for the modifier to refer to.
2. Put the modifier as close as possible to the word it explains.
3. Solve the problem by rewriting the dangling modifier as a dependent clause.

Chapter Review

I. Circle the modifier and draw an arrow from it to the word it modifies.

1. Making a pizza, the chef flipped the dough into the air.
2. To learn to play the violin, a fellow must have patience and neighbours who really like him.
3. To work up a sweat, Reynaldo jogs four kilometres.
4. Since starting college, Su Mei has learned the meaning of hard work.
5. While filling the gas tank, the attendant told us about the new show in town.
6. Barking furiously, the puppy chased the cat.
7. Pretending to be asleep, she listened to the transistor radio.
8. Before finding a parking space, they had driven around the block three times.
9. Not paying attention, the students dozed off.
10. To relax, you can put your feet up and read a good book.

II. Fill in the blank with an appropriate subject.

1. Barking and wagging his tail, ________________ showed his affection for his master.
2. Swerving to the left, ________________ hit a lamppost.

3. To be a movie star, ________________ need good looks and talent.
4. When lost in a strange city, ________________ always use my CB to get directions.
5. In northern Saskatchewan, ________________ is generally very cold, and there is always a lot of snow.
6. Playing his role, ________________ persuaded the audience that he really was Hamlet.
7. After dialing the wrong number, ________________ asked the operator for assistance.
8. When scrambled with cheese and onions, ________________ are absolutely delicious.
9. At the age of sixty, ________________ retired from her job.
10. Using his professional knowledge, ________________ repaired our leaky tap.

III. Complete these sentences.

1. By sending her children to camp, ________________
2. To make a Spanish omelet, ________________
3. After realizing he had made the wrong turn, ________________
4. When Kitty voices her opinion, ________________
5. When feeling depressed, ________________
6. Thinking of you, ________________
7. On being appointed president of the club, ________________
8. While working in that restaurant, ________________
9. To cancel your appointment, ________________
10. During her career as a newscaster, ________________
11. Ordering everyone around, ________________
12. Scrubbing the kitchen floor, ________________
13. To lend me a hand in this job, ________________

14. After vacationing in Canada, ______________________________

15. At the age of twelve, ______________________________

16. Expecting to see her boyfriend,______________________________

17. To change engine oil, ______________________________

18. When looking up a word in the dictionary, ______________________________

19. Seeing his arch rival, ______________________________

20. To show me that you love me,______________________________

IV. Write *C* if the sentence is correct as it stands. Write *D* if it contains a dangling modifier and underline the word that the modifier is supposed to modify. If the sentence contains no such word, put a circle around the *D*.

_______ 1. Risking his life, the passengers were saved by the captain.

_______ 2. Speeding on his motorcycle, the police officer gave him a ticket.

_______ 3. To make a good impression, you should wear a tie.

_______ 4. After crossing the finish line, the officials awarded a medal to the winner.

_______ 5. To learn to play a musical instrument, lessons are helpful.

_______ 6. Before going down into the cave, our backpacks were secured.

_______ 7. After lighting his cigarette, the match went out.

_______ 8. Seeing my wife, I raced to her arms.

_______ 9. Before losing your temper, you should find out exactly what happened .

_______ 10. When cooked properly, I love to eat chicken.

V. All the following sentences contain dangling modifiers. Rewrite each sentence, eliminating the dangling modifier.

1. Forgetting his meal ticket, lunch was not given to the student.

____

2. Before pruning the trees, the blades had to be sharpened.

____

3. To get the student rate, certain requirements must be met.

____

4. When playing the guitar, finger picks are often used.

____

5. Driving at night, his vision was impaired.

____

6. While making the frappe, the blender broke.

____

7. At the age of six, my finger was fractured.

____

8. Sailing on the lake, her hat blew away.

____

9. To lose weight, a diet must be followed.

____

10. To play golf, a set of clubs is necessary.

____

11. Before hitting the jackpot, a good-luck dance was performed.

____

12. While laid up in a cast, the nurse told me to take it easy.

____

13. Since firing Ben, business has improved.

____

14. By considering the options, a decision was made.

____

15. Being a pirate, a patch covered his right eye.

____

16. Foaming at the mouth, the dogcatcher chased the rabid dog.

____

17. Exploding in brilliant colours, the crowd watched the fireworks on Canada Day.

____

18. To put the car in reverse, the stick shift must be used.

____

19. When tired and hungry, a ham and cheese sandwich really hits the spot.

____

20. In setting a table, forks, knives, and spoons must be placed correctly.

____

VI. Rewrite the following passages, correcting any sentences which contain dangling modifiers.

On arriving in Canada, the sights and sounds amazed Pierre. Having travelled alone, so many people hurrying around and shouting came as a jolt to him. Coming from a small village in the south of France, so much commotion had never before been witnessed by the young traveller. And being only eight years old and a bit nervous, his luggage seemed to be his only companion. On this trip, his cousins in Quebec City would be his hosts. After looking for them at the gate, and not being able to find them, an attendant took him to the information booth. Over the loudspeaker, Pierre's cousins were paged. To locate them, an announcement had to be made twice by the attendant. Then, running through the terminal, from the other end of the building, Pierre recognized his relatives. Feeling relieved, Pierre ran to them and escaped the crazy crowds of Canada.

____

____

____

____

____

____

____

____

____

____

____

____

____

____

____

To throw a successful party, several factors must be taken into consideration. When making up a list of people to invite, they should be compatible. After deciding on the guests, the amount of food and drink must be decided. If preparing a fruit punch, a large bowl and a ladle are necessary. To save money, a fruit punch is often better than serving everyone individual cocktails. Preparing the food in advance is also a good idea. When planning the meal, the number of guests must, of course, be considered. By cooking ahead of time, a lot of bother may be avoided. To make a suggestion, lasagna is always a favourite. When a host serves punch and lasagna, you can be almost certain that the party will be a success.

As a way of fighting the high cost of travel and of conserving fuel, smaller automobiles are common. On the highway, mileage is improved in a small car. In the city, when driving in traffic, gasoline is saved. After an average of 15 000 kilometres of rolling on the roads, the driver should bring his small car in for a tuneup. After receiving the proper care, any car owner will find that his vehicle is ready for continued efficient use. When you think about it, the day of the big car is gone.

CHAPTER 8

Pronouns and Faulty Pronoun Reference

Suppose I run into you in the hallway and say, "Hey, I saw Bill and Jim yesterday, and he has a great new job!" Your response will probably be, "*Who* has a great new job? Bill or Jim?" If I answer, "Bill, of course," you will be quite justified in saying that there is no "of course" about it. From my original sentence, you could not possibly tell whether "he" referred to Bill or to Jim. This is an example of *faulty pronoun reference.*

A *pronoun* is a word that can be substituted for a noun. Pronouns are valuable because they save a lot of clumsy repetition. Instead of saying, "That's Virginia's dorm. Virginia lives on the second floor, and Virginia keeps a cat in Virginia's room," we can say, "That's Virginia's dorm. She lives on the second floor, and she keeps a cat in her room."

But like other parts of a sentence, pronouns must be used correctly. Otherwise the meaning of the sentence will not be clear. The basic rule is simple: Make sure the pronoun refers clearly to the noun whose place it takes in a sentence.

POINT 1 A pronoun may be used as the subject of a sentence.

- *Remember:* A subject tells who or what is taking part in the action described by the verb.

Ronnie works on a farm.

Ronnie is the subject of the sentence.

He works on a farm.

The pronoun, *he*, takes the place of *Ronnie*, and becomes the subject.

> **Shirley and Ruth** went to the movies.
> **They** went to the movies.

The pronoun, *they*, takes the place of *Shirley and Ruth*, and becomes the subject.

Pronouns as subjects were discussed in Chapter 3, Point 2. Look back to that section if you need to refresh your memory.

Exercise: Point 1

Rewrite each of the following sentences, using a single pronoun as the subject.

1. Andy's parents are going on a vacation.

   They are going on a vacation.

2. You and I will haul this stuff to the dump.

   ____

3. Brenda is learning how to water-ski.

   ____

4. The car antenna has been snapped in half.

   ____

5. The union members are planning a strike.

   ____

6. My uncle served in Holland with the Canadian army.

   ____

7. Mary's parents are celebrating an anniversary.

   ____

8. Sally, Art, and I spent the day at the Glenbow Museum.

   ____

9. His sister is going for her Ph.D. at Dalhousie University.

   ____

10. Weightlifting gives Fritz great pleasure.

    ____

POINT 2 A pronoun may be used as the *object* of a verb in a sentence.

An *object* is a word (or a group of words) that is affected by the action of a verb.

To determine the subject of a sentence, we ask who or what performed the action. To determine the object of a sentence, we ask who or what was affected by the action.

Steve rode the horse.

Who or what performed the action? Steve rode the horse; therefore *Steve is* the subject. Who or what was affected by the action? The horse was affected by Steve's action; therefore *the horse* is the object.

Cathy cooked breakfast.

Can you identify the subject and the object in this sentence?

Objects are also used following such words as *in, on, by, at, to, for, around, between, near, among, through, upon.*

Gene went to the game.

Gene is the subject; *game* is the object.

The rabbit ran through our yard.

Rabbit is the subject; *yard* is the object.

You already know what pronouns can be used as subjects. For objects, you must use a different set of pronouns.

Subjects	Objects
I	me
you	you
he	him
she	her
it	it
we	us
you	you
they	them

▸ To take the place of a noun that is affected by the action of a verb, always use an object pronoun. Use object pronouns following such words as *in, on, by,* and so on.

Jack repaired the broken **window.**

Jack is the subject; *window* is the object.

Jack repaired **it.**

Jack is the subject; *it* is the object.

He repaired the **window.**

He is the subject; *window* is the object.

He repaired **it**.

He is the subject; *it* is the object.

Marcia spoke to **Mr. Otis**.

Marcia is the subject; *Mr. Otis* is the object.

Marcia spoke to **him**.
She spoke to Mr. Otis.
She spoke to **him**.

Exercise: Point 2

Rewrite the following sentences, changing all the nouns to pronouns.

1. Lori hit George with a stick.

   She hit him with it.

2. I wrote a poem about my girlfriend.

   ____

3. The twins starred in the school play.

   ____

4. Ms. Alexander bought that sofa.

   ____

5. Robbie paid for that suit.

   ____

6. The police officer told Jim and Carl to move their van right away.

   ____

7. Lou and Barbara called Danielle and me.

   ____

8. Danielle and I called Lou and Barbara.

   ____

9. Do you smoke that hand-carved pipe?

   ____

10. Honesty is important to Jane and Max.

    ____

Review Exercise: Points 1 and 2

Fill in the blank with a pronoun that can take the place of the noun given in the parentheses.

1. ____We____ (Al and I) bought ____them____ (those records) yesterday.

2. ________ (Jane White) used to be married to ________ (Joe Brown).

3. ________ (the toy) is a present from ________ (my grandmother).

4. ________ (my brothers) confronted my mother about ________ (the situation).

5. ________ (Sridath) planted ________ (flowers) in his garden.

6. ________ (Some officials) claim that ________ (marijuana) is bad for your health.

7. ________ (Petra) purchased ________ (a clock radio) for ________ (her father).

8. ________ (the ashtray) is filled with ________ (cigar butts).

9. ________ (Viktor) took ________ (the picture) of ________ (Pearl and Amos).

10. ________ (Joey and I) met near ________ (the river).

POINT 3 **Often a sentence contains both a noun and a pronoun that refers to the noun. To decide whether to use a subject pronoun or an object pronoun. Look at the pronoun's relation to *its own verb*.**

Carla brought the ice cream and the boys thanked her.

The pronoun *her* refers to Carla. *Carla* is the subject of the verb *brought*, but *her* is the object of the verb *thanked*. Therefore an object pronoun is needed.

Usually, you can *hear* the correct choice of pronoun. You would never write:

> Carla brought the ice cream and the boys thanked *she.*

> I saw Mel yesterday and he told me about his trip.

The pronoun *he* is the subject of *told,* so a subject pronoun is needed.

Exercise: Point 3

Fill in the blank with the appropriate pronoun, and underline the word to which it refers. Mark *S* or *O* above the noun and the pronoun to show whether each is a subject or an object. Some sentences have more than one blank.

1. The boat drifted for three weeks before the Canadian coast guard found it.
2. I entered a dress in the design contest and ________________ won second prize.
3. Martha and I are going to Mexico this summer; her cousins will join ________________ there.
4. Tom and his friend just left for Camrose, where ________________ hope to find summer jobs.
5. If ________________ can find the money, Dolores hopes to go back to school next year.
6. Larry has gotten interested in skate boarding; it seems as if everyone is trying ________________ .
7. Willie's adviser told ________________ that he has to pass this course if ________________ wants to be a physical therapist.
8. Sandra had a flat tire last night. ________________ had to change ________________ in the pouring rain, while other cars kept passing ________________ .
9. I want to go to the movie, but I have a big test in consumer economics tomorrow. Oh, well, I'll be back in time to study for ________________ .
10. I need to get a notebook and some pens at the bookstore. Having spent all my money on that trip yesterday, I'll have to charge ________________ .

POINT 4 **When a sentence contains two or more nouns, place the pronoun as close as possible to the noun it refers to, and make sure the reference is clear.**

When the fans met the players, they were excited.

Who was excited? Was it the fans or the players? We cannot tell, because *they* could refer to either *fans* or *players.* We could rewrite the sentence this way:

The fans were excited when they met the players.

Now we know that the fans were the ones who were excited. Or

The players were excited when they met the fans.

In this case, *they* refers to *players.*

On the other hand, what about this sentence?

When Dave met the players, they were excited.

Now it is clear that the players were excited. *Players* is the only noun in this sentence to which *they* can refer.

Sentences with *told, said to,* and similar words need to be fixed differently.

Cindy told Marie that she was jealous.

Whom does the pronoun *she* refer to? Was it Cindy or Marie who was jealous? We cannot tell. In this sentence, there is nowhere else to put the pronoun *she.* We might rewrite it like this:

Cindy told Marie, "I am jealous."

Now it is clear that Cindy is the one who is jealous. The pronoun *I* refers to Cindy. Or, on the other hand,

Cindy told Marie, "You are jealous."

You refers to Marie, so now it is Marie who is jealous.

The words inside the " " marks in these sentences are *quotations.* The " " marks, or *quotation marks,* tell us that these are the exact words the person spoke. We will have more to say about quotations in Chapter 11.

Exercise: Point 4

All the following sentences contain faulty pronoun references. Rewrite each sentence, making the pronoun references clear. There may be more than one correct way to rewrite the sentence. Choose one.

1. Stan told Barbara that she would be elected class president.

   Stan told Barbara, "You will be elected class president."

2. He added pepper and salt and then some more of it.

   ____

3. When the Blue Bombers played the Lions, they won.

____

4. Before Ms. Rae adopted Marie, she lived in an orphanage.

____

5. When Bill finally approached his father, he felt great.

____

6. When the car hit the telephone pole, it was damaged.

____

7. When my mother scolded my little sister, she was quite upset.

____

8. Paul told his nephew that he would be great Canadian some day.

____

9. The doctor told her patient that she would have to take some time off.

____

10. When the boys asked the girls to dance, they were embarrassed.

____

Review Exercise: Points 1–4

Underline the pronoun in each of the following sentences and draw an arrow from it to the noun it refers to. Mark *S* in the blank if the pronoun is used as a subject or *O* if it is used as an object. (Some sentences have more than one pronoun.)

___O___ 1. The counsellor called one of the boys and sent him to find Jim.

______ 2. Lee called and said she will be here by seven.

______ 3. The traffic gets very bad on Sherbrooke St. around nine in the morning; Anita avoids it by leaving early.

______ 4. The premier was glad when his bill was passed; he had put a lot of work into it.

______ 5. Eddie said to Ivan, "You're a real friend to stand by me this way."

______ 6. The vase broke when the wind knocked it over.

_______ 7. Craig acted shy when Gail asked him to dance.

_______ 8. Dave and Sandy, can you lend a hand with this box of books?

_______ 9. Carol told her parents that she was leaving home.

_______ 10. The carton had to be taped when the bottom of it fell out.

POINT 5 Be sure that pronouns refer to a single noun and not to a whole idea.

Such words as *it, this, that,* and *which* should not be used to refer to a whole idea.

The weather was going to be beautiful, which made me very happy.

Which, in this example, refers to an entire idea rather than to a single noun. This is a faulty pronoun reference. The sentence may be rewritten:

I was very happy that the weather was going to be beautiful.
Barney said he is sure that Charles can't do the work. **This** is untrue.

What is untrue? Is it untrue that Barney is sure, or is it untrue that Charles can't do the work? The faulty pronoun reference makes it impossible to tell. The sentence may be rewritten as follows:

It is untrue that Barney said he is sure Charles can't do the work.

or

Barney was mistaken when he said he is sure that Charles can't do the work.

Exercise: Point 5

Write *C* if the pronoun reference is correct or *F* if the pronoun reference is faulty. Underline the pronoun *(it, this, that,* or *which),* and circle the word or whole idea it refers to.

__F__ 1. The class show was a great success, which greatly pleased all who worked on it.

_______ 2. He hadn't heard about the change in plans, which caused him to be late.

_______ 3. It made her angry that the mattress did not arrive on the day it was supposed to.

_______ 4. People continue to drive after drinking. This is ridiculous.

_______ 5. Every Canadian has the chance to be whatever he or she chooses. This is one of the basic concepts of democracy.

_______ 6. Buses never seem to keep to the schedules anymore. It is really getting out of hand.

_______ 7. I miss my family, and that is why I go home for the holidays every year.

_______ 8. She takes a ballet lesson every Thursday, which helps to strengthen her leg muscles.

_______ 9. When I was younger, my mother always bugged me about keeping my room clean. But this changed as I grew older and more mature.

_______ 10. He always carries a calculator with him, which makes his work a lot easier.

POINT 6 Be sure that a pronoun has a word, and not an unexpressed idea, to refer to.

To get a job in a department store, you have to dress the way **they** tell you to.

Who are *they?* Are *they* a department store? We have here a faulty pronoun reference, because *they* does not refer to any particular word in the sentence. Instead, it refers to an idea that has not been expressed. The sentence may be rewritten:

To get a job in a department store, you have to dress the way the managers tell you to.

Kate *is* always happy to see me, but **it** rarely shows.

To what word does *it* refer? Remember, pronouns refer to nouns. Is *happy* a noun? Since there is no noun for *it* to refer to, the pronoun reference is faulty. The sentence may be rewritten as follows:

Kate is always happy to see me, but her happiness rarely shows.

Her happiness has taken the place of *it.*

I don't mind going to the dentist's office, because **he** is so friendly.

Is *he* a dentist's office?

Because the dentist is so friendly, I don't mind going to his office.

Exercise: Point 6

All the following sentences contain faulty pronoun references. Identify the word to which the pronoun *should* refer by answering the question following each sentence.

1. Joseph is nervous about the upcoming event, but *it* doesn't show.

   What is *it*? his nervousness

2. Whenever I swim in Lake Huron, *they* always nip at my feet.

   Who are *they*? ______

3. Paula bought some red dye for her hair so she could become *one*.

   What is *one*? ______

4. He joined the fraternity at Western because *they* enjoy the same things he does.

   Who are *they*? ______

5. Although he made *one*, he was intimidated by all the home-run hitters in the lineup.

   What is *one*? ______

6. Some teachers feel that their students are lazy, and that *it* is the result of too many hours spent watching television.

   What is *it*? ______

7. To avoid getting penalized for a late return, you have to send *them* your income tax forms by April 30.

   What are *they*? ______

8. The concert was sold out, so we will have to see *them* some other time.

   Who are *they*? ______

9. Her sandwich was stale, but *it* was because she had not wrapped it properly.

   What is *it*? ______

10. When we flew to Europe, I was surprised at how quickly *it* went.

    What is *it*? ______

Review Exercise: Points 1–6

To make use of the work you have done in the last two exercises, choose five sentences from the Point 5 exercise and five sentences from the Point 6 exercise, and rewrite them correctly in the following space. Number the sentences you choose by point number and sentence number.

1. *(5,1) Everyone who worked in the class show was pleased that it was a great success.*

2.

3.

4.

5.

6.

7.

8.

9.

10.

HOW TO AVOID TROUBLE WITH PRONOUNS

1. To decide whether you should use a subject or an object pronoun, think of the pronoun's relation to *its own verb*.
2. Be clear about which noun in the sentence each pronoun refers to.
3. Use a pronoun to refer to a single noun, not a group of words.

Chapter Review

I. Circle the correct pronoun given in the parentheses.

1. (I, me) plan to improve my grades next semester.
2. (She, her) sent (I, me) a package in the mail.
3. Have you seen (he, him) lately?
4. Ling is somewhere around; have you seen (she, her)?
5. The commanding officer gave (him, he) a real bawling out.
6. They told (us, we) to look for (they, them) after the show.
7. (They, them) invited (we, us) over for cocktails.
8. I will never speak to (they, them) again.
9. Adrian chose (he, him) and (I, me) for teammates.
10. The bullies on the beach were bothering (we, us).
11. (We, us) don't know what is good for (we, us).
12. Federico saw (she, her) standing on the corner.
13. (They, them) will have to figure that out for themselves.
14. Maxine tried to visit (he, him) in the hospital, but the nurses would not let (she, her) in.
15. (He, him) and (I, me) are on the same bowling team.
16. Either (she, her) or (I, me) will have to save the seats while (he, him) gets the popcorn.
17. (We, us) wanted our luggage returned to (we, us).
18. Oksana has an amusing hobby; (her, she) collects toy hippopotamuses.
19. (He, him) is the best driver I know.
20. Both (we, us) and (they, them) had the chance to appear on a television game show.

II. Fill in the blank with an appropriate pronoun.

1. After spending two hours in the sun, ________________ discovered that her back was badly burned.

2. We noticed that the turtle's shell was pink and purple, and we realized that ______________________ had been painted.

3. Since the family moved to a new apartment, ______________________ have been happier than ever.

4. The children were frightened when the pony chased ______________ .

5. When Tony dated ______________________ , Sylvia was only sixteen years old.

6. Marco admitted that ______________________ was the one who made the phony phone call.

7. It was our turn to get the hot dogs, so ______________________ piled into Alan's car.

8. Theresa said to Judy, "______________________ are the only one who will understand my problem."

9. Cheryl discovered that her new job with its overwhelming demands was simply too much for ______________________ .

10. Barry found his Swiss army knife in the drawer with a pile of T-shirts on top of ______________________ .

III. Write *C* if the pronoun reference is clear or *F* if it is faulty. Be prepared to defend your answers.

_______ 1. Tom had had enough of school, which is why he decided to join the Royal Canadian Navy.

_______ 2. He used a hacksaw instead of a wood saw to cut through the wire fence. This is an example of clear thinking.

_______ 3. Donna is able to design and sew her own clothes. It is one way to save money.

_______ 4. Jake told his brother that he ought to get out and enjoy the fresh air.

_______ 5. Ted threw the plate through the window and broke it.

_______ 6. After I talked with the therapist, she told me to come back once a week for consultation.

_______ 7. A rolling stone gathers no moss, which is why one must always be on the go.

_______ 8. There is never enough time to see all my friends when I come to town. It is a real shame.

_______ 9. Jim told his father that he should learn to type.

_______ 10. Sue has always enjoyed helping people, and she plans to study medicine when she completes her undergraduate studies.

_______ 11. I have a bucket, but it has a hole in it.

_______ 12. He joined a commune because they share everything there.

_______ 13. Life is peaceful on a farm, which is one good reason to escape the rat race of the city.

_______ 14. After I heard Leona Boyd play the guitar, I decided that that was what I wanted to be.

_______ 15. Wheat is one grain from which they make bread.

_______ 16. There is relatively little traffic in the sky, which is one reason air travel is safer than driving.

_______ 17. I scored twenty points because I was very good at it.

_______ 18. When he worked with clay, he could mold it beautifully.

_______ 19. Gus told Jerome that he was an expert marksman.

_______ 20. Mike told Alice that she was the most intelligent person he had ever met.

IV. Rewrite the following sentences, eliminating any faulty pronoun references.

1. I changed my mind about buying a motorcycle, which pleased my wife.

____

2. When he put the saw on the shelf, it fell down.

____

3. Betty told Jenny that she was the best cook in the world.

4. I bought a new pair of sneakers, but my old ones are still pretty good, so I always wear them.

5. We could not find a parking space, which was why we were late.

6. Gene loves nature. That is why he moved there.

7. She told her sister that she had found true love.

8. I brought the broken tool to the hardware store because I don't know how to do it.

9. In Moosonee they have plenty of snow.

10. As soon as I pumped up the tires, I went for a ride on it.

11. She appeared in a play at the Stratford Festival, which was her debut.

12. When I used that coupon, it drove my wife crazy.

13. Vincent told Stephen that he was awarded a medal of honour.

14. Rudy said that he had heard I was moving to Nova Scotia. This is untrue.

15. He pays a great deal of attention to his children, which is what makes him a good father.

16. Oscar is happiest when he is working, but it never shows.

17. I knew the president of the company, which is how I got the job.

18. Sally told her mother that her plans were outrageous.

19. When I went to the supermarket, I was happy to see that they had gone down in price.

20. Two plus two equals four, which is an elementary fact in mathematics.

V. Rewrite these passages, eliminating any faulty pronoun references.

When I first learned to drive a car, it was a harrowing experience. I took ten weeks of lessons at a driving school, which were very helpful. But it was not until I was preparing for my road test that I found out how inexperienced I really was. That was really the problem.

In my last trial run, I backed the car out of my driveway and hit a lamppost, but it was not badly damaged. That was only the beginning. I finally got the car moving smoothly, and was nervous about running into something else, but I didn't let it show. I was cruising along at 40 kilometres per hour with the radio playing, which always helped me to calm down. A police officer who was patrolling the neighbourhood must have thought I was going too slowly and pulled me over. We talked for a few minutes, and it turned out to be rather helpful: he suggested I use the headlights while driving at night.

When I was informed of the rally, it was an exciting event. As soon as I heard about the demonstration, I got them ready. They had shiny leather tops, brand-new laces, and thick rubber soles, which put me into the right frame of mind for walking. I really believed in the cause, which was why I looked forward to the march with great anticipation. Sometimes I get weary during a long walk, but I never let it show. Besides, this was a truly important demonstration! When I slid my feet into my shoes, this time they did not ache at all.

The nine-to-five workday, which millions of Canadians experience five times a week, may be slowly dying out, which would make many people very happy. Employers are telling their employees that they could use some extra time to themselves. A four-day workweek may be with us shortly, and they are pleased to have the chance to spend more time with their families. Fathers and mothers will be able to take up new hobbies and pursue new interests, and it will serve to improve the health of many people. This applies to both physical and mental health. Working fewer hours would make millions of people very happy, but it would have to go along with a promise of no drop in income. There are still some problems in setting up the shortened working schedule, but they are confident that as the need for it becomes more apparent, it will come about.

CHAPTER 9

Faulty Parallelism

Many sentences contain what we might call *parallel thoughts.* For example, you might say, "Lee had a great time scuba-diving and water-skiing on her vacation." *Scuba-diving* and *water-skiing* are parallel thoughts; that is, they are both things that Lee had a great time doing. By expressing both of them with *-ing* words, the sentence emphasizes this parallelism. A clumsier way of saying the same thing might be, "Lee had a great time scuba-diving and also she water-skied during her vacation." Here the two parallel thoughts are expressed in nonparallel forms of words, and the sense of their parallel relationship is weakened.

POINT 1 When elements are parallel in thought, use parallel forms to express them.

cooking, eating, cleaning

All the elements in this series are *-ing* words; they are arranged in a parallel structure.

to cook, to eat, to clean

All the elements are *to* forms of verbs; their structure is parallel.

have cooked, have eaten, have cleaned

Again, a parallel structure.

pretty, tall, friendly

All are words that are used to describe a person. These modifiers are arranged in a parallel structure.

If one form of a verb is mixed with another form of the same verb in a sentence, the parallel structure is lost:

cooking, to eat, have cleaned

Now the elements are of different forms; there is no parallel structure in this series.

▸ *Remember:* When you make any kind of list, put all the items in the same form.

Exercise: Point 1

Fill in the blank with the correct form of the verb given in the parentheses. The first verb in the series will tell you which form to use. Be sure to maintain parallel structure.

1. dancing, singing (sing), laughing (laugh)
2. to blend, ______ (mix), ______ (stir)
3. pushed, ______ (pull), ______ (shove)
4. have written, ______ (stamp), ______ (send)
5. fed, ______ (swallow), ______ (digest)
6. building, ______ (paint), ______ (whitewash)
7. rose, ______ (sink), ______ (reappear)
8. to love, ______ (honour), ______ (obey)
9. drove, ______ (park), ______ (pay)
10. living, ______ (laugh), ______ (love)

POINT 2 **Balance a noun with a noun, a verb with a verb, a modifier with a modifier, and so on.**

Whenever possible, words of the same kind should be used to do the same kinds of jobs in a sentence.

She is **charming** and **beautiful.**

In this sentence, *charming*, an *-ing* word, is balanced with *beautiful.* They are in parallel structure, however, because they are both modifiers; that is, they both describe a person.

She **is charming** and **has beauty**.

Both phrases describe her, but *charming* is a modifier, whereas *beauty is* a noun. Therefore, the sentence has now lost its parallel structure.

We like **tacos** and **to eat enchiladas**.

Tacos is a noun; *to eat enchiladas* is a combination of a verb form and a noun. Is this sentence in parallel structure?

We like tacos and enchiladas.

Does this sentence have parallel structure? What words are parallel? What kind of words are they?

We like to eat tacos and enchiladas.

Although this sentence may appear to have faulty parallelism, it actually does have a parallel structure. In this case, *tacos* and *enchiladas* are objects of the verb *to eat.* What do we like to eat? We like to eat tacos and we also like to eat enchiladas.

Exercise: Point 2

Add one element to each series. Make sure that the new element is parallel to those provided.

1. hungry, thirsty, tired
2. proud, brave, ____
3. brunette, brown-eyed, ____
4. weaving, crocheting, ____
5. bought, traded, ____
6. to replace, to repair, ____
7. playing baseball, playing football, ____
8. exciting, fantastic, ____
9. planting, reaping, ____
10. dreamed, desired, ____

POINT 3 Use parallel constructions for words joined by such connectors as *and, but, nor, or.*

I enjoy **reading, writing,** and **conducting** experiments in a laboratory.

Note that the three elements are all *-ing* words. This sentence contains proper parallelism.

Our baby is **cute** and **behaves well**.

In this example, the parallelism is faulty. *Cute* is a modifier; *behaves well* is a form of a verb. This sentence may be rewritten as follows:

Our baby is **cute** and **well behaved**.

Now we have two modifiers describing the baby; the parallelism is proper.

Whenever I try to talk to him he is crabby, busy, or doesn't know what to say.

Crabby and *busy* are both modifiers, but *doesn't know what to say* is a form of a verb. It would be hard to find a modifier that would take the place of the verb form here. Instead, the sentence might be rewritten thus:

Whenever I try to talk to him he is crabby or busy or else he doesn't know what to say.

Now *crabby* and *busy* are parallel modifiers joined by *or,* whereas *he is* and *he does know* are parallel subjects and verbs joined by *or else.*

Exercise: Point 3

Complete the following sentences by filling in the blanks. Be sure to maintain parallel structure. Underline the original part of the sentence to which your addition is parallel.

1. Eduardo has always enjoyed fishing and ___hunting___.
2. You can see the moon and ________________ in the sky tonight.
3. As an accountant, Phyllis adds and ________________ figures all day long.
4. I will probably be washing the dishes or ________________ when you arrive.
5. He is old but ________________.
6. Filling the gas tank and ________________ are two of the responsibilities of a gas station attendant.

7. A teacher expects his students to do their homework, to attend classes regularly, and ________________ .
8. Before she left, she combed her hair, polished her fingernails, and ________________ .
9. When customers are not satisfied, they return the merchandise or ________________ .
10. The day is sunny, hot, and ________________ .

Review Exercise: Points 1–3

All the following sentences contain errors in parallel structure. Revise and rewrite the sentences in the space provided.

1. Put the cheese between two slices of bread and frying it.
   Put the cheese between two slices of bread and fry it.
2. He was a good lecturer, a kind man, and he worked hard.
   ____
3. A lifeguard supervises the beach, is flirting with girls, and rescues swimmers who are having difficulty.
   ____
4. Lynn is preparing her résumé, reading the want ads, and she will go for interviews.
   ____
5. A good friend is thoughtful, truthful, and he supports you.
   ____
6. I enjoy seeing shows, to read a good book, and going to the movies.
   ____
7. To be a doctor, one must have ambition, persistence, and be willing to work long hours.
   ____
8. The cat purred, meowed, and cleaning itself.
   ____
9. He was forced to pawn his watch, sell his radio, and trying to find a new job.
   ____

10. To be or not being; that is the question.

____

POINT 4 Use parallel structure with such constructions as *either. . .or, neither. . .nor, not. . . but, not only. . .but also, both. . .and.*

Either **going for a ride** or **to lie in the sun** is my idea of a good time.

This sentence may be rewritten,

Either **going for a ride** or **lying in the sun** is my idea of a good time.

Now the two elements are in a parallel structure.

Not only was he a great man, but also an excellent writer.

What is wrong with the parallelism here? *Was he a great man* contains both a subject—*he*—and a verb—*was; an excellent writer* contains neither. This is an especially common error. The sentence may be rewritten as

He was not only a great man but also an excellent writer.

Now the subject and verb have been moved out of the parallel sections, and there is proper parallelism between *a great man* and *an excellent writer.* Or

Not only was he a great man but he was also an excellent writer.

Now each clause has a subject and a verb; again there is proper parallelism.

Exercise: Point 4

Write *P* if the sentence has proper parallelism or *X* if the parallelism is faulty.

_______ 1. Either you come here or I will go there.

_______ 2. He is neither fair nor aiming to please.

_______ 3. Janet is not only a good tennis player but also a fine golfer.

_______ 4. The dog is both noisy and he chases all the other animals on the block.

_______ 5. I can't decide whether to laugh or to cry.

_______ 6. Pete not only failed the test but also was caught trying to cheat.

_______ 7. Neither Josh nor I care to remain here.

_______ 8. He is both a gentleman and a scholar.

_______ 9. To be a good parent, one must be dedicated, caring, and want the best for his children.

_______ 10. Either I am crazy or I heard that phone ring.

POINT 5 Make sure that *parallel groups of words* in a sentence have parallel structure.

> I promise **to be a good husband** and **that I will help clean the apartment.**

The two groups of words do not have a parallel structure in this sentence. One begins with the *to* form of a verb, and the other does not. This sentence may be rewritten as follows:

> I promise **that I will be a good husband** and **that I will help clean the apartment.**

Now the two elements are parallel. Note how the form of the first has been changed to go along with the second.

> **By changing the oil myself,** and **because I know how to do tune-ups,** I save money on the care of my car.

Again the two separate elements of this sentence do not coincide. There is no parallel structure. The sentence may be rewritten as follows:

> **By changing the oil myself** and **by doing my own tune-ups,** I save money on the care of my car.

> She got a new job **with a higher salary, increased benefits,** and **she also works fewer hours than before.**

may be changed to

> She got a new job with a **higher salary, increased benefits,** and **shorter working hours.**

Exercise: Point 5

Cross out the part of the sentence that is not parallel and write the correction in the space above it.

1. Our house is located near the bus station, the laundromat, and ~~is within walking distance of a~~ *the* supermarket.
2. By taking lessons and because she practises daily, Andrea has become a fine violinist.
3. My dream is to have a good job, a family, and buying a house in the country.

4. Washing my car, removing the rust, and to get a good finish takes time.
5. He said that he would stop by our house, to deliver the package, and that he would eat dinner with us.
6. I bought a car with whitewall tires, leather seats, and it has an AM-FM radio.
7. She asked me where I went to school and my degree.
8. Waiting for the bus and to become a bit nervous, Hal started biting his nails.
9. I promise to dress properly and that I will arrive on time.
10. Doris wants to be a violinist, a music teacher, or she will learn to conduct.

Review Exercise: Points 1–5

All the following sentences lack parallel construction. Rewrite the sentences, eliminating the errors.

1. He accepted the money, promised to spend it wisely, and was going for a ride in his car.

   He accepted the money, promised to spend it wisely, and went for a ride in his car.

2. Not only was she intelligent, but also she had a good sense of humour.

   ____

3. They went to the Okanagan Valley on their vacation for camping and to have fun.

   ____

4. The book is boring and is too long.

   ____

5. Her coat has six brass buttons, flared sleeves, and there is a detachable hood.

   ____

6. Eating breakfast, eating lunch, and to eat dinner are my three favourite activities of the day.

   ____

7. Therese was either angry or she was just irritable.

____

____

8. The fullback is strong, big, and runs with speed.

____

____

9. We went to the concert with Fred, with Jane, and Zelda came along also.

____

____

10. They were interested in buying the air conditioner, but not willing to spend so much money.

____

____

HOW TO AVOID FAULTY PARALLELISM

1. Remember that elements that are parallel in thought should be expressed in parallel forms.
2. Use parallel structure for elements joined by such words as *and, but, or nor, either. . .or, neither. . .nor, not. . .but, not only. . .but also.*
3. Make sure parallel groups of words in a sentence have parallel structure.

Chapter Review

I. Circle the word or phrase that maintains the parallel structure in each sentence.

1. I enjoy working hard, getting paid well, and (to get a sense of satisfaction, achieving a sense of satisfaction).
2. He admitted to robbing the store and (escaping in the green Ford, that he escaped in the green Ford).
3. She achieved her fame by working hard and (having good luck, she was lucky).
4. Isamu hates to get up in the morning, to brush his teeth, and (combing his hair, to comb his hair).

5. I admire his talent, his ambition, and (his ability to keep cool, he was able to keep cool).
6. The drummer kept the beat, the guitarist played the melody, and (the singing was done by the piano player, the piano player sang).
7. She went either with my sister, with my brother, or (by herself, alone).
8. The bull was snorting and (charging at us, started to charge at us).
9. In grammar school I learned to read, to write, and (arithmetic, to do arithmetic).
10. My aunt was charming, helpful, and (kind, always doing kind things).

II. Cross out the element in each series that is not parallel to the other two.

1. standing in line
   to cash a cheque
   speaking to my friend
2. on my own
   in the forest
   looking out for bears
3. short
   ugly
   with pimples
4. looking outside
   was in the room
   wanted to open the window
5. in the city
   on a subway
   riding
6. to get undressed
   taking a shower
   watching television
7. by raking the leaves
   mowing the lawn
   by trimming the shrubs
8. sturdy
   made of wood
   has compartments for pencils
9. green eyes
   a long, curling tail
   on the sofa
10. to meet the neighbours
    telling stories
    talking outside

III. Complete the following sentences by filling in the blanks. Be careful to maintain parallel structure. Underline the original part of the sentence to which your addition is parallel.

1. It is my ambition to be successful and ________________ .
2. Franz can speak both English and ________________ .
3. She said that she would be on either the 7:00 bus or ________________ .
4. The brown puppy was wagging its tail and ________________ .
5. The cabinet she built is made of pine and ________________ .
6. We strolled under the boardwalk ________________ .
7. He wants to move to Brandon and ________________ .

8. Judy kept a rabbit's foot, a four-leaf clover, and a _______________ in her drawer.
9. When we visited Toronto, we rode the streetcars, went to Ontario Place, and _______________ .
10. When left alone, he gets sad, lonely, and _______________ .

IV. Each of the following sentences has an error in parallelism. Write a corrected version of each sentence in the space provided.

1. He admitted the crime and that he deserved to get caught.

   ____

2. We were disappointed with our grades but understanding them.

   ____

3. Batting, throwing, and to field are important skills in baseball.

   ____

4. The dog dug up the bone and finding it to his liking.

   ____

5. Ramon knows that he should work on his writing and to improve his spelling.

   ____

6. His lunch included soup, a roast beef sandwich, a peach, and there was also dessert.

   ____

7. I respected his intellect, his strength, and he was also very funny.

   ____

8. It would make my day complete to see you, going to a movie, and to have dinner with you.

   ____

9. That cigarette has a harsh taste and is probably stale.

   ____

10. Marianne spends her day attending classes, she studies, and to listen to music.

   ____

11. The day was sunny, bright, and with low humidity.

____

12. The dean told the teacher that classes were suspended and to allow the students to go home.

____

13. She could read on a bus, in an elevator, or when she waited in line at the bank.

____

____

14. The camper learned how to tie a knot, how to start a fire, and horseback riding.

____

15. That car with four-wheel drive can get out of mud, of snow, and deep potholes.

____

16. There were news items about the rising price of coffee, the increased crime rate, and how we are running short of energy.

____

____

17. The grass turned brown and was needing water.

____

18. Going for a walk in the evening and to meet a friend on the street is a simple and great pleasure.

____

19. I wish I knew more about croquet and how to play badminton.

____

____

20. Stupid questions anger me and I am losing my temper.

____

V. Compose a sentence, using the elements provided. If the elements are not parallel, make them so.

1. watching the ball game

   eating hot dogs

   ____

2. that we had won Loto 649

   that we had become instant millionaires

   ____

3. to catch a butterfly

   running

   jumping

   ____

4. cooked our dinner

   then cleaned the dishes

   ____

5. to save money

   to buy presents

   ____

6. to go to the dance

   choosing a partner

   dancing

   ____

7. to listen to the radio

   putting my feet up

   relaxing

   ____

8. that he could stand no more

   that he would lose his temper

   ____

9. thin

   flimsy

   ____

10. keeping good notes

    to use a tape recorder

    ____

11. with my buddies

    to Commonwealth Stadium

    ____

12. applying for a job

    scheduled an interview

    ____

13. steep

    dangerous

    slippery

    ____

14. on Mother's Day

    on Father's Day

    Canada Day

    ____

15. laughing

    happy

    ____

16. around the corner

    in aisle three

    ____

17. if I got the job

    when I would start working

    ____

18. to build a fire

    roasting marshmallows

    ____

19. that I was her best friend

    that she wanted to read me her poetry

    ____

20. to have friends

    to be free

    ____

VI. Rewrite each passage, eliminating any cases of faulty parallelism.

A library is a good place to spend an afternoon and relaxing. You can read the newspaper from any major city, spend time looking for a good novel, or listening to a record. Librarians can tell you where to find a particular book and a quiet place to read it. Many libraries have display halls where you can observe artwork or just strolling around.

People find many different things to do in the library. There is usually someone studying or to write a research paper; there are those who read periodicals and those just chatting with a friend. All things considered, the library is an excellent place for meeting people, to read, or to relax.

When we heard that we had won the lottery, we wanted to jump for joy, scream our lungs out, and patting each other on the back. We immediately made plans for a car that we could rent, dining, and dancing. We went wild, spending the evening eating the best food we had ever tasted, drinking only the finest wines, and we rode to the top of the CN Tower to get a dramatic view of Toronto. Finally at around 3:00 a.m. we decided that we were pooped, that we had to go home, and we wanted to climb into bed.

Sir Frederick Banting was one of Canada's most famous doctors. Not only was he a war hero, he also was the co-discoverer of insulin. You use insulin to treat diabetes.

In 1920, he writing down an idea to aim at isolating the secretion from the pancreas. And that he receives support from Dr. J. MacLeod, assisted by Dr. Charles Best. In the winter of 1921–22, they discovered insulin. Banting is the principal discoverer because he was beginning the research, he was prominent in its early use, and to fight for recognition. Banting was winning the Nobel Prize in 1923, and knighted in 1934.

Banting's discovery both gave diabetes victims a new chance at life. During his lifetime, he is the country's most famous living Canadian.

CHAPTER 10

Shifts in Number, Person, and Tense

Suppose you were watching a ball game on television when something went wrong with the set and the image began to jump all over the screen. You'd probably be quite annoyed. It would be pretty hard to keep track of the action if you couldn't tell where the player was going to be from one eyeblink to the next. If you couldn't fix the picture, you'd probably give up and turn off the set.

Something similar can occur in writing. If I say, "First you turn this knob, then one presses this lever, and finally we open the lid," you may get the idea, but you're likely to be a bit dizzy. There's too much jumping around in the sentence – from *you*, to *one*, to *we*. You can follow the instructions a lot more easily if I say, "First you turn this knob, then you press this lever, and finally you open the lid." Now all the subjects are *you*. There is a kind of parallelism in this sentence that was missing from the first sentence. Like the parallelism we studied in Chapter 9, it makes the sentence clearer and easier to understand.

This chapter is concerned with some of the jumps, or *shifts*, that often occur in sentences. Like the jumping image on the television screen, they get in the way of understanding. However, like faulty parallelism, they are easy to avoid once you know what to watch out for.

POINT I ***Number*** **refers to the number of units referred to. In English grammar, there are only two numbers: singular and plural.**

Singular refers to *one:*

the student
a cow
the population
I, me, my, mine
you, your, yours
he, she, him, her, his, hers, it, its

Plural refers to *more than one:*

the women
men
vegetables
we, us, our, ours
you, your, yours
they, them, their, theirs

Exercise: Point 1

Write *S* if the example is singular or *P* if it is plural.

_______ 1. a romantic novel

_______ 2. an everyday problem

_______ 3. the members of Parliament

_______ 4. a drive-in movie

_______ 5. my relatives

_______ 6. dancing

_______ 7. cigar boxes

_______ 8. the news

_______ 9. somersaults

_______ 10. potato chips

POINT 2 Be sure to keep number consistent throughout a sentence.

A man should be dedicated to **their** job.

Their is plural; if it is used to refer to *a man,* which is singular, the sentence will contain a faulty shift in number. The correct version would be

A man should be dedicated to **his** job.

A woman should be dedicated to **her** job.

Woman is singular, and so is *her.*

Men should be dedicated to **their** jobs.

Men and *their* are both plural.

Women should be dedicated to **their** jobs.

If a personal subject is not specifically female, the masculine forms *he, him,* and *his* are customarily used. This is not meant to slight women; it is simply a matter of accepted usage and style.

A **doctor** is responsible to **his** patients.

In this sentence, *doctor* is used in its general sense. That is, we are not speaking about any doctor in particular. On the other hand, if we are speaking about Doctor Karen Mills, we might write:

The **doctor** is responsible to her patients.

If you are using a word in its general sense and want to avoid suggesting a masculine slant, you can sometimes solve the problem by making the sentence plural:

Doctors are responsible to **their** patients.

To refer to a singular, nonliving thing, use *it* or *its.*

The **book** is in **its** place on the shelf.

The **books** are in **their** places on the shelf.

Books is plural; it takes the plural pronoun *their.*

- Keep in mind the principles of correct pronoun reference. For a review of pronoun reference, turn to Chapter 8.

Exercise: Point 2

Circle the correct word given in the parentheses. Underline the word (or words) to which the circled word refers.

1. A reporter should always write (his, their) stories objectively.
2. If a driver is careful, (he, they) will avoid accidents.
3. A model should always look (their, his) best when (he, they) is being photographed.
4. Breakfast cereals are tasty, and (it, they) supply vitamins and minerals.
5. The headmaster works in (his, their) office.
6. A disc jockey plays records; also, (she, they) reads commercials.
7. A teacher should be familiar with (his, their) material; moreover, (they, he) should be able to present it in a clear manner.
8. Our boss is vacationing in (her, their) trailer.
9. My grandmother is making (her, their) special soup.
10. The fans are waiting in line for (his, their) turn.

Review Exercise: Points 1 and 2

Rewrite the following sentences, correcting any faulty shifts in number.

1. A successful comedian tries to get a sense of their audience.

   A successful comedian tries to get a sense of his audience.

2. A person should try to understand their limitations.

3. I was looking for my hat, but I could not find them.

4. You have two chances, so use it wisely.

5. A teacher grades papers, and sometimes they also write comments.

6. A lawyer advises their clients, but their fees are often excessive.

7. Athletes often get his back massaged.

8. The radio is broken, but they can be repaired.

9. Ms. Kanter is cooking their special pot roast.

10. A party can be a lot of fun, but they must be well planned.

POINT 3 There are only three *persons* in English grammar. Each person may be either singular or plural.

First person – used to indicate the person who is speaking or a group which includes that person. First-person words are

Singular	Plural
I, me, my, mine	we, us, our, ours

I am a sailor.
We are trying to change our lives.

Second person—used to indicate the person spoken to. Second-person words are

Both Singular and Plural
you, your, yours

you had better stop bothering me.

Marty, **you** had better stop bothering me.
You are all invited to the party.

The forms of the second person are the same in both singular and plural.
Third person—used to indicate the person or persons spoken about. Third-person words are

Singular	Plural
he, him, his she, her, hers it, its	they, them, their, theirs

Words such as *one, anyone, everyone, everybody,* and *nobody* are also third-person. As we saw in Chapter 3, such words are singular. *Note: All nouns* are third-person.

She is an excellent athlete.
I want to speak with **him**.
One must be careful these days.
Mr. Martinez works in the department store.
A **bird** sat on my windowsill.

Exercise: Point 3

Write *1* if the word is in the first person, *2* if it is in the second person, or *3* if it is in the third person.

__3__ 1. the flowers

______ 2. I

______ 3. your parrot

______ 4. she

______ 5. it

______ 6. you

______ 7. Sir John A. Macdonald

______ 9. the shopping center

______ 10. anyone

POINT 4 Be sure to keep person consistent throughout a sentence.

When you write a sentence, choose *one person* to write in, and *stick with it.* It is confusing to shift person in the middle of a sentence, a paragraph, or an essay.

Note: Be especially careful of shifts from the third person to the second.

> A **clerk** should always count change aloud or you are liable to make a mistake.

Clerk is third person; *you* is second person. This shift in person in the middle of the sentence makes its meaning unclear. This sentence may be rewritten as follows:

> A **clerk** should always count change aloud or **he** is liable to make a mistake.

Now both a **clerk** and **he** are in the third person. If you are not sure why *he* is used, check Point 2.

> In writing a paper, **one** should always keep **your** basic point in mind.

Again we see a shift from the third person—*one*—to the second person—*your.* This sentence should be revised:

> In writing a paper, **one** should always keep **his** basic point in mind.

However, *one* should be used very sparingly. If you use it often, your writing is likely to sound stiff. It is sometimes better to rewrite the sentence, eliminating *one:*

> In writing a paper, you should always keep your basic point in mind.

Exercise: Point 4

Circle the correct word given in the parentheses. Make sure there is no shift in person in the sentence.

1. A person can run for public office if (he, you) meets certain requirements.
2. If he were really my friend, (he, you) wouldn't have made that remark.
3. If one is running for office, (he, you) should always tell the truth.
4. One could ask her a question and (you, he) would never get an answer.
5. Anyone can quit smoking if (he, you) really puts (his, your) mind to it.
6. She sat in the sun for three hours, and (you, one) can't do that without getting a severe burn.
7. You can do it if (one, you) put your mind to it.
8. The bowler scored seven strikes in a row; (one, you) has to be skillful to do that.
9. After we left, (we, you) felt that (we, you) wanted to visit again.
10. A lawyer should advise (his, your) clients carefully.

Review Exercise: Points 1–4

All the following sentences contain shifts in number or person. Rewrite the sentences, correcting the errors, in the space provided.

1. A good businessman is always helpful to your clients.

   A good businessman is always helpful to his clients.

2. The student who studies hard is sure to find satisfaction for themselves.

   ____

3. A roller coaster is exciting to ride, but some think they are dangerous.

   ____

4. She likes to watch television, but you should spend some of your time reading.

   ____

5. A person should brush their teeth after every meal.

   ____

6. A son may sometimes try to take after their father.

   ____

7. Sherry always keeps their chequebook balanced.

   ____

8. A butcher must be careful not to back into his meat slicer, or you may get a little behind in your work.

   ____

9. Mt. Logan in the Yukon are Canada's highest mountains.

   ____

10. A wise person looks ahead to the future; they do not get themselves forever tied up in the past.

    ____

POINT 5 Be sure to keep tense consistent throughout a sentence.

A sentence, a paragraph, or an essay should be written in one tense. Do not shift tenses (from past to present, or present to past) in the middle of a sentence. If you need to review verb tenses, look back at Chapter 2.

He **calls** my name and **told** me to stand.

Calls is in the present tense; *told* is in the past tense. The shift in tense in the middle of the sentence results in an incorrect and misleading expression. The sentence may be rewritten as follows:

He **calls** my name and **tells** me to stand.

(both verbs are in the present tense) or

He **called** my name and **told** me to stand.

(both verbs are in the past tense).

In my haste I **tripped** over the skateboard and **fall**.

Again, we see a shift in tense. This sentence may be rewritten as

In my haste I **tripped** over the skateboard and **fell**.

or

In my haste I **trip** over the skateboard and **fall**.

Exercise: Point 5

Underline the first verb in each sentence. Then circle the correct form of the verb given in the parentheses. Make sure there is no shift in tense in the sentence.

1. She gave him good advice, but he (ignore, ignored) her.
2. I lost my library card, so I (get, got) a new one.
3. I could not find my way, so I (ask, asked) for help.
4. It was one of the weirdest experiences I ever (have, had).
5. The police officer stopped him because he (is, was) jaywalking.
6. I miss you and (want, wanted) you.
7. When I tell her that I (love, loved) her, she is happy.
8. She asked, "Are you coming?" and I (says, said), "No."
9. We stayed for the entire show and then (go, went) out for ice cream.
10. The road was rocky, but because he (is, was) driving carefully, we (arrive, arrived) safely.

Review Exercise: Points 1–5

All the following sentences contain shifts in number, person, or tense. Rewrite the sentences, correcting any errors, in the space provided.

1. We bought an air conditioner, so we stay cool all last summer.

   We bought an air conditioner, so we stayed cool all last summer.

2. He was a man who always put your best foot forward.

   ______

3. A teacher must prepare their lesson plans every night.

   ______

4. She berates her brother and hit him, too.

   ______

5. A great chef will never tell you their secret recipes.

   ______

6. Everyone who was at the Queen's Plate had your fanciest clothes on.

   ______

7. I saw her at a distance, and then I run to her.

   ______

8. A politician must know how to address their constituency.

   ______

9. If one intends to get an A in the course, you will have to work hard.

   ______

10. Explorers founded Montreal before he discovered the prairies.

   ______

CONFUSING SHIFTS TO AVOID

Make sure your sentences do not contain shifts in

1. Number – singular or plural.
2. Person – first, second, or third.
3. Tense – past, present, or future.

Chapter Review

I. Circle the correct word given in the parentheses. Make sure there is no shift in number, person, or tense.

1. A fashion designer has (his, their) work cut out for (him, them).
2. When you know the answer raise (your, his) hand.
3. She was hired yesterday and (celebrates, celebrated) last evening.
4. Whenever he sneezes, he (causes, caused) quite a ruckus.
5. Children should respect (his, her, their) parents.
6. The golfer measured the putt and tapped (his, your) ball in for a par.
7. A car should be serviced regularly or else (it, you) will not run well.
8. We went skiing at Lake Louise, had drinks before a fireplace, and (get, got) to know each other better.
9. When a baby cries, it often means that (he, they) wants (his, their) dinner.
10. Some people never get (their, your) car tuned.
11. Man's best friend is (his, your) dog.
12. Don't lose (your, his) cool!
13. We go for a ride, have a picnic, and then come home and (have, had) another party.
14. I came, I saw, I (conquer, conquered).
15. A computer is useful to (his, its) owner.
16. The rock group wrote most of (its, their) songs.
17. Food is very expensive today; also, heating costs (are, were) higher.
18. She ran out of the room and (says, said), "I am leaving."
19. As Canadians, we are supposed to have the opportunity to improve (their, our) future.
20. The singer signalled for (her, their) musicians to pick up the tempo.

II. Fill in the blank with an appropriate word. Make sure there is no shift in number, person, or tense.

1. A person may get his hair cut, or ____________________ may get it styled.

2. A doctor should be sympathetic with ______________________ patients.
3. We ate and ______________________ until we were full.
4. A dog is man's best friend; ______________________ always comes when ______________________ calls.
5. I missed the bus, so I ______________________ for another.
6. Children should respect ______________________ parents.
7. If you cross the street in the middle of the block, ______________________ have to be very careful.
8. A public official should heed the opinions of ______________________ constituents.
9. The building inspector expressed ______________________ opinion that the old house should be torn down.
10. The dog chased the man and ______________________ his leg.
11. One should exercise ______________________ right to vote.
12. A student should try to hand in ______________________ papers on time.
13. The principal called the teachers in for a meeting and addressed ______________________ on methods of discipline.
14. The car swerved and ______________________ a telephone pole.
15. A person should try to make ______________________ dreams come true.
16. People should try to make ______________________ dreams come true.
17. You are my best friend, for ______________________ always listen when I have problems.
18. The bus driver wanted the exact change, but we ______________________ not have it.
19. She wanted ______________________ boss to give ______________________ a raise.

20. Go tell Aunt Rodie that the old gray goose ______________________ dead.

III. Circle any words in the following sentences that represent faulty shifts in number, person, or tense. Then, in the space provided, write what type of shift takes place.

1. If an employer is considerate, they are likely to get along well with their employees.

   Shift in ______________________

2. We swam, sailed, and picnicked, and then decide it was time to go home.

   Shift in ______________________

3. A professor may be exciting or boring; it depends on how you present your material.

   Shift in ______________________

4. A father should teach your children right from wrong.

   Shift in ______________________

5. I do all the work around here, and I never got a compliment.

   Shift in ______________________

6. Bicyclists must be sure that his tires have the proper air pressure.

   Shift in ______________________

7. One should be honest with your friends.

   Shift in ______________________

8. He built that house with your own bare hands.

   Shift in ______________________

9. Shakespeare's poetry is beautiful; they are an example of the form known as the sonnet.

   Shift in ______________________

10. I was playing the guitar and use an amplifier.

    Shift in ______________________

IV. All the following sentences contain faulty shifts in number, person, or tense. In the space provided, rewrite the sentences to eliminate the errors.

1. First you read the novel, then he wrote the paper.

   ____

2. A sportscaster should be objective, but they always seem to root for the home team.

____

3. If a student studies regularly, they will not have to cram the night before a test.

____

4. She enjoys reading, but she disliked writing.

____

5. One must participate in class discussion, or your grade will suffer.

____

6. Anyone can learn home repair if you concentrate.

____

7. Hansel and Gretel finally found his way home.

____

8. She counts to ten before she lost her temper.

____

9. Pilots always try to make her passengers feel at ease.

____

10. A person can educate themselves if they put their minds to it.

____

11. King Arthur ate with all of their knights at the Round Table.

____

12. Every morning she washes her face, brushes her teeth, and combed her hair.

____

13. I am sentimental whenever you hear old favourite melodies.

____

14. Almost anyone can learn to use the computer if you take lessons.

____

15. He whines whenever he did not get his way.

16. Many taxpayers need an accountant to figure out your returns.

17. I don't enjoy shopping for clothes because you have to spend so much time in dressing rooms.

18. If one intends to quit your job, he should give two weeks' notice.

19. A pediatrician must like children, because they deal with them every day.

20. I went to the Royal Winnipeg Ballet and see some beautiful costumes.

V. Rewrite these passages, eliminating any faulty shifts in number, person, or tense.

If one intends to be a writer, you must first learn the great task of self-discipline. Most novelists, or poets, or dramatists do not work in an office; he often works at home. If he is unable to rid himself of distractions, they will probably find that they do very little work. There are always plenty of reasons or excuses not to write, but if the writer is able to set his mind to their work, he will not bother them. Some writers make schedules for themselves; others chose to work when they were inspired. Whatever the case, the point remained the same: if one wants to write, you write; if one does not, you don't.

Today, news programs and magazines were quite the rage. Everywhere you look, I can see news of this strike or that tax increase thrown at you. A newspaper should be objective, but they always seem to inject their own opinion into the stories. Because of the subjective nature of the news, more and more magazines find its way onto the newsstands. Moreover, these magazines often produced more in-depth accounts of the news. I suppose every form of the news media has their place.

I work in a bank in Surrey, and when you have that type of job, you have to be willing to wake up at a very early hour. Each morning, I drive to work, park my car, and walked a block to work. I get a lunch break every day at noon, and they love to eat at the delicatessen around the corner. I worked at the bank for over a year, and decided that I had had enough. After looking around for a new job, I found one where you had to be at work by 6:00 a.m. This job was in a restaurant where you had to stand up all day, and after six months, I decided to go back to the bank. The manager was very nice to me and says, "You can have your old job back if one promises to stay at least two years." I take the job, and I enjoyed an extra hour of sleep every morning.

PART III

Punctuation

CHAPTER 11

Period, Question Mark, Exclamation Mark, Quotation Marks

When we talk, we do not merely recite a string of words. We pause or let our voices rise or fall in pitch or put extra stress on some words. If I say, "She wants to marry him," I drop the pitch of my voice at the end. The listener knows from this that I have simply told a fact. But if, instead, I raise my voice and put extra stress on the word "marry," the listener knows I am expressing surprise. The sentence has become an exclamation: "She wants to *marry* him!" A change in the tone of my voice has made the same set of words into a completely different kind of sentence.

In writing, of course, we cannot use changes in sound to help express our meaning. Instead, we use *punctuation marks*—periods, commas, question marks, and so on. A few simple rules will help you use them correctly and effectively.

POINT 1 Use a *period* at the end of a sentence that makes a statement.

We went to the movies last night.

This sentence makes a clear statement; that is, it *states* a piece of information. It is followed by a *period.*

She said that she was an Aquarian.

Again we have a sentence that makes a statement. Note the period at the end.

James wanted to know if he could come with us.

Although this sentence *sounds* as if it is asking a question, it is not. It is making a statement about someone else's question. This kind of statement is sometimes called an indirect question. However, since it is still a statement, we still use the period at the end.

Exercise: Point 1

Write *S* if the sentence makes a statement or *X* if it does not. If the sentence *does* make a statement, put a period in its proper position.

__S__ 1. They promised to arrive on time.

______ 2. The humidity bothers me

______ 3. Will you speak to her for me

______ 4. The repairman asked whether we had fooled around with the plug

______ 5. Why

______ 6. Prince Edward Island is Canada's smallest province.

______ 7. I bought a new needle for my record player

______ 8. Let's build a bonfire tonight

______ 9. They danced the tango

______ 10. Why do you treat me this way

POINT 2 Use a *period* after an abbreviation.

co.	Mr.	Ont.
viz.	Dr.	Oct.
etc.	Ms.	Mon.
ff.	Mrs.	Man.

Some abbreviations consist of the first letters of several words. In this case, put a period after the abbreviation of each word:

C.P.A.	Ph.D.
M.D.	M.A.
B.C.	P.E.I.

Certain agencies or organizations have abbreviations which do not require a period:

CIDA	CAW
YMCA	CAA
SPCA	NATO

If an abbreviation comes at the end of a sentence that makes a statement, only one period is necessary.

He studies biology, chemistry, physics, etc.
She moved from Ontario to B.C.

Metric measurements are indicated by international symbols, not abbreviations. Therefore no periods are required:

cm^2	mm	km/h
kg	C	L

Too many abbreviations can confuse the reader. What is your reaction to this example?

> On Sat., Dec. 4, I test drove a 2nd hand Buick. At speeds over 65 km/h, it got only 5 km/L. The engine has a lot of h.p. By 9:00 p.m., I had decided to buy the car. It cost $6,050 F.O.B. Oshawa. Since I am a C.A. (with a B.A. in accounting) I had no trouble estimating my monthly payments.

Review Exercise: Points 1 and 2

Add periods where they are necessary in the following sentences.

1. Dr. Mitchell cancelled my appointment,
2. *Ms* magazine is very popular reading these days
3. A PhD is an advanced degree
4. Combine 57 g butter with 114 g sugar
5. Now I get it
6. Mrs Ames raised an objection
7. I have been instructed to report on Sept 30
8. Gen. Burns was a great man
9. There are never enough hours in the day
10. The room measured 5 m^2

POINT 3 Use a *question mark* after a direct question.

> Were you invited to the party?

The direct question is followed by a question mark.

> He is your brother, isn't he?

Again the direct question, *isn't he,* is followed by a question mark. However, you *should not* use a question mark if the question in the sentence is asked *indirectly.*

> He asked whether the new job offered a higher salary.

This is an indirect question, like the example under Point 1. In this type of sentence, use a period instead of a question mark.

> Does the new job offer a higher salary?

Now the sentence has been changed so that the question is asked *directly.* Note that the end punctuation has been changed to a question mark.

Exercise: Point 3

Write *C* if the sentence is punctuated correctly or *X* if it is punctuated incorrectly.

___C___ 1. Will the rain never stop?

_______ 2. He asked her if she would marry him?

_______ 3. Have you ever pondered the fate of the earth.

_______ 4. She is your closest friend, isn't she?

_______ 5. Can you tell me why you did that.

_______ 6. We wondered whether the movie would be shown on television?

_______ 7. To be or not to be, that is the question?

_______ 8. Are you going to study chemistry tonight.

_______ 9. He wondered if she would call?

_______ 10. You live in Saskatchewan now, don't you.

POINT 4 Use an *exclamation mark* after an expression or statement that shows strong feeling, including a forceful command.

The exclamation mark should not be overused. It gives real emphasis to individual expressions when used carefully.

> Fire!
> Get out of here!

This expression shows strong feeling and deserves an exclamation mark.

> Unemployment must end!
> We've made it!

When the exclamation mark is overused, it tends to take the emphasis away from the expressions that really need it.

> I had a great time today! All of my friends came over to my house! We played records and danced all afternoon! Then we had a barbecue!

As you can see, too many exclamation marks make the passage sound almost ridiculous.

Exercise: Point 4

The following paragraph contains far too many exclamation marks. Circle the ones you think should be kept, and cross out the others. You should have no more than two or three exclamation marks when you finish.

> The alarm clock was shrieking! I woke up with a start! When I looked at the clock, it said 8:30! Oh, no! I had meant to set it for 7:30! Now I'd never get to the bus stop on time! I jumped out of bed, yanked on my clothes, and grabbed a couple of doughnuts from last night's party! They would have to do for breakfast; I couldn't even take time to make coffee! With the doughnuts in one hand and my coat in the other, I dashed out the door and ran down the street! The bus was coming! I would never make it! Then, at the last minute, the traffic light turned red! The bus had to wait! I put on a last burst of speed and made it to the bus stop just as the bus rolled up! As I scrambled aboard, panting, the driver grinned! "I saw you coming," he said! "I would have waited for you!" I ought to have thanked him, but the way he grinned made me want to hit him instead! I collapsed into the nearest seat, puffing like an overweight elephant! It didn't matter — I had caught the bus!

Review Exercise: Points 1–4

Insert the proper punctuation at the end of each sentence.

1. Working by candlelight can be inspiring.
2. Has the mail arrived yet
3. She asked him if he would like to go out for dinner
4. We do not take credit cards here
5. I would like a corned beef sandwich
6. Are you still taking violin lessons
7. Good grief, he's having a heart attack
8. Is there any reason to continue
9. You had better comb your hair and straighten your tie
10. I hope I don't have any cavities

POINT 5 **Use *quotation marks* to enclose the exact words of a speaker or writer.**

> She said, "I am finally ready to go."

The exact words of the speaker have been placed inside the quotation marks.

The politician said, "There will be no new taxes. I will see to it that the crime rate declines. I will be a representative of the people."

Note that the entire speech, even though it consists of more than one sentence, is enclosed by *one set* of quotation marks.

A new paragraph should be begun whenever there is a change of speaker:

"Doctor, I think I'm a dog," the patient said.

"Lie down on the couch and we'll talk about it," replied the doctor.

The patient looked sad, and said, "Oh no, I'm not allowed on the couch."

Note that in this example, a new paragraph was begun each time the speaker changed. Quotation marks were used any time the exact words of the speaker were written.

However, you should *not* use quotation marks if the quotation is indirect, that is, if the exact words of the speaker are not used:

She said that supper is almost ready.

This indirect quotation does not require quotation marks.

She said, "Supper is almost ready."

We have added quotation marks and removed the word *that.*

Make sure that the quotations themselves begin with a capital letter:

The professor announced, "There will be an exam next Wednesday."

Use *There* instead of *there.*

However, if the quotation is split, as in the following sentence, you should not begin the second part with a capital letter:

"We'll see the movie," he said, "and then we'll go out for dessert."

Two sets of quotation marks are needed here to separate the speaker's words from *he said*.

Two sets of quotation marks are also needed to separate the speaker's words from *she said*, but this example is not a split quotation; it consists of *two* quotations by the same speaker.

"I'm cold," she said. "Please hand me my sweater."

Exercise: Point 5

Place quotation marks where they are needed in each of the following sentences.

1. The teller said, "I'm sorry, but your cheque has bounced."
2. I'll never lie again, he said I promise.
3. This assignment is due Tuesday, the teacher announced.
4. I warned him to drive slowly on the icy roads.
5. Do you know the answer? the teacher asked.

6. The doctor said, Take two aspirins and go to sleep.
7. Carol asked me if she could have a ride home.
8. You can't get there from here, said the tour guide.
9. I am telling the truth, he said. Then he added, I know you won't believe me.
10. Why don't you and Jane come for dinner, she asked.

POINT 6 **(a) Periods and commas are always placed *inside* quotation marks; (b) question marks and exclamation marks are placed *outside* quotation marks except when the quotation itself is a direct question or an exclamation; (c) semicolons and colons are placed outside the closing quotation marks.**

He said, "I enjoy working on automobile engines."
"I enjoy working on automobile engines," he said.

Note the comma in the second sentence. When the end of a quoted statement comes before the end of the whole sentence, its period is replaced by a comma.

I said, "Tell me that you love me."
"Tell me that you love me," I said.

Did you say, "We are going away together"?

The entire sentence is a question, but the quoted material itself is a statement.

She asked, "Are you coming?"

The quotation itself is a direct question; therefore the question mark is placed *inside* the quotation marks.

"Are you coming?" she asked.

Again the quotation itself is a direct question.

He yelled, "Get out!"

The quotation itself is an exclamation; the exclamation mark is placed *inside* the quotation marks.

Did you notice that in three of the last four sentences, one punctuation mark has been dropped? For instance, "We are going away together" is a statement, but there is no period or comma at the end of it. Why not? When the end of a quotation comes at the end of the whole sentence, only the *stronger punctuation mark* is used. Question marks and exclamation marks are strong; periods and commas are weak. A question mark is usually stronger than an exclamation mark. When both the whole sentence and the quotation are statements, only one period is used, inside the quotation marks.

Also, have you noticed that in every example we have seen so far, a *comma* follows the word just before a direct quotation? Look back over the previous examples and note how the comma is used in this way.

Notice in the following example how the semicolon is used in relation to quotation marks. In Chapter 5, Point 2, you learned how a semicolon can connect two independent clauses; more information on the semicolon and the colon will be provided in Chapter 12.

> "The only seats left," shouted the usher, "are in the first row"; by then, however, we had settled into comfortable seats in the middle of the theatre.

Here are some more examples of sentences with quotations. They are all correctly written. See if you can tell why certain punctuation is used in each case. If you have difficulty, reread Points 5 and 6.

> Gail asked, "Whose record is this?"
> "Will you come if I ask you nicely?" he inquired.
> Did you say, "Cows have three legs," or am I crazy?
> Roger screamed, "So this is my destiny!"
> "Time!" the coach shouted.
> I said, "These phone bills are getting out of hand."
> "I have always been a loner," the old man whispered.
> Fire anyone who says, "I'm too tired"!
> Was it you who asked, "Is anybody home?"

Exercise: Point 6

Write *C* if the sentence is punctuated correctly or *X* if it is not. Rewrite the incorrect sentences, correcting the punctuation.

__X__ 1. Joyce said, "I think I have a cold".

Joyce said, "I think I have a cold."

____ 2. "Do you love me," he asked?

____

____ 3. "Mend your ways!" I screamed!

____

____ 4. Billy asked, "Why is it always me."

____

____ 5. I can't believe you actually said, "Fishing is for the birds."; you have a weird sense of humor.

____

____ 6. "Does this car need oil"? the attendant inquired.

____

_______ 7. "Out, damn Spot," she screamed, throwing her dog out the door!

____

_______ 8. "I am trying not to lose my temper," said Mr. Yevchenko.

____

_______ 9. Did you shout, "Bargains galore!"?

____

_______ 10. Cries of "Help"! echoed through the building.

____

POINT 7 **Use quotation marks to enclose the title of a short work such as a story, essay, short poem, song, or radio or television program.**

We heard "Beauty and the Beast" on the radio.
"A Trip to the Coast" was written by Alice Munro.
Have you ever read Pratt's "The Shark"?

Note that what appears in the quotation marks is the *exact* title. If there is no punctuation in the title itself, there should be no punctuation within the quotation marks.

For longer works such as novels, plays, movies, newspapers, full-length books, and magazines, use underlining instead of quotation marks. In printed material, the names of such works usually appear in italics.

Have you seen *Pulp Fiction*?
I read about the blackout in the Fredericton *Gleaner.*
During the semester we will read Richler's *The Apprenticeship of Duddy Kravitz.*

Exercise: Point 7

Use quotation marks or underlining where necessary in each of the following sentences.

1. Last night we saw *The Diviners* on television.
2. Before my vacation I read Europe on Ten Dollars a Day.
3. Grammar Review is the first part of Troubleshooting.
4. I read an article entitled In Praise of Canadian Heroes.
5. My essay was titled The Decline of Canadian Culture.
6. Surfacing is one of Atwood's most enjoyable novels.

7. O Canada is Canada's national anthem.
8. The Canadian edition of Time magazine contains many interesting articles.
9. Dorothy Livesay wrote a poem entitled The Three Emilys.
10. Alannis Morisette's first hit CD was Jagged Little Pill.

Review Exercise: Points 5–7

The following sentences contain errors in the use of quotation marks or other elements covered in Points 5–7. Rewrite each sentence, making the necessary corrections.

1. Annie asked are you going to sing that song again?

   Annie asked, "Are you going to sing that song again?"

2. I plan to read The Diviners this summer.

3. "Are you my friend or aren't you," she asked?

4. The time is right he said for us to move on.

5. One of Oscar Peterson's earliest compositions was Canadiana Suite.

6. She said that "she would be studying all night."

7. Ahmed said Come visit us next weekend.

8. "Before I go", she said, "Let me ask you one question?"

9. Do you read Maclean's she asked.

10. Get that car out of my driveway, the man hollered.

HOW TO PUNCTUATE SENTENCES

1. Use a *period* at the end of a statement or an indirect question and at the end of an abbreviation.
2. Use a *question mark* after a direct question.
3. Use an *exclamation mark* after an expression of strong feeling.
4. Use *quotation marks* to enclose a direct quotation.

Chapter Review

I. Write *C* if the sentence is punctuated correctly or *X* if it contains any error in punctuation.

_______ 1. "Do you want to have a good time" he asked?

_______ 2. I wrote a poem this summer titled The Voyageurs.

_______ 3. Ms Katz has seventeen cats.

_______ 4. She wanted to know whether the sauce was too spicy?

_______ 5. Will you join us?

_______ 6. "I don't care," she said, "and I will not change my mind."

_______ 7. "Are you a man she inquired or a mouse?"

_______ 8. "You must be kidding!" she cried.

_______ 9. Did you ask her if she was in the right seat.

_______ 10. "What"?

II. Punctuate the following sentences.

1. I am spending more time in the library these days
2. Have you ever eaten smelts
3. Don't try any funny business with me
4. I wonder why they say blondes have more fun
5. The show is on Channel 5
6. He has a lighter with his initials on it
7. Did you say that you were driving to Cape Breton this summer
8. The bellboy asked whether we needed any help with our bags
9. Dr. McCarthy is the new chairman

10. Mira is working toward her Phd
11. What kind of fool am I
12. Get lost, Buster
13. Where were you on the night of June 3
14. Should I wait for her
15. Let's go, Tiger Cats
16. She asked whether she could expect a raise
17. Have you heard about Shollet and Luis
18. A rolling stone gathers no moss
19. Sgt Anderson is an excellent detective
20. Should we call you Ms. Burns or Mrs Burns

III. Add or change punctuation where necessary in each of the following sentences.

1. I'm thinking. Give me some time! Enrico snapped.
2. Suzanne asked, Will there be an essay question on the test?
3. We're late, she cried, hurry up
4. The movie Ben Hur is considered a classic.
5. The short story The Window is from Mrs. Golightly and other Stories.
6. The metric system is too confusing, he complained.
7. Don't you get the joke? she asked.
8. Block that kick, the crowd chanted rhythmically.
9. His mother pleaded, Finish your vegetables. There are people starving in India.
10. Why don't you come up and see me sometime? she sang.
11. Get lost! we screamed at the hoodlums.
12. The lyrics are Chestnuts roasting on an open fire, Jack Frost nipping at your nose.
13. The doctor asked, Are you feeling better?
14. This won't hurt a bit, the nurse said as he stuck the needle into my arm.

15. What is your hurry, asked the old timer?
16. Paul Anka wrote the song My Way for Frank Sinatra.
17. I heard her say, This is the worst party I've ever been to.
18. Hold it right there! the police officer shouted.
19. I hate peas, wailed the child!
20. Run a mile a day, she advised, and you're sure to feel better.

IV. Complete these sentences. Be sure to use all necessary punctuation marks.

1. Sunita asked ______________________________
2. The little boy cried______________________________
3. Inez asked her brother______________________________
4. She wondered if ______________________________
5. As I always say ______________________________
6. Ms. Yee said______________________________
7. He responded by saying ______________________________
8. Do you know that song ______________________________
9. My favourite movie is ______________________________
10. The doctor warned us ______________________________

V. All of the following sentences contain errors in punctuation. Rewrite each correctly in the space provided.

1. "I love scary movies my sister informed us."

   ____

2. Dr. Gomez is an M D

   ____

3. "Where do you think you're going," my mother asked.

   ____

4. I wonder, he said, if the economy will ever improve.

   ____

5. My sister said that "she was going to run off to the Orient."

   ____

6. Why must you always complain, I asked her?

7. *The End of the World is* a short story by Mavis Gallant.

8. Full speed ahead shouted the captain.

9. What's the deal, he whispered.

10 Was it you who said I'm definitely not hungry?

11. "I'm working as a file clerk this summer he said."

12. Was it you who asked "that stupid question?"

13. "There's no green cheese up here," said the astronaut

14. There's a Hippo in my Tub was a very popular children's song.

15. "Get out of my life, she cried, I've had enough!"

16. While I'm away he said please water my plants.

17. Why are you so good to me, she sighed?

18. You fool screamed the man whose car I had just hit.

19. Will I ever be able to learn programming Thomas asked?

20. "You will be a great writer", his teacher told him.

____

VI. Rewrite these passages, correcting any errors in the usage of periods, question marks, exclamation marks, and quotation marks.

"This is the third paper of the semester that you have turned in late said Professor Martin and you are simply going to have to change your work habits." I know said Bruce, and I promise to change my ways. Mr. Martin said, Don't tell me your dog chewed up the paper. What happened. "I don't have a dog, replied Bruce, but I do have a little brother. "And he tore it up? Mr. Martin asked." "No, said Bruce," but he wrote it for me, and since his spelling was so bad, it took me two whole days to correct it."

____

____

____

____

____

____

____

____

____

____

____

____

____

____

____

Three men were stationed in the farthest reaches of the Yukon, and their supply of whiskey was running low. Two of the men felt that they could take advantage of the third, so they told him to go out into the blizzard and buy some more whiskey in the nearest town. The third man said I will go only if you promise to save the last drop of this remaining whiskey for me. Don't worry the others said we promise. I will definitely not go if you drink that last drop the third man said. We promise, we promise, the others assured him. With that, the third man left. A day went by Two days went by A week and then two weeks went by. The two men figured that the third must have died in the blizzard and decided "to drink the last bit of whiskey." They took the bottle down from the shelf, said Cheers, and were about to indulge when the third man flung the door open. I told you he announced I wasn't going to go if you drank that last drop!

CHAPTER 12

Semicolon and Colon

Now we come to two punctuation marks that, are used only within sentences, never at the end. They are the *semicolon* (;) and the *colon* (:). As you can see, they look very much alike, and people often get them confused. However, they are used in quite different ways. You have already learned one way to use semicolons, in Chapter 5. Just for a refresher, we will review that way and then go on to some new ones.

POINT 1 Use a *semicolon* to separate two independent clauses.

If you need to review independent clauses, look back at Chapter 4, Point 3, and Chapter 5, Point 2.

The movie started late; we had enough time to buy popcorn.

In this sentence we have two independent clauses; that is, each clause can stand alone as a complete sentence, since it has a subject and a verb. The two clauses are separated by a semicolon.

The record was scratched; I returned it the next day.

Again we have two independent clauses separated by a semicolon.

My sister calls me once a week; we have a good relationship.

Exercise: Point 1

Each of the following sentences contains two independent clauses. Separate the two clauses with a semicolon.

1. My family vacationed in Alberta; we visited Lake Louise and Banff.

2. The baseball game was exciting it went into extra innings.
3. We always see the latest horror films we like being scared.
4. Mary lost her I.D. card she couldn't get the student rate.
5. The lawn was overgrown Dave volunteered to mow it.
6. Firefighters have to be brave they risk their lives almost every day.
7. We got the mortgage we bought the house.
8. I will use a road map I will not lose my way.
9. The Mariposa Folk Festival was given outdoors it was at the end of June.
10. He talks to his house plants they just don't want to grow.

Note: Sometimes you may wonder whether to put a semicolon at the end of one line or the beginning of the next. *Never* put a semicolon at the beginning of a line. You should write

> He was late for dinner every night for a week;
> I was really getting fed up.

not

> He was late for dinner every night for a week
> ; I was really getting fed up.

Follow this rule with all punctuation marks except opening quotation marks.

POINT 2 Do not use a semicolon when two independent clauses are joined by such connecting words as *and, but, for, nor, or, so, yet.*

> I wanted to play for the team; but I was cut.

The semicolon is used incorrectly in this sentence. Two independent clauses are connected by the word *but.* The sentence may be rewritten as follows:

> I wanted to play for the team; I was cut.

(now we have two independent clauses joined by only a semicolon) or

> I wanted to play for the team, but I was cut.

(a comma has been substituted for the semicolon). This gives us a sentence like those discussed in Chapter 5, Point 1.

> She got an A on her final; so she threw a party.

Again we have an incorrect use of the semicolon. Can you see why? This sentence may be rewritten:

She got an A on her final; she threw a party.

However, if the clauses are joined by stronger connecting words, such as *also, however, therefore, then, otherwise, nevertheless,* and *moreover,* you should use a semicolon.

Bottle-cutting can be great fun; however, one must have great patience.

Two independent clauses are joined by a semicolon and the connecting word *however.* This sentence is complete and correct as it stands. Finally, note the placement of the comma after *however.*

Exercise: Point 2

Write *C* if the semicolon is used correctly or *X* if it is used incorrectly. Be prepared to explain your answers.

__X__ 1. That is a difficult question; but I can tell you the answer.

______ 2. I sat on the beach for five hours; I got an awful sunburn.

______ 3. We bought a huge bagful of groceries; then we cooked a stupendous dinner.

______ 4. We gave it our best; yet we still finished second.

______ 5. He was not happy about the decision; nor did he accept it quietly.

______ 6. I think; therefore I am.

______ 7. It is a shame; moreover, it is a disgrace.

______ 8. A disc jockey must know a lot about popular music; and he must be able to sell products.

______ 9. You have treated me unfairly; nevertheless, I remain your friend.

______ 10. The garbage disposal was clogged; so we had to scrape out the orange rinds.

Review Exercise: Points 1 and 2

Rewrite the following sentences, using a semicolon in each one. Remember to put commas where they are needed.

1. The weather was miserable it rained all day.

The weather was miserable; it rained all day.

2. The cabinet is handcrafted it is made of oak.

____

3. Mr. Ryan got a new job however he is not very happy in it.

____

4. We went skiing last weekend in the Gatineaus the snow was perfectly packed.

____

5. I witnessed the accident therefore I will testify in court.

____

6. Alice missed a week of class nevertheless she passed the exam.

____

7. I enjoy reading novels of the occult however I find the movies boring.

____

8. Reporters have strict deadlines they work under great pressure.

____

9. Raking leaves is spiritually rewarding it is also exhausting.

____

10. I have planted a garden I expect tomatoes by the end of the summer.

____

POINT 3 Use semicolons to separate items in a series when the items (a) have internal punctuation or (b) are long.

Ordinarily commas are used to separate items in a series, but in the two instances just stated, a semicolon is less confusing.

> We visited Hull, Quebec, Rimouski, and Granby, Quebec.

Hull, Quebec, is one town, but from the way the sentence is punctuated we might just as well be talking about Hull *and* Quebec City. The sentence doesn't distinguish between punctuation *within* a series item and punctuation at the *end* of an item. A better version would be

> We visited Hull, Quebec; Rimouski; and Granby, Quebec.

Now it is clear just what towns we are talking about.

The importance of semicolons is even more obvious when the items are longer:

> We visited Hamilton, Ontario, where we went to Dundurn Castle, Niagara Falls, where we took a boat ride under the falls, and St. Catharines, Ontario, where we spent the afternoon at the university.

The semicolons make clear what happened where.

> We visited Hamilton, Ontario, where we went to Dundurn Castle; Niagara Falls, where we took a boat ride under the falls; and St. Catharines, Ontario, where we spent the afternoon at the university.

Exercise: Point 3

Put semicolons where necessary in each of the following sentences.

1. I read in the newspaper about the premier's efforts to lower automobile insurance rates the latest troubles in the Middle East and a new program for providing hot meals for the elderly on holidays.
2. In my refrigerator are the remains of a bacon, lettuce, and tomato sandwich, which I made two weeks ago, some cheddar cheese, which could probably be used for penicillin, a fried egg, and two bottles of beer, which I should probably drink to forget about the sad state of my refrigerator.
3. Nancy has lived at three different addresses: 86 Hutcherson Square, Buckingham, Quebec, 21 Renfield Crescent, Dorval, Quebec, and 714 Welland Avenue, Brooks, Alberta.
4. Our neighbourhood council has resolved that street lights will be turned on every evening at 7:30 that parents should keep a close watch on their children to see that vandalism declines and that a recycling drop-off point will be established at the corner of Northend and Pleasant Streets.
5. The terms of the contract stated that the work must be finished by August 15 that payment would be made in two installments, one by September 30, the other by December 30 and that all work must be presented in a manner judged acceptable by the employer.

POINT 4 Use a *colon* to introduce a list following a noun that names the list.

I have three favourite foods: chocolate bars, potato chips, and diet cola.

Note the placement of the colon. It introduces a list and follows a noun, *foods*, that names the list.

In the last two months, Nathan has read four books: a mystery, a romance, a spy thriller, and a cookbook.

Books is the noun that names the list to follow; therefore a colon is used to introduce the list. Why have semicolons been used to separate the items in the series? Do not be tempted to write this sentence as follows:

Nathan read: a mystery, a romance, a spy thriller, and a cookbook.

This sentence is punctuated incorrectly because there is *no noun* that names the list.

Exercise: Point 4

Write *C* if the colon is used correctly or *X* if it is used incorrectly. Circle the noun, if there is one, that names the list.

__C__ 1. I bought two CDs: "Thankful" by the Holly Cole Trio and "One Track Mind" by TBTBT.

_____ 2. The teacher said: that there would be an exam and that we had better study.

_____ 3. My talents: guitar playing, cooking, carpentry.

_____ 4. We packed: swimsuits, suntan lotion, plastic cups, and a thermos filled with lemonade.

_____ 5. I was worried about: my financial state, my health, and my future.

_____ 6. Uses of the semicolon: to separate items in a series and to join two independent clauses.

_____ 7. Vices: gambling, smoking, and drinking.

_____ 8. We were: ready, willing, and able.

_____ 9. Cups are made of: glass, clay, or plastic.

_____ 10. Types of cups: glass, clay, and plastic.

POINT 5 **Use a colon to set off a list or statement that is introduced by the words *the following* or *as follows*.**

> The crooks stole the following: a television set, a radio, a camera, and a silver serving platter.

The list of items is preceded by a colon because it is introduced by the phrase *the following*.

> The teacher instructed us as follows: "Read the chapter carefully, take notes, reread the chapter, and finally, reread your notes."

The statement is introduced by the words *as follows* and a colon.

Review Exercise: Points 4 and 5

Write *C* if the colon is used correctly or *X* if it is used incorrectly. If the sentence is faulty, rewrite it in the space provided.

__X__ 1. Every morning I eat: cereal, eggs, and toast.

Every morning I eat cereal, eggs, and toast.

_____ 2. She has promised: to love, to honour, and to cherish.

____

_____ 3. We took the following: a tent, two sleeping bags, and a lantern.

____

_____ 4. I am learning: to drive, to swim, and to type.

____

_____ 5. Important English skills: grammar, spelling, and punctuation.

____

_____ 6. Equipment necessary for tennis: sneakers, tennis balls, and a racquet.

____

_____ 7. Directions: north, east, south, west.

____

_____ 8. Line up: two by two, and in order of your height.

____

_______ 9. Steps in cooking spaghetti: boil the water, add the spaghetti, cook for ten minutes, and drain.

____

_______ 10. She directed us as follows: "Go three blocks south, turn to the right, and look for a mailbox with a picture of a collie on it."

____

HOW TO USE A SEMICOLON

1. To separate two independent clauses, unless the clauses are joined by a weak connecting word.
2. To separate items in a list, when the items are long or have internal punctuation.

HOW TO USE A COLON

1. To introduce a list following a noun that names the list.
2. To set off a list or statement that is introduced by *the following* or *as follows*.

Chapter Review

I. Write *C* if the sentence is punctuated correctly or *X* if it is punctuated incorrectly.

_______ 1. The firefighter rescued the baby; however, the building was destroyed.

_______ 2. We will invite: Jack and Jill from the hill.

_______ 3. I like you: I want you to like me.

_______ 4. We forgot the following: a toothbrush, a shaving kit, and a good book to read.

_______ 5. Sports: baseball, football, basketball, golf.

_______ 6. Hamlet had to make a choice: to be or not to be.

_______ 7. I'd love to meet her; but I am busy tonight.

_______ 8. He is usually unlucky at games: however, he won tonight.

_______ 9. Sophia has four brothers: Tommy, Sal, Joe, and Robert.

_______ 10. You are in trouble; and you know it.

II. Circle the correct punctuation mark given in the parentheses.

1. The car has a flat tire (; :) there is a spare in the trunk.
2. I didn't finish the assignment (; :) I was too busy.
3. That dress comes in three colours (; :) red, blue, and yellow.
4. We've never travelled so much (; :) it's fun.
5. He told me the following (; :) that he was fed up with the city and that he was moving to the country.
6. I'm exhausted (; :) moreover, I still have more to study.
7. Carl has only two desires (; :) to be rich and to be famous.
8. Linda had two jobs before this one (; :) waitress and grounds keeper.
9. Russian dressing is good (; :) nevertheless, I prefer Italian.
10. We were late for the concert (; :) the usher made us wait until the first number had been completed.
11. John Donne once wrote, "Ask not for whom the bell tolls (; :) it tolls for thee."
12. They drove through three provinces (; :) Alberta, Manitoba, and Saskatchewan.
13. You cook with love (; :) therefore, your dinners are wonderful.
14. We went horseback riding in the afternoon (; :) then we settled down to an evening of food and good talk.
15. Human needs (; :) food, clothing, and shelter.
16. I don't enjoy flying (; :) nevertheless, we flew to Europe last summer.
17. Norm used to smoke cigarettes (; :) now he smokes a pipe.
18. Intramural sports are great (; :) they give you a chance to exercise without high-pressure competition.
19. Ingredients for a salad (; :) lettuce, tomatoes, carrots, and peppers.
20. You have been given three wishes (; :) make them carefully.

III. In each of the following examples, draw one line under the first independent clause and two lines under the second independent clause. Then put a semicolon or other punctuation where it is necessary.

1. We bought tickets well in advance therefore we got good seats.
2. I would love to go however I am too tired.
3. Choose one essay question answer it in 500 words or less.
4. I keep losing my ball-point pens I should get one with a clip.
5. Our team won the championship we were awarded a trophy.
6. You must learn to control your temper it can get you into trouble.
7. My favourite actress starred in the movie she gave a great performance.
8. A calendar watch can be a great convenience however it has to be reset once a month.
9. A sense of humour is important try to develop one.
10. I get hay fever attacks every August however, they do not bother me much with my new allergy pills.

IV. In each of the following examples, underline the noun that names the list, and supply a colon where necessary.

1. I have two reasons to be depressed my girlfriend left me, and I'm developing dandruff.
2. Shakespeare wrote plays in different styles comedy, tragedy, and history.
3. We had a great dinner veal, spaghetti, green beans, and wine.
4. Aspects of a novel plot, character, setting, theme, and tone.
5. Our teacher stressed two points that we should attend class regularly and that we should hand assignments in on time.
6. Janos has two pairs of sneakers one for tennis and one for basketball.
7. You will receive the following a demonstration lesson and a free career brochure.
8. We went to two stores today Wal-Mart and Zellers.
9. I have written three parts of my essay already the first word, the second word, and the third word.
10. Choose one main dish chicken chow mein or chop suey.

V. Write five sentences of your own, using semicolons.

1. ______

2. ______

3. ______

4. ______

5. ______

VI. All the following sentences contain errors in the use of semicolons or colons. In the space provided, rewrite the sentences to correct the errors.

1. Janet works in the Library of Parliament: she is a page.

______

2. You don't understand: I apologize for my thoughtlessness.

______

3. That store sells: jeans, jeans, and more jeans.

______

4. I have been to that part of town once; but I will never go back.

______

5. He was arrested on the following charges; assault and battery and armed robbery.

______

6. Beatrice exercises daily; and it shows in her fine physique.

______

7. Call me anytime: I'm here when you need me.

______

8. Birds fly; fish swim; and snakes crawl.

______

9. He sang as follows; off-key and very loud.

______

10. The cast rehearsed for weeks: still they were nervous on opening night.

______

11. There's no business like show business: I should know.

12. She appeared calm: on the inside, though, she was scared.

13. It was Pierre's fault: he is such a klutz.

14. Tomorrow is her birthday: she'll be twenty-five.

15. We watch: the news and the business report every night.

16. He is responsible for; tending the garden, painting the house, and washing the car.

17. The jury announced its verdict as follows guilty of first-degree murder.

18. First the leaves turn colours: then they fall.

19. I want bigger muscles: therefore; I lift weights.

20. Omer doesn't take care of his teeth: consequently, he gets at least six cavities a year.

VII. Rewrite the following passages, correcting any errors in the use of semicolons or colons.

The team was in trouble: it had dropped from first place to last in three weeks. The manager called a meeting of the players at which the following issues were discussed; the importance of developing a winning attitude, whereby the players would place the goals of the team over their individual achievements, the imposition of a strict curfew so that the players would be well rested for the games, the problem of teammates competing among themselves for higher salaries and greater coverage in the newspapers, and last but not least, the general lack of hustle and determination on the part of the team's stars.

My friends and I recently spent a day driving around the Maritimes trying to hit as many hamburger joints as we could in 16 hours. Our travels took us to the following places; Halifax, Nova Scotia, where we prepared our stomachs with thick shakes and French fries, Truro, Nova Scotia, where we indulged in double cheeseburgers, Amherst, Nova Scotia, where we settled for soft drinks, Borden, Prince Edward Island, where we each downed a filet of fish, and finally to Charlottetown, P.E.I., where we celebrated with chicken sandwiches; we ate dessert at the quick lunch bar at Holland College in Charlottetown.

CHAPTER 13

Comma

Commas are the most used and most frequently misused punctuation marks. Basically the comma is used to signal a pause. It can help make the meaning of a sentence more clear, but if it is used carelessly, it can cloud the meaning of a sentence entirely. The most important rule of thumb regarding commas is to use a comma only when you are sure you need it.

POINT 1 Use *commas* to separate three or more items in a series.

I enjoy baseball, basketball, and tennis.

In this sentence, the items in the series are separated by commas. Note that the comma follows the item. Since the last item is the last word of the sentence, there is no need to put a comma after it; it is followed by a period.

She knows how to sing, dance, and play the piano.

Again the items in the series are separated by commas.

We bought groceries and liquor.

Note that there are no commas in this sentence. There are only two items in the series; therefore, no comma is required.

Exercise: Point 1

Put commas where necessary in each of the following sentences.

1. She was lonely, depressed, and nostalgic.
2. Kathy planted tulips daffodils and roses.

3. It is hot and muggy today.
4. He stormed out of the house went for a walk and came back the next morning.
5. I've been to South America Central America and Europe.
6. Bend me shake me break me; do anything you want.
7. The letter was signed sealed and delivered.
8. We strolled along the beach and gathered shells.
9. This library has books books and more books.
10. For lunch we had soup salad and a sandwich.

POINT 2 **Use a comma between two independent clauses if they are connected by such words as *and, but, for, or, nor, yet, so.***

This is something that has been covered before, but it will be useful to review it now.

> I wanted to go, but I didn't have enough money.

This sentence contains two independent clauses; they are separated by a comma.

> I was hired for the job, and I start work Monday.

Again we have two independent clauses, which are connected by a comma and *and.* Note that the comma *precedes* the connecting word.

> You should pay your bills when they are due, or you will have to pay an interest charge.

Two independent clauses are connected by a comma and *or.* Note the placement of the comma.

When connecting independent clauses in this way, be sure to use the comma *plus* the connecting word. The use of the comma without the connecting word creates a serious error in sentence structure — the run-on sentence. Go back to chapter 5 if you need to review run-ons.

> Trish ran for office and was elected.

In this sentence there is no comma because we do not have two independent clauses. There is only one subject, *Trish*; the two verbs refer to the same subject.

> He tried his best but failed.

Is this sentence correct as it stands?

Exercise: Point 2

Put commas where necessary in the following sentences.

1. He thinks he should be a star, but he really isn't very talented.
2. I can type very fast but I make a lot of mistakes.
3. That's the way it goes and you will have to accept it.
4. Brenda tries to rush me yet I always take my time.
5. She had a cold so she stayed in bed all day.
6. I'm taking flying lessons but I can't seem to get the hang of making turns.
7. Randy will graduate from Capilano College this year and he hopes to get a job in the clothing industry.
8. Friendship is simple yet complex.
9. Be truthful with me or I will leave you.
10. He is very bright but can't seem to get his head together.

Review Exercise: Points 1 and 2

All the following sentences contain errors in comma usage. In the space provided, rewrite the sentences to correct the errors.

1. Joe, Sue and Anne were invited to the party.

   Joe, Sue, and Anne were invited to the party.

2. We hoped the humidity would end but it didn't.

   ____

3. There were cows, and horses roaming around the field.

   ____

4. I ate pizza and she ate a salad.

   ____

5. We spoke seriously, yet insincerely.

   ____

6. She used parsley, garlic and tarragon in the sauce.

   ____

7. She is superstitious and her husband is a nervous wreck.

____

8. We got to the concert on time but we left at the intermission.

____

9. Reading writing and arithmetic are the basics of education.

____

10. We sang laughed and danced all night long.

____

POINT 3 **Use a comma after a long introductory phrase or clause. Use a comma after a short introductory phrase if it is necessary to avoid unclear meaning.**

When the time comes, everything will be settled.

When the time comes is a dependent clause. As we saw in Chapter 4, Point 4, a dependent clause at the beginning of a sentence is usually followed by a comma.

All through the long drive, my mind kept going back to last night's conversation.

All through the long drive is not part of the main idea.

While eating, the group discussed plans for the afternoon.

Without a comma, it might look as though someone were eating the group.

As captain, Cho decided the lineup.

Again, without a comma there could be confusion. But

At eight o'clock he opened the doors.

Here there is no real danger of confusion, so a comma is not needed.

The words *yes* and *no* are generally followed by a comma when they begin a sentence. So are words such as the following:

however	of course	by the way
in fact	incidentally	well

No, there is no need for concern.
However, you will have to talk to your adviser.
Well, I haven't seen her in three weeks.

It is important for a writer to develop a good ear if he is to use commas efficiently. Learn to listen to your words. If a sentence seems to have a natural pause, it *may* need a comma.

Exercise: Point 3

Put commas where necessary in each of the following sentences.

1. After the party ended, we cleaned the apartment.
2. Yes we have no bananas.
3. As I said before the lecture is cancelled.
4. Not wanting to go I said I wasn't feeling well.
5. Since you wanted popsicles I bought some.
6. By the way you have been promoted.
7. Whenever I hear that CD I feel better.
8. As I feared the end is near.
9. Thinking about the past I always get melancholy.
10. Unfortunately your plan will never work.

Another Exercise: Point 3

Write five sentences of your own, using introductory phrases.

1. ______________________________
2. ______________________________
3. ______________________________
4. ______________________________
5. ______________________________

POINT 4 Use commas on both sides of a word (or group of words) that interrupts the flow of the sentence.

The fact is, Bob, that I feel quite unhappy about it.

Bob interrupts the flow of the sentence and therefore is set off from the rest of the sentence with commas.

Croissants, for example, are delicious with coffee.

For example interrupts the flow of the sentence and therefore is set off with commas.

Other expressions that are generally set off with commas include

however	in fact	at any rate
of course	to tell the truth	I think
therefore	by the way	finally

We are, of course, pleased with your grades.

Note the placement of the commas.

Your last letter, by the way, was very puzzling.
Ricky, not knowing what the question was, was dumbfounded.

In the preceding sentence, the interrupting phrase adds information to or comments on the situation. It is set off with commas.

I am sorry, sir, for what I have done.

The interrupting word, *sir,* tells us to whom the statement is being made.

Exercise: Point 4

Put commas where necessary in each of the following sentences.

1. I told you once, Margie, and I will not tell you again.
2. Bliss Carman for example wrote beautiful poems.
3. I think therefore that we should adjourn immediately.
4. My grandmother strangely enough bought a motorcycle.
5. Watch out Hubert!
6. I believe on the other hand that there is too much violence on television.
7. Her illness of course is the reason for her absence.
8. Jogging as it turns out has helped me lose weight.
9. Your theory I am certain is worthy of more consideration.
10. A car if it is not tuned regularly is likely to break down.

Review Exercise: Points 1–4

Put commas where necessary in each of the following sentences.

1. At the barbeque, we had hamburgers, hot dogs, and chicken.
2. We saw the game at the Pacific Coliseum and we watched the highlights on television.
3. After we finished eating Harry and Gail went for a walk.

4. I am asking you Mr. Maxwell to give me a direct answer.
5. A bagel with cream cheese makes a great snack.
6. The manager however refused to listen to the demands of the employees.
7. During her road test Trudy had to parallel park back up and make a U-turn and park the car on a hill.
8. He made copies of the article and circulated them among the students.
9. Without taking much time Pat answered all the questions on the test.
10. A parent if he wants his child to do well in school should encourage him to work his hardest.

Another Review Exercise: Points 1–4

All the following sentences contain errors in the use of commas. Rewrite the sentences, correcting the errors, in the space provided.

1. The poet spoke to the audience, and answered questions.

   The poet spoke to the audience and answered questions.

2. Before making up her mind Linda asked her counsellor for advice.

   ____

3. We cast our votes as usual, just before the polls closed.

   ____

4. By the way Mom happy Mother's Day.

   ____

5. Reading, *The Hockey News*, is my favourite way to relax.

   ____

6. In addition, to mastering the use of commas you have, improved your vocabulary.

   ____

7. I am have always been and always will be your best friend.

   ____

8. Those wind chimes are lovely but, they are too expensive.

   ____

9. Never before in my life, have I met such a man.

____

10. That puppy, with the floppy ears, is mine.

____

POINT 5 Use commas to set off nonessential material.

Nonessential material, simply defined, is material that may be interesting but is not absolutely necessary for the main idea of the sentence. That is, any material that can be left out of the sentence without changing the main idea is nonessential.

> Mr. Turner, who was defeated in the election four years ago, is running for office again.

The material set off by commas is nonessential; that is, the main idea of the sentence would not be changed if that material were omitted.

> A hiccough remedy that usually works is hard to come by.

There is no nonessential material in this sentence. Do not be tempted to write this sentence as follows:

> A hiccough remedy, that usually works, is hard to find.

This is incorrect because the group of words *that usually works* is essential to the meaning of the sentence. If this group of words were omitted, the sentence would read, "A hiccough remedy is hard to find." An important part of its meaning would be lost.

> *The Blue Wall*, which is about policemen, was written by Carsten Stroud.

If we omit the nonessential material between the commas, the sentence would read: *The Blue Wall* was written by Carsten Stroud. The main idea of the original sentence still stands; the group of words *which is about policemen* is nonessential.

> Carsten Stroud's *The Blue Wall* is about policemen.

In this sentence there is no nonessential material.

Exercise: Point 5

Put commas where necessary in each of the following sentences.

1. His car, which had been repaired at Moe's Garage, broke down again.
2. My sister an Aquarian was born in January.
3. Mr. Thomas the coach of our football team called practice off for today.
4. Her suggestion that we feed the cats was reinforced by a chorus of meows.

5. This cottage which was built in 1901 is our favourite vacation spot.
6. The tea kettle that I bought at the bazaar is an antique.
7. Tomorrow June 20 is our wedding anniversary.
8. Joey smiling like a fool looked ridiculous.
9. The kerosene lamp which we always use in an emergency came in very handy.
10. The job that you applied for has been filled.

Another Exercise: Point 5

Write five sentences of your own in which you use commas to set off nonessential material.

1. ______________________________
2. ______________________________
3. ______________________________
4. ______________________________
5. ______________________________

Review Exercise: Points 1–5

All the following sentences contain errors in the use of commas. Rewrite each sentence, correcting the error, in the space provided.

1. A fool, and his money, are soon parted.

   A fool and his money are soon parted.

2. It is I think the best way to solve the problem.

   ____

3. Chicken soup which some people believe can cure diseases, is delicious.

   ____

4. He can play the flute, the clarinet the oboe and the trumpet.

   ____

5. After a while even the most exciting entertainment can become boring.

   ____

6. That in fact is exactly the reason I am here.

___

7. As sure as I'm breathing you're a double for my brother.

___

8. Backgammon a game which involves gambling, is very popular.

___

9. A nuclear plant, which some people feel is destructive to the environment has been built in Pickering Ontario.

___

10. We browsed, in the bookstore, for an hour.

___

POINT 6 **Use a comma after every item in an address or date.**

610 South Street, London, Ontario
Apt. 5, Wellington Arms, 1515 Broadway, Ottawa, Ont.
Sunday, January 1, 1978
On March 8, 1977, we were married in Sherbrooke, Quebec

A one-item address or date is an exception to this rule:

May 5 is my brother's birthday.
The house at 412 Fisher Street is the one that people say is haunted.

Exercise: Point 6

Put commas where necessary in each of the following sentences.

1. Paul was born on September 3, 1953.
2. Renee works at Mohawk College Fennel and West 5th St. Hamilton Ontario.
3. The paper is due on Monday May 15.
4. The play opened on September 1 1985 at the Arts and Culture Centre Prince Phillip Drive St. John's Newfoundland.
5. We celebrated our anniversary July 19 in Yellowknife North West Territories.

Write one sentence in which you tell when and where you were born.

___

Review Exercise: Points 1–6

All the following sentences contain errors in the use of commas. Rewrite the sentences, correcting the errors, in the space provided.

1. There were no runs two hits and two men left on base.

   There were no runs, two hits, and two men left on base.

2. That guy, in the blue suede shoes, is really wild.

3. After deliberating for two hours the jury reached a verdict.

4. Toby Al and Dave have moved to Thunder Bay Ontario.

5. Biology the study of living things is my favourite subject.

6. I have, after much thought reached a decision.

7. We walked, and talked all night long.

8. I'm afraid it will rain although I hope it doesn't.

9. I have up until now, handed in my assignments on time.

10. Are you sure pal that you want to come along?

HOW TO USE COMMAS

1. Use them to separate three or more items in a series.
2. Use them between two independent clauses joined by a weak connecting word.
3. Use them after introductory material when it is long or the meaning might otherwise be unclear.
4. Use them to set off nonessential material or words that interrupt the flow of the sentence.

Chapter Review

I. Write *C* if the sentence is punctuated correctly or *X* if it contains an error in comma usage. Be prepared to explain your answers.

_______ 1. We have never since we moved here had to lock our doors.

_______ 2. As Socrates said, "Know thyself."

_______ 3. I brush my teeth, twice a day.

_______ 4. The bread, that you were baking, is burned.

_______ 5. Yes, sir, I know what you mean.

_______ 6. This couch, which we bought at a flea market is very comfortable.

_______ 7. On December 5 I will be twenty-six years old.

_______ 8. You must, however have a library card.

_______ 9. Do you know what I mean, or are you confused?

_______ 10. When the time is right you will know it.

II. Put commas where necessary in each of the following sentences.

1. This section therefore will be closed.
2. Hey wait!
3. While waiting for the bus we told each other jokes.
4. Why Mr. Carl must you be so rude?
5. The television set which was stolen last week was found in the basement of a warehouse.
6. The store is located at 520 Elm Street Chatham New Brunswick.
7. We must if we are ever to change our ways begin today.
8. I'd love to go to The Citadel but she won't let me.
9. Sometimes when I am feeling blue a good record can lift my spirits.
10. You know of course that our television is broken.
11. In a sense you are right.
12. We plan if the weather is good to go swimming tomorrow.

13. He had always wanted to participate in the Olympics but he had never trained properly for the trials.
14. The recipe directs you to mix the batter with one egg add the premeasured packet of chocolate chips and bake the mixture for forty-five minutes in an oven set at 120° C.
15. Time as it always does has a way of changing things.
16. While showering I sing to myself.
17. The novel which by the way I have never read is supposed to be excellent.
18. A sandwich if made with whole wheat bread is delicious and healthful.
19. There has never been as far as I can remember such a destructive storm.
20. Well how do you like that!

III. Here are four rules governing the use of commas:

(1) Use commas to separate items in a series.

(2) Use a comma between two independent clauses if they are connected by one of the weak connecting words.

(3) Use a comma after a long introductory phrase or clause and after a short introductory phrase if it is needed to make the meaning clear.

(4) Use commas around words that interrupt the flow of a sentence and around nonessential material.

All the following sentences are punctuated *correctly*. Write the *number* of the rule that applies to the use of the comma in each sentence.

_______ 1. One of my friends, Edina, is planning to get married.

_______ 2. The scarecrow, which was made of straw, was dragged to the ground.

_______ 3. I watered the plants, fed the dog, and cleaned the kitchen.

_______ 4. They had a golden opportunity, but they could not capitalize on it.

_______ 5. As a student of the arts, I am required to go to the museum once a week.

_______ 6. The dean, however, was willing to listen to the demands of the student committee.

_______ 7. Since I hurt my back, I have never shovelled snow.

_______ 8. Dorothy, in her early years, was a dancer.

_______ 9. The pitcher, who was brought up from the minor league last week, threw a shutout.

_______ 10. We visited my parents, my wife's parents, and my sister.

_______ 11. I will not repeat myself, so you had better listen carefully.

_______ 12. This, of all things, you call a surprise!

_______ 13. I'm sorry, Dad, for banging up the car.

_______ 14. We played chess, checkers, and cribbage.

_______ 15. So, after all that, you want to apologize!

_______ 16. Shopping wisely, we bought sheets and pillowcases that matched.

_______ 17. And now, for my final number, I will play a piece by Glenn Gould.

_______ 18. Have you ever, in your whole life, met such a man?

_______ 19. This, above all, is what is important.

_______ 20. I met her in the morning, and I married her in the evening.

IV. Write sentences of your own, using the rule indicated by the number in the parentheses. The numbers refer to the rules in the previous exercise. If, for example, you are directed to write a sentence using (1), you should apply the rule that states, "Use commas to separate items in a series."

(1) ____

____

(1) ____

____

(2) ____

____

(2) ______________________________

____

(3) ______________________________

____

(3) ______________________________

____

(4) ______________________________

____

(4) ______________________________

____

V. All the following sentences contain errors in the use of commas. Rewrite the sentences, correcting the errors, in the space provided.

1. Waving her wand the princess performed some magic.

____

2. Never never will you get away with that.

____

3. I had a bacon lettuce and tomato sandwich for lunch.

____

4. Who in your opinion is the world's greatest athlete?

____

5. Her latest poem, is superb.

____

6. As of next week the prisoner will be a free man.

____

7. His answer which was wrong made the class laugh.

____

8. That dog barking at the tree, is mine.

____

9. We were wed on April 17 1977.

____

10. When our guests arrived we greeted them at the door.

11. Once upon a time there was a dog who could fly.

12. We met as usual at the corner of Yonge, and Bloor.

13. I waited, for nearly a month for your letter.

14. It is my choice however to travel alone.

15. For once try studying.

16. You are mine and I am yours.

17. Write to me at 65 Market Street Banff Alberta.

18. You are all prepared I'm sure for the test.

19. Ice cream if it is made at home is very good.

20. As long as I live I will love to dance.

VI. Rewrite the following passages, correcting any errors in comma usage.

When we spent the day at my grandmother's cottage, on the beach, we had a great time. My wife and I, together with two friends, drove about sixty kilometres, from our home to the small two-room beach house which had been built over a hundred years ago. We stopped at a small market, to pick up some food, for sandwiches, and ate as soon as we arrived at the cottage. We spent the rest of the day, eating drinking sunning ourselves going for walks and swimming. By the time the sun went down we were thoroughly exhausted. Isn't it strange I ask you that doing nothing can make someone so tired?

Liberal arts contrary to what some people think provides a good basis for an education. It is important I believe for every student to be well grounded in such subjects as art history science, politics and English. These subjects give students a good idea, of what has been accomplished in the history of the world, and what is yet to be accomplished. By the time one completes a full program in liberal arts he or she will be ready to live with vigour, and vitality.

PART IV

Mechanics

CHAPTER 14

Capital Letters

One of the ways to make important words stand out is to *capitalize* them — that is, begin them with a capital letter. There are a lot of rules for capitalization. However, they will be easier to learn if you keep in mind that most of them have to do with *names:* names of people, names of magazines, names of places, and so on. For instance, you would write,

John Morrison
Canadian Living
Winnipeg, Manitoba

Moreover, as you can see, capitalization usually has to do with very *specific* names. We would write

Yukon College	but	a two-year college
Ottawa Rough Riders	but	the football team

There are few other uses of capital letters. For instance, you probably know already that the word *I* is always capitalized and that the first word of every sentence is capitalized. But keep in mind the principle of specific names. With this to help, you should not have much trouble learning when and when not to capitalize.

POINT 1 Capitalize the first, last, and important words in a title.

More Joy in Heaven

In the title of this movie, the first word, the last word, and the important word *Joy* begin with capital letters. *In* is not quite as important as the other words and is therefore not capitalized.

Roughing It in the Bush
The Man from Glengarry

▸ *Remember:* In a sentence, the title of a work of some length should be underlined or italicized. (See Chapter 11, Point 7)

Exercise: Point 1

Circle any letters that should be capitalized in the following sentences.

1. have you ever been to the art gallery of ontario?
2. i read an article entitled "offra harnoy: world-class cellist."
3. one of Freud's most important books is called *the interpretation of dreams.*
4. We saw the Shaw Festival's production of *peter pan.*
5. i have a book called *how to grow beautiful house plants.*

Another Exercise: Point 1

Write five sentences of your own in which you use titles. Be sure to use capital letters when necessary.

1. ______________________________
2. ______________________________
3. ______________________________
4. ______________________________
5. ______________________________

POINT 2 Capitalize the names of specific persons, places, languages, nations, and nationalities.

Alice J. Brock	English
Mr. Farnsworth	Italian
Sydney, Nova Scotia	Metis
St. Lawrence River	American
Oriental	Canadian
French Canadian	Etobicoke
Latin America	France

He works at the hardware store on Mill Street.

Mill Street, the name of a specific place, is capitalized.

We went canoeing on the Mackenzie River.

Again the name of a specific place is capitalized.

Ms. Warren can speak English and French.

A specific person's name is capitalized; names of languages are capitalized.

Names of races used to be capitalized, but today they frequently are not. You will be on fairly safe ground if you capitalize *Oriental* and *Indian,* but do not capitalize *white* and *black.* The words *Chicano* and *Caucasian* are usually capitalized, but some writers prefer not to capitalize them. Whichever you choose to do, be consistent about it within each piece of writing.

Exercise: Point 2

Circle any letters that should be capitalized in the following sentences.

1. the fowlers always spend their vacation in victoria.
2. mel gave up his united states citizenship when he moved to canada.
3. joe perry has moved to red deer, alberta.
4. does tori know how to speak german?
5. venezuela, argentina, mexico, and most of latin america have been free countries since they rebelled against spain.
6. lou takes great pride in his italian-canadian heritage.
7. the school is going to offer a course in native canadian history next semester.

Another Exercise: Point 2

Write five sentences of your own in which you use capital letters to name a specific person, place, language, or nationality.

1. ______________________________
2. ______________________________
3. ______________________________
4. ______________________________
5. ______________________________

POINT 3 Capitalize names of days of the week, months, and holidays: do not capitalize names of the seasons.

Thanksgiving falls on the second Monday of October.

The names of a holiday, a day of the week, and a month are capitalized.

It has been a hard winter.

The name of a season, *winter*, is not capitalized.

Summer brings heat and humidity.

Summer is capitalized only because it is the first word of the sentence.

Next Monday is Victoria Day.

The name of the holiday contains two words — both are capitalized.

Exercise: Point 3

Circle any letters that should be capitalized in the following sentences.

1. september 21 is the first day of autumn.
2. i am on the road on monday and thursday.
3. canada day falls on july 1.
4. we visit my family on the first sunday of every month.
5. september and october are the loveliest months of the year.

Another Exercise: Point 3

Write five sentences of your own in which you use capital letters in the names of days of the week, months, and holidays.

1. ______________________________
2. ______________________________
3. ______________________________
4. ______________________________
5. ______________________________

Review Exercise: Points 1–3

All the following sentences contain errors in the use of capital letters. Rewrite the sentences, correcting the errors, in the space provided.

1. i read *the progress of love* last spring.

   I read The Progress of Love last spring.

2. barry smith works in edmonton, but he lives in st. albert.

3. on monday we will discuss shakespeare's play *king lear*.

4. i travel to the mountains every autumn.

5. lina was born in the united states but she lives in manitoba and considers herself a canadian.

6. the police found the stolen car in norfolk county.

7. have you read the article "in search of the canadian identity"?

8. be careful on april fool's day.

9. she is reading a book about canada's first nations peoples.

10. last summer we visited nova scotia, new brunswick, and newfoundland.

POINT 4 Capitalize the first word of a direct quotation.

My teacher said, "This is a brilliant answer!"

The first word of the direct quotation, *This*, is capitalized.

"Are you planning to move?" she asked.

Again the first word of the direct quotation is capitalized.

She wanted to know whether dinner was ready.

There is no direct quotation in this sentence.

If you need to review the use of quotation marks in these sentences, look back at Chapter 11, Point 5.

Exercise: Point 4

Circle any letters that should be capitalized in the following sentences.

1. john asked lucy, "will you come to the dance with me?"
2. the pharmacist said, "here is your prescription."
3. "when will we get our tests back?" i asked.
4. "you are all invited to the victory party," the candidate announced.
5. "please pick up some tomatoes," she said.

Another Exercise: Point 4

Write five sentences of your own in which you use capital letters to begin direct quotations.

1. ____________________
2. ____________________
3. ____________________
4. ____________________
5. ____________________

POINT 5 Capitalize words of family relationship when they are used as names.

Are you coming, Mother?

Mother, a word of family relationship, is capitalized because it is used as a name.

My husband's Uncle Mike came to visit us.

Uncle is used as part of a name.

Come on, Dad, let's go to the ball game.

However, if a *possessive* word is used before the word, the word should not be capitalized. Such possessives include *my, our, your, his, her, its, their, Bill's, the doctor's* and similar words.

My mother is coming.
Our uncle came to visit us.
We went to the ball game with Steve's dad.

Exercise: Point 5

Circle any letters that should be capitalized in the following sentences.

1. Happy Birthday, sister.
2. I'm not eating these lima beans, mom.
3. my aunt is a champion at poker.
4. Have you heard from uncle ebenezer?
5. My brother is also my best friend.
6. I heard that ed's father used to play professional baseball.
7. My grandmother married a man half her age.
8. Is it true that father knows best?
9. I visited grandpa mac in his office.
10. abby's cousin lisa is very pretty.

POINT 6 Capitalize words such as *college, doctor,* and *building* when they are part of the names of specific people or things.

I am a student at Victoria College.

Victoria College is the name of a specific thing; therefore, it is capitalized.

She has an appointment with Dr. Miller.

Dr. Miller is a specific person.

Professor Chapman teaches that course.

Professor Chapman is a specific person.

We went to the top of the Calgary Tower.

The *Calgary Tower* is the name of a specific thing.

When such words are not part of specific names, they should not be capitalized.

I am a student in college.
She has an appointment with the doctor.

Our professor teaches that course.
We went to the top of the building.

Exercise: Point 6

Circle any letters that should be capitalized in the following sentences.

1. We took a boat ride on the fraser river.
2. The ice cream shop is located on franklin drive.
3. She teaches literature at acadia university.
4. He has been our mpp for twelve years.
5. Mr. ramlall our professor.
6. He expects us to call him professor ramlall.
7. She was the architect for the wilson county courthouse.
8. Have you ever visited stanley park in vancouver?
9. They went swimming in lake of the woods.
10. They went swimming in great bear lake.

Review Exercise: Points 1–6

All the following sentences contain errors in the use of capital letters. Rewrite the sentences, correcting the errors, in the space provided.

1. dr. meyer's office is on queen street.

   Dr. Meyer's office is on Queen Street.

2. on the first night of Chanukah, we visited grandma and grandpa.

   ____

3. we went to Nathan Phillips Square on new year's eve.

   ____

4. our teacher is from the iberian peninsula.

   ____

5. "when will you hand in that paper?" the Professor asked.

   ____

6. i answered, "i will hand it in next tuesday."

____

7. I read an article in *byte* magazine.

____

8. Next winter we will ski in the french alps.

____

9. does your Brother still work at the Plant?

____

10. In the Fall we will go camping at long point provincial park.

____

Another Review Exercise: Points 1–6

Write your own sentences, using the word given in the parentheses. Use the word *exactly* as it appears.

1. (River)_______________________________________
2. (grandmother) _________________________________
3. (Sister) ______________________________________
4. (Winter) _____________________________________
5. (building)_____________________________________

POINT 7 Capitalize events in history, movements, and periods.

The War of 1812 was an important event in Canadian history.

The War of 1812, an event in history, is capitalized.

The Impressionists did much to change people's thinking about art.

Impressionists refers to a group of artists who were part of the movement called Impressionism.

Much of our terrain was formed during the Ice Age.

Ice Age refers to a period in history.

The years after World War I are known as the Roaring Twenties.

Exercise: Point 7

Circle any letters that should be capitalized in the following sentences.

1. the constitution act was signed in 1982.
2. life was exciting in the frontier age.
3. the raid on dieppe was thought by many to be a tragedy.
4. Leonardo da Vinci was an important figure during the renaissance.
5. the throne speech was delivered by the governor general.

Another Exercise: Point 7

Write five sentences of your own in which you use the names of historical events, movements, or periods.

1. ____________________
2. ____________________
3. ____________________
4. ____________________
5. ____________________

POINT 8 **Capitalize the names of specific school courses, but do not capitalize general words that refer to the courses.**

I take Spanish 10 and Chemistry 101.

The names of these specific courses are capitalized.

I am studying history, foreign language, and mathematics.

No specific course is mentioned in this sentence.

I take Spanish and chemistry.

Spanish is capitalized because it is the name of a language; *chemistry* is not capitalized because there is no mention of a *specific* course.

Exercise: Point 8

Circle any letters that should be capitalized in the following sentences.

1. She is studying english with professor ross.

2. do you expect to take german 101 next semester?
3. Sarath plans to major in anthropology.
4. i wanted to take english 2a, but my advisor suggested i take basic composition.
5. He got an A on his physics final.

Another Exercise: Point 8

Write sentences of your own in which you name five courses you have taken in your academic career.

1. ______________________________
2. ______________________________
3. ______________________________
4. ______________________________
5. ______________________________

Review Exercise: Points 1–8

All the following sentences contain errors in the use of capital letters. Rewrite the sentences, correcting the errors, in the space provided.

1. the hotel frontenac in Quebec City is more than One Hundred years old.

   The Hotel Frontenac in Quebec City is more than one hundred years old.

2. aunt tilly is preparing her annual holiday dinner.

   ____

3. next winter we will ski in the laurentians.

   ____

4. "why didn't you fill that prescription?" dr. cohen asked.

   ____

5. do you refer to niagara falls, canada, or to niagara falls, new york?

   ____

6. anett got a B in biology 2a last term.

   ____

7. so, mom, do you think i should buy a ford or a chevy?

____

8. canada entered world war II after germany attacked poland.

____

9. can we try that new french restaurant?

____

10. were you whale watching near trinity bay, newfoundland?

____

WHEN TO USE CAPITAL LETTERS

1. Capitalize the names of specific persons, places, languages, nations, nationalities, and some races.
2. Capitalize the names of days of the week, months, and holidays (but not seasons).
3. Capitalize the first, last, and important words in a title.
4. Capitalize the first word of a direct quotation.
5. Capitalize the first word of a sentence.
6. Capitalize the word *I*.

Chapter Review

I. Write *C* if the sentence makes correct use of capital letters or *X* if it contains an error in the use of capital letters.

_______ 1. Let's go to the museum after we visit parliament hill.

_______ 2. Mr. Anderchek has been named dean of the College.

_______ 3. he is the lieutenant governor of Ontario.

_______ 4. The conductor said, "Tickets, please."

_______ 5. I will be an english major.

_______ 6. Next Friday is her Thirteenth Birthday.

_______ 7. Aunt Martha is sally's favourite relative.

_______ 8. Oh, mom!

_______ 9. muskoka is beautiful in the Autumn.

_______ 10. I own two dogs, a labrador retriever and a wheaton terrier.

II. Circle any letters that should be capitalized in the following sentences.

1. He is my uncle from brandon.
2. the professor asked, "who knows the answer to this question?"
3. I always buy *la presse* on sunday.
4. victoria is the capital of british columbia.
5. the boutique is located on willis avenue.
6. don't capitalize every letter you see!
7. i just finished reading *the lark in the clear air.*
8. Did you see the football game on labour day?
9. When, dad, will you ever understand me?
10. Zelda lives a zesty life in zanzibar.
11. mr. Allesandrino, our biology teacher, is also coach of the basketball team.
12. The vancouver grizzlies is a new NBA franchise.
13. You can find the book you want at the Kelowna public library.
14. For the second time, I flunked economics 101.
15. "I live near the bow river," he said.
16. Rajesh plans to join the rcmp.
17. in october the leaves begin to fall.
18. When we were in ottawa we visited the parliament buildings.
19. She teaches spanish at Lethbridge high school.
20. He was born in north bay, and he lives in selkirk, manitoba.

III. Write sentences of your own, using the word given in the parentheses. Use the word *exactly* as it appears.

1. (Captain) ____________________
2. (summer) ____________________
3. (Uncle) ____________________
4. (March) ____________________
5. (history) ____________________

6. (Revolution) ______________________________

7. (Dad) ______________________________

8. (mother) ______________________________

9. (Autumn) ______________________________

10. (Park) ______________________________

IV. Circle the correct word given in the parentheses.

1. Last (summer, Summer) I worked in a gas station.
2. My (father, Father) served in World War II.
3. My sister learned to play (volleyball, Volleyball) in (high school, High School).
4. She asked me, "(why, Why) must you treat me this way?"
5. I think (Doctor, doctor) Aho is a veterinarian.
6. I have been studying (latin, Latin).
7. Did you write a letter to your (aunt, Aunt)?
8. Our (teacher, Teacher) is not here today.
9. I hope the (flames, Flames) win the Stanley Cup.
10 We went sailing on the Hudson (river, River)
11. Many (Metis, metis) people live on the (Prairies, prairies).
12. We're going to Vancouver over the Labour Day (weekend, Weekend).
13. "How," I said, "(do, Do) you expect to pass that exam?"
14. Many fairy tales begin, "Once upon a (time, Time)."
15. He learned to play the (bagpipes, Bagpipes) in Scotland.
16. (winter, Winter) is my favourite season.
17. Life was very different in the Middle (ages, Ages).
18. My (sister, Sister) has dropped out of (school, School).
19. It's (greek, Greek) to me!
20. He asked me (whether, Whether) I planned to get a haircut.

V. All the following sentences contain errors in the use of capital letters. Rewrite the sentences, correcting the errors, in the space provided.

1. "Lucy In the Sky With diamonds" is a Beatles' song.

2. he was born in wasaga beach, and he has lived there all his life.

3. i would like to drive a rolls royce.

4. I'm only asking you, dad, to give me another chance.

5. The Babysitter pleaded, "behave yourself."

6. My Grandfather will be ninety years old next month.

7. The ottawa senators are in the national hockey league.

8. Let's see the fireworks on Victoria day!

9. albert's aunt alberta has arrived.

10. We ate dinner in the restaurant at the top of the Building.

11. Is there a Doctor in the house?

12. when you are in Winnipeg, visit the centennial arts centre.

13. Come on, horatio, you're holding us up.

14. i asked Dr. Aresta if I could changeably appointment.

15. Mario is the Manager of a big department store.

16. Mail the form to john doe, anytown, canada.

17. i read the bestseller called *borderline.*

18. Everyone wants to know When the stock market will improve.

19. My Brother exclaimed, "so this is your apartment!"

20. John Polyani won the nobel prize for chemistry.

VI. Rewrite the following passages, correcting any errors in capitalization.

many people think of Hockey as the great Canadian game. And why not? Fans get to sit in beautiful arenas such as the calgary saddledome, eat Hot Dogs, watch an exciting event, and Yell Their Lungs Out. All the fun and excitement typifies the Spirit of Canada. A Canadian author, scott young, has examined the international ice hockey game in his book titled *war on ice*. It makes great reading for the serious and even the not-so-serious fan.

if you need someone to fix something in your apartment or house, don't call me! i have read *The Book Of Home Repair,* and still cannot manage to hang a picture or fix a leaky faucet. whenever something goes wrong in my home, i always call my Uncle, who is a whiz at such things. last Fall — i believe it was around thanksgiving — our garbage disposal overflowed. as usual, i called my Uncle, who said, "this is getting a bit out of hand. you can't expect me to drive all the way from yarmouth to fix your garbage disposal!" seeing as we lived in digby, he was right. i called a Plumber instead, who charged me a hundred dollars for the job; the Lake on the kitchen floor vanished, but i vowed i would either learn something about home repair or move to yarmouth.

CHAPTER 15

Spelling

Spelling — ugh! How do you ever know whether something is spelled right or not? And who cares, anyway, as long as the word can be understood?

Fortunately or unfortunately, such people as teachers and bosses do seem to care about correct spelling. And it's not just fussiness; often a word is harder to understand if it's not spelled in the way people are used to seeing it. So it's worthwhile making the effort to learn the rules for correct spelling.

Of course, there are a lot of cases that aren't covered by the rules. English-language spelling is full of irregularities. Many of them can be learned only by using them often enough so that they become familiar. In the meantime, perhaps the best spelling rule is this: *When in doubt, check the dictionary.*

Still, there are *some* rules that hold for most words. The most basic rules are given in this chapter, and if you master them you will be able to avoid many common errors. Also included in the chapter is a list of frequently misspelled words, which you may find it helpful to memorize.

A final point: In using many of the following rules, you will need to be aware of the difference between vowels and consonants. Five letters of the alphabet are known as *vowels a, e, i, o,* and *u.* All other letters are consonants.

POINT 1 **Use *i* before *e*
Except after *c*
Or when sounded as *a*
As in n*ei*ghbour or w*ei*gh.**

i before e	*ei after c*	*ei when sounded as a*
believe	receive	eight
chief	ceiling	vein
niece	deceive	sleigh
thief	conceive	freight

This rule works in most cases, but there are a few exceptions you should memorize:

either	height
neither	leisure
weird	seize

Exercise: Point 1

Write *C* if the word is spelled correctly; if it is spelled incorrectly, write the proper spelling in the space provided.

1. preist ______________ priest ______________
2. reign ______________
3. reciept ______________
4. wieght ______________
5. retreive ______________
6. die ______________
7. peice ______________
8. fiegn ______________
9. sliegh ______________
10. height ______________

POINT 2 **In putting an additional ending on a word, drop a *final silent e* when the ending begins with a vowel; keep a final silent *e* when the ending begins with a consonant.**

Endings Beginning with Vowels	Endings Beginning with Consonants
-ing	-ly
-ure	-ent
-ion	-ness
-ance	-ty
-able	-ful
-ed	-less
-ish	

1. Drop the *e* when the ending begins with a vowel:

   love + ing = loving
   please + ure = pleasure

recreate + ion = recreation
resemble + ance = resemblance
move + able = movable
scare + ed = scared
peeve + ish = peevish

2. Keep the *e* when the ending begins with consonant:

like + ly = likely
arrange + ment = arrangement
white + ness = whiteness
nine + ty = ninety
hope + ful = hopeful
care + less = careless

There are, however, some exceptions to this rule. As always, it is wise to check with a dictionary. The exceptions:

notice + able = noticeable
change + able = changeable
dye + ing = dyeing (This differs from die + ing = dying.)
awe + ful = awful
true + ly = truly

Exercise: Point 2

Form each of the following words.

1. entire + ly = entirely
2. come + ing = ______
3. improve + ment = ______
4. guide + ance = ______
5. love + less = ______
6. smoke + ed = ______
7. safe + ty = ______
8. like + able = ______
9. use + ful = ______
10. complete + ion = ______

Review Exercise: Points 1 and 2

All the following sentences contain spelling errors. Rewrite the sentences, correcting the errors, in the space provided.

1. Fernando wieghs 94 kilograms.

   Fernando weighs 94 kilograms.

2. You will need a stepladder to paint that cieling.

3. Your pleasure is my pleaseure.

4. Nghia bears a great likness to her mother.

5. We expressed our condoleences at the funeral.

6. The hobo scrambled aboard the frieght train.

7. She always speaks sincerly about the most delicate of issues.

8. This is one wierd party!

9. I was truely amazed at the endurance of marathon swimmers.

10. One pays a price for being fameous.

A letter that behaves a bit differently from most others is *y*. The following rules will cover most situations involving this letter.

POINT 3 **Change *y* to *i* when it is preceded by a consonant and followed by any letter other than *i*.**

try + ed = tried	*but*	try + ing = trying
greasy + er = greasier		forty + ish = fortyish
merry + ly = merrily		
plenty + ful = plentiful		
penny + less = penniless		

Exception: In most cases, change y to *ie* when it is preceded by a consonant and followed by the ending *-s*.

try + s = tries
baby + s = babies
hurry + s = hurries

Do not change *y* when it is preceded by a vowel.

stay + s = stays
play + ed = played
enjoy + able = enjoyable

Exceptions: a few common words:

day + ly = daily
gay + ly = gaily

Exercise: Point 3

Form each of the following words by using the rules you have learned in this step.

1. gully + s = gullies
2. worry + ed = ______
3. happy + ness = ______
4. repay + ing = ______
5. attorney + s = ______
6. stray + ed = ______
7. fry + ing = ______
8. necessary + ly = ______
9. apply + ed = ______
10. lonely + est = ______

POINT 4 **Add *-s* to form the plural of most nouns; add *-es* when the plural has an extra syllable, unless the singular ends in a silent *e*.**

Same Number of Syllables

Singular	Plural
step	steps
picture	pictures

Singular	Plural
radio	radios
key	keys
flower	flowers
boy	boys

Note that all these examples have been changed from singular to plural merely by adding *-s.*

Most words that have an extra syllable in the plural are words in which the singular form ends in an *s*-like sound.

Extra Syllable in Plural

Singular	Plural
bush	bushes
fox	foxes
mattress	mattresses
spice	spices

Note that all these examples have been changed from singular to plural by adding *-es*, except the last, which already has a silent *e* in the singular.

Some words, such as *tomato* and *potato*, do not follow the rule. The plural forms of these words are *tomatoes* and *potatoes*. As always, it is a good idea to check with a dictionary when you are in doubt.

Certain other nouns do not follow a regular pattern in changing from singular to plural. It is wise to memorize the following list of common irregular plural nouns, but you should also remember to consult the dictionary whenever you have a question about how to use a word.

Singular	Plural
wife	wives
life	lives
knife	knives
man	men
woman	women
crisis	crises

Exercise: Point 4

Form the plurals of the following words by adding *-s* or *-es*.

1. girl ______ girls ______
2. typewriter ____________
3. church ____________

4. trace ______
5. cigar ______
6. apartment ______
7. porch ______
8. bus ______
9. ache ______
10. tax ______

Review Exercise: Points 1–4

All the following sentences contain spelling errors. Rewrite the sentences, correcting the errors, in the space provided.

1. Norman was curseing his fate.

   Norman was cursing his fate.

2. I have already applyed to three graduate schools.

   ______

3. I'm looking for a peice of the action.

   ______

4. His whole apartment is lighted by gas lampes.

   ______

5. There are three different styles of couchs to choose from.

   ______

6. That is a great wieght off my shoulders.

   ______

7. We are looking ahead hopfully to the next election.

   ______

8. Richard is pursueing a new career.

   ______

9. Honey, you are my shineing star.

   ______

10. This sandwich is just aweful.

   ______

POINT 5 **Double a *final single consonant* before an ending beginning with a vowel when both of the following occur: (1) a single vowel precedes the consonant, and (2) the accent is on the last syllable.**

hop + ing = hopping	
Final single consonant?	*p*
Single vowel precedes consonant?	*o*
Ending beginning with a vowel?	*i*
Accent on last syllable?	*only one syllable*

omit + ed = omitted	
Final single consonant?	*t*
Single vowel precedes consonant?	*i*
Ending beginning with a vowel?	*e*
Accent on last syllable?	*yes*

corner + ed = cornered	
Final single consonant?	*r*
Single vowel precedes consonant?	*e*
Ending beginning with a vowel?	*e*
Accent on last syllable?	*no*

Since the accent is not on the last syllable in *corner,* we do not double the *r* to form *cornered.*

keep + ing = keeping	
Final single consonant?	*p*
Single vowel precedes consonant?	*no*
Ending beginning with a vowel?	*i*
Accent on last syllable?	*only one*

Since *keep* does not meet one of the requirements (it has *two* vowels preceding the final consonant), we do not double the *p* to form *keeping.*

walk + ed = walked

Can you tell why this word is not spelled *walkked?*

Exercise: Point 5

Form each of the following words by using the rules you have learned in Point 5.

1. control + ed = controlled
2. admit + ing = ____________________
3. begin + ing = ____________________
4. small + est = ____________________

5. scream + ing = ____________________
6. develop + ed = ____________________
7. suffer + ing = ____________________
8. fish + ing = ____________________
9. puff + ed = ____________________
10. stir + ing = ____________________

Review Exercise: Points 1–5

All the following sentences contain spelling errors. Rewrite the sentences, correcting the errors, in the space provided.

1. This is a chapter about speling.

   This is a chapter about spelling.

2. I am admiting no fault whatsoever.

   ____

3. We visited Ripley's Beleive it or Not Museum.

   ____

4. Tomorrow we will go horseback rideing.

   ____

5. I have resistted greater temptations in the past.

   ____

6. Those bananas are roting!

   ____

7. Come to this office immediatly!

   ____

8. This corner is the busyest one in Estevan.

   ____

9. Everyone benefitted by his generosity.

   ____

10. All waiters should report to the dineing room.

    ____

HOW TO AVOID COMMON SPELLING ERRORS

1. Remember the rules for using *ie* or *ei*.
2. Keep in mind the rules for dropping final letters when you add an ending to a word.
3. Remember that you may need to change *y* to *i* or *ie* when adding an ending.
4. Be sure you know whether to add *-s* or *-es* to change a word from singular to plural, and *use your dictionary!*

Words Frequently Misspelled

1. absence
2. accept
3. across
4. address
5. almost
6. already
7. always
8. among
9. answer
10. athlete
11. beginning
12. business
13. college
14. coming
15. committee
16. competition
17. counsellor
18. criticism
19. criticize
20. decision
21. definite
22. definition
23. describe
24. description
25. desperate
26. discipline
27. divide
28. eighth
29. eliminate
30. embarrassed
31. escape
32. etc.
33. exaggerate
34. excellent
35. experience
36. extremely
37. familiar
38. finally
39. foreign
40. forty
41. friend
42. government
43. guarantee
44. immediately
45. independence
46. independent
47. intelligence
48. interest
49. interfere
50. judgment
51. knowledge
52. laboratory
53. length
54. library
55. licence
56. marriage
57. mathematics
58. meant
59. necessary
60. ninety
61. ninth
62. occasionally
63. occur
64. opinion
65. opportunity
66. paid
67. particular
68. performance
69. possess
70. possible
71. preferred
72. prejudice
73. preparation
74. pressure
75. privilege
76. probably
77. professor
78. realize
79. recommend
80. relieve
81. religious
82. repetition
83. rhythm
84. ridiculous
85. sacrifice
86. safety
87. scene
88. schedule
89. science
90. separate
91. similar
92. sophomore
93. straight
94. succeed
95. surprise
96. temperature
97. together
98. tragedy
99. unusual
100. Wednesday

Chapter Review

I. Write *C* if the word is spelled correctly. If it is misspelled, rewrite it correctly in the space provided.

1. radioes ____
2. arrangeing ____
3. location ____
4. fortyeth ____
5. controllable ____
6. blotted ____
7. developped ____
8. recieve ____
9. unstoppable ____
10. bushs ____
11. paling ____
12. greif ____
13. eightyeth ____
14. livly ____
15. trying ____
16. despairring ____
17. ladderes ____
18. associateion ____
19. liesure ____
20. entirety ____

II. Form the following words by using the rules you have learned in this chapter.

1. get + ing = ____
2. guide + ing = ____
3. satisfy + ed = ____
4. spy + s = ____

5. run + ing = __________
6. seize + ure = __________
7. party + ing = __________
8. relieve + ed = __________
9. like + ness = __________
10. hope + less = __________
11. pray + ing = __________
12. time + ed = __________
13. spite + ful = __________
14. toy + ing = __________
15. guide + ance = __________
16. manage + ed = __________
17. marry + ed = __________
18. pit + ed = __________
19. chop + ed = __________
20. pity + able = __________

III. Form the plurals of the following singular nouns:

1. goat __________
2. baby __________
3. guitar __________
4. envelope __________
5. woe __________
6. tree __________
7. history __________
8. taco __________
9. church __________
10. glass __________

IV. Circle the correctly spelled word given in the parentheses.

1. Can't you accept (criticism, critisism)?
2. She gets (embarassed, embarrassed) when she drops something.
3. Try to avoid (carless, careless) spelling errors.
4. It (pays, payes) to shop at Arthur's.
5. You are not a very (friendly, freindly) person.
6. His temper is (uncontrolable, uncontrollable).
7. It is your (privilige, privilege), not your right!
8. The students (seized, siezed) the administration building.
9. I enjoyed my (sophomore, sophmore) year best of all.
10. She is (emploied, employed) by Weston bakeries.

V. All the following sentences contain spelling errors. Rewrite the sentences, correcting the errors, in the space provided.

1. Ken sliped on the ice and broke his ankle.

____

2. My girlfriend spendes too much time studying.

____

3. The lamp broke into hundreds of peices.

____

4. Forget it; it is niether my business nor yours.

____

5. I'll be fliing high if I get good news.

____

6. The administration has adoptted a new policy on energy.

____

7. Camping in New Brunswick was such a pleaseure.

____

8. She is the fairest and lovliest child I know.

____

9. The criminal was sentenced to ninty years in prison.

10. You have embarased me with your remark.

11. Church and state must be seperated.

12. "Discribe the man you saw," said the detective.

13. This is your third abcence from class this week.

14. I admited my secret passion.

15. Welcome to the nieghbourhood!

16. The weather around here is so changable.

17. We have gone to four partys allready this week.

18. I can't stand shoping for shoes.

19. The stringes are broken and have to be replaced.

20. I am a very happyly married man.

VI. Rewrite the following passages, correcting any misspelled words.

Late summer is truely a lovly time of the year. After being fryed by the heat and drenchhed by humidity, many people feel that it is a great releif to expirience the cool evenings that promise the comming of autumn. As the cool weather returnes, people seem to regain much of the energy that they had lost dureing the hot and stickey monthes of July and August. There are all kinds of outdoor activityes: baseball gams, barbequs, campfirs. It is as if the cool breezs bring with them a fresh and new feeling for life.

There is probaly no greater thrill or privelege than watching the birth of your own child. Manny of my freinds have acepted the responsability of takeing part in the proces, particularly by acting as an asistant to the doctor. These husbands have helped thier wifes with breathing and relaxashun techniques. Above all, they get the definate plesure of witnesing what is surly the most amazing act of all.

Possessives and Contractions

A useful little mark that handles two quite different chores in modern-day English is the *apostrophe* ('). It marks the place where letters have been dropped out of a word to form a *contraction*, and it also serves along with *s* to show *possession*. (A few centuries ago, these two uses were more closely related than they are now. We won't go into that, though.)

The value of both contractions and possessives is that they let us express things more quickly and in fewer words than we could without them. We say *I'll* instead of *I will*, *they haven't* instead of *they have not*, and *Ed's book* instead of *the book of Ed*.

There are a few things you need to keep in mind, however, in using these forms. One is that apostrophes are rather easily misplaced, and putting one in the wrong spot can sometimes change the meaning of the word. So can leaving out an apostrophe. *We'll* has quite another meaning than *well*. And if I write, *the boy's doughnut*, we have one boy and one doughnut — a reasonable situation. But if I write, *the boys' doughnut*, we have several boys and one doughnut. In this situation, there could be quite an argument if the boys are hungry!

The other thing to be careful about is that some contractions sound just like some possessive words, but they aren't spelled the same. So in writing, it's important to keep in mind what kind of a word you're using.

The rules about possessives and contractions are fairly simple. If you master them, you will be able to use these forms competently in your writing.

POINT 1 To determine ownership, ask, "Who owns what?"

the radio of Cindy

To determine ownership, we ask *who owns what*. Cindy owns the radio.

the car of George

Who owns what? George owns the car.

friends of mine

Since one doesn't really *own* friends, we can ask, "Who has what?" The answer: "I have friends."

Do not get confused: The radio does not own Cindy; the car does not own George, friends do not have me.

Exercise: Point 1

For each of the following phrases, determine who owns what.

1. the house of mine ______ I own the house. ______
2. The whistle of the police officer ______
3. the leotard of the dancer______
4. the headlights of the car ______
5. the newspaper of my father ______
6. the credit card of my mother______
7. the ring of my wife______
8. the power of the engine ______
9. the dolls of my baby sister ______
10. the fountain pen of Aretha______

POINT 2 Use -*'s* to form the possessive of most singular nouns.

Cindy owns the radio.

Once we have determined that Cindy owns the radio, we can apply the *'s rule*. The sentence may be rewritten as follows:

It is Cindy's radio.

Cindy is a noun that does not end in -*s*. Therefore, we can add -*'s* to *Cindy*, making *Cindy's*. *Cindy's* is the possessive form of the noun.

The car belongs to George.

may be rewritten

It is George's car.

Here are some more examples:

the hairstyle of my sister

becomes

my sister's hairstyle

the power of the engine

becomes

the engine's power

Note: In these examples *Cindy, George, sister,* and *engine* are all singular nouns. For a review of the terms *singular* and *plural,* turn to Chapter 1, Point 1.

Exercise: Point 2

Change these phrases into possessives by using -'s.

1. the idea of my mother ___my mother's idea___
2. the plants of Judy ______
3. the copy machine of the library ______
4. the choice of the people ______
5. the job of the detective ______
6. the mail of the camper ______
7. the pants of Sam ______
8. the money of the bookie ______
9. the rattle of the baby ______
10. the paper route of the boy ______

POINT 3 Use only an apostrophe to form the possessive of plural nouns ending in *-s.*

the boat of the boys

This phrase has a noun ending in *-s*. The boat belongs to the boys. To form the possessive, we need only add an apostrophe after the noun we wish to make possessive. The phrase may be rewritten as follows:

the boys' boat

Note that the possessive is not written *boys's.* In this phrase, there is more than one boy.

It is *extremely important* to be able to distinguish the following:

boy
boy's (belonging to one boy)
boys
boys' (belonging to more than one boy)

Here are some more examples:

clothing for girls	girls' clothing
the noise of the cars	cars' noise
the sound of the bells	bells' sound

Note that all the preceding examples have words that end in *-s*. An exception to this rule is that if a *singular* word ending in *-s* has only *one syllable,* you should use -'s to form the possessive.

the dog of Charles	Charles's dog
the desk of the boss	the boss's desk

Be aware, also, of plural nouns that do not end in *-s*. These words, such as *men, women,* and *children,* are made possessive by adding 's to the end.

the center for children	the children's center
clothing for women	women's clothing

Exercise: Point 3

Change these phrases into possessives by adding an apostrophe.

1. the crying of the babies *the babies' crying*
2. the home town of my cousins ____________
3. the chairs of the barbers ____________
4. the slant of the rooftops ____________
5. the smell of the cigars ____________
6. the duration of the exhibits ____________
7. the offices of the professors ____________
8. the running shoes of the men ____________
9. the salaries of the players ____________
10. the legs of the tables ____________

Review Exercise: Points 1–3

Rewrite the following sentences, adding apostrophes where necessary.

1. Johns mother belongs to the Professional Womens Club.

   John's mother belongs to the Professional Women's Club.

2. Have you read Marks essay on sexual freedom?

3. The womens marathon is the next event.

4. Is this Carlos raincoat?

5. Have you ever been to a worlds fair?

6. The publishers wanted to buy Marthas manuscript.

7. One of Torontos popular meeting places is Yorkville.

8. Mr. Dickens daughter will be married next week.

9. The managers lineup card was taped to the dugout wall.

10. The Canadiens home arena is The Forum.

Before going on, we might note a common kind of expression that is not exactly a possessive but behaves just like one:

> I will be there in less than an hour's time.

(that is, in time *of* less than an hour, or a time *lasting* less than an hour). Since *an hour* is singular, this expression behaves just like a singular possessive.

> She took a three weeks' vacation.

Three weeks is plural, so the expression behaves like a plural possessive.

POINT 4 Be sure to distinguish between plurals and possessives.

▸ *Remember:* plural refers to number, and specifically, to more than one. Plural words do not necessarily show ownership.

Possessives may, of course, be either singular or plural. Do not be tempted to "overcorrect" by adding apostrophes to plurals as well as possessives.

Plural	Possessive
boys (more than one boy)	boys' (belonging to more than one boy)
girls (more than one girl)	girls' (belonging to more than one girl)
boats (more than one boat)	boats' (belonging to more than one boat)

The following chart may help you understand the relationships among singular, plural, and possessive forms.

Singular	Singular Possessive	Plural	Plural Possessive
tree	tree's	trees	trees'
girl	girl's	girls	girls'
athlete	athlete's	athletes	athletes'
man	man's	men	men's
child	child's	children	children's
year	year's	years	years'

Can you use each of these different forms in a sentence?

Exercise: Point 4

Circle the correct word given in the parentheses.

1. Keep those (animals, animals') in their cages.
2. We visited both (professors, professors') offices.
3. What are the (titles, titles') of your courses?
4. What are your (courses, courses') titles?
5. Those rotted (trees, trees') will have to go.
6. They are my (parents, parents') parents.
7. The scientist clipped those (bugs, bugs') wings.
8. Two (candles, candles') provide all the light in this room.
9. They are the (stars, stars') of the show.
10. They are the (shows, show's) stars.

POINT 5 Do not use an apostrophe with possessive modifiers or pronouns.

Possessive *modifiers* come *before* a noun and describe it. They are

my	our	whose
your	your	
his, her, its	their	

Note that none of these words takes an apostrophe. Possession is built into them.

This is my dog.	*never*	This is my's dog.
This is your dog.	*never*	This is your's dog.
This is his dog.	*never*	This is his' dog.
This is her dog.	*never*	This is her's dog.
Whose dog is this?	*never*	Whose' dog is this?

Possessive *pronouns* are used when the possessive word is *separated from* the name of the thing possessed. They are

mine	ours	whose
yours	yours	
his, hers	theirs	

Note that these words are very similar to the possessive modifiers. Be careful not to get them confused. Again, none of them takes an apostrophe.

The magazine is ours.	*never*	The magazine is our's.
The magazine is yours.	*never*	The magazine is your's.
The magazine is hers.	*never*	The magazine is her's.
Whose is this magazine?	*never*	Whose' is this magazine?

Possessive words are used to take the place of possessives formed from nouns. Therefore, the sentence

Joe's teacher is always late for class.

may be changed to

His teacher is always late for class.

Likewise, the sentence

I ran into a friend of **Peggy's.**

may be changed to

I ran into a friend of **hers.**

Be very careful when using the possessive words *its, whose, your,* and *their.* Always remember that these words are used strictly to show possession.

The stereo has lost **its** power.

The power "belongs" to the stereo.

Whose apartment is this?

The apartment belongs to someone.

This is **your** life.

The life belongs to you.

The kids are brushing **their** teeth.

The teeth belong to them.

Exercise: Point 5

Fill in the blank with an appropriate possessive modifer or pronoun.

1. It is ______his______ decision to make.
2. We will have to change ____________ approach.
3. That sewing machine is ____________ .
4. The storm had taken ____________ toll.
5. ____________ beautiful garden is this?
6. What can I do to make you change ____________ mind?
7. They are taking ____________ children to the Royal Winnipeg Ballet.
8. I bought it, so it is ____________ .
9. I must be losing ____________ mind.
10. I am sorry, sir, but that coat is not ____________ ; it is ____________ .

Review Exercise: Points 1–5

Rewrite the following sentences, correcting any errors with possessives.

1. The childrens play group meets once a week.
   ______The children's play group meets once a week.______
2. Mr. Jones car needs to be washed.
   ____
3. Great writers messages are sometimes misunderstood.
   ____
4. That seat is not yours'; it is mine.
   ____

5. The superintendents apartment was vandalized last night.

____

6. Now it is someone elses game to win or lose.

____

7. Whose' ten-speed bicycle are you using?

____

8. The teachers union supported the strike.

____

9. Do you understand the reasons' for my decision?

____

10. The Athabaska River overflowed it's banks.

____

POINT 6 **A contraction (two words condensed into one) is formed by replacing a letter (or group of letters) with an apostrophe.**

When forming a contraction, you should make sure that the apostrophe goes in the exact place where the letter would have been.

I am	I'm

Here the apostrophe takes the place of *a*.

you are	you're	I would	I'd
he is	he's	he would	he'd
she is	she's	they would	they'd
it is	it's	are not	aren't
we are	we're	cannot	can't
you are	you're	does not	doesn't
they are	they're	do not	don't
there is	there's	have not	haven't
he has	he's	should not	shouldn't
she has	she's	could not	couldn't
they have	they've	would not	wouldn't
I will	I'll	let us	let's
she will	she'll	where is	where's
he will	he'll	will not	won't
I had	I'd	they had	they'd
he had	he'd		

Remember *won't* in particular. It is an exception to the rule for forming contractions.

Contractions are used frequently in everyday speech. It is usually better *not* to use them in writing, unless you want to sound "chatty." Although they are little more than time and space savers, it is important to use them correctly if you use them at all.

Note: Ain't is sometimes heard as a contraction of several expressions—*am not, is not, are not, has not, have not.* It should *not* be used in writing, except in direct quotations.

Exercise: Point 6

Rewrite the following sentences, changing the underlined words into contractions.

1. He has never been to summer camp before.

   He's never been to summer camp before.

2. I will buy the chips if you will make the dip.

   ____

3. They would have arrived on time if they did not have a balky car.

   ____

4. I am sorry, but this time it is not my fault.

   ____

5. She will never know what hit her.

   ____

6. I would have chosen a different colour.

   ____

7. Let us work together for a change.

   ____

8. He would not mind if you combed his hair with a rake.

   ____

9. I have not been to the dentist in three years.

   ____

10. Patti does not plan to be an Avon lady all her life.

    ____

POINT 7 Do not confuse contractions with possessives.

There is an important difference between

Possessive		Contraction
your	and	you're
its	and	it's
their	and	they're
whose	and	who's

your means *belonging to you*
you're means *you are*

its means *belonging to it*
it's means *it is*

their means *belonging to them*
they're means *they are*

whose means *belonging to whom*
who's means *who is*

These pairs of words look similar and sound exactly alike. Make sure you have a reason for using one or the other in a sentence. Always determine whether you want a contraction or a possessive.

Exercise: Point 7

Circle the correct word given in the parentheses.

1. (Its, It's) a beautiful day for a drive in the country.
2. (Whose, Who's) bright idea was that?
3. This is (your, you're) problem, not mine.
4. Do you approve of the way they raise (their, they're) children?
5. My soda has lost (it's, its) fizz.
6. (Whose, Who's) the leader of the New Democratic Party?
7. (Your, You're) a good man, Charlie Brown.
8. (Their, They're) never going to be able to straighten out (their? they're) finances.
9. (Its, It's) a sure bet!
10. (Whose, Who's) going to pay for all this damage?

Review Exercise: Points 1–7

Rewrite the following sentences, adding apostrophes where necessary.

1. Were hoping that shell pass her English exam.

   We're hoping that she'll pass her English exam.

2. Its Russ car, and hell be angry if you drive it.

3. The days work isnt done yet.

4. The Regina Symphonys performance was outstanding.

5. Is the responsibility yours or Tims?

6. Lately weve been keeping a hawks eye on our diets.

7. That actress lines should be rewritten.

8. Thats Ernies problem, not mine.

9. Cheryls motorcycle isnt running smoothly these days.

10. Its never too late to say youre sorry.

HOW TO AVOID MISTAKES IN POSSESSIVES

1. In forming a possessive from a noun, think of the rules for deciding whether to add -' or -'s
2. Never use an apostrophe with a possessive modifier or pronoun.

HOW TO AVOID MISTAKES IN CONTRACTIONS

1. Note where you have removed letters to form the contraction. and be sure to put the apostrophe exactly there.
2. Be careful not to confuse contractions with possessives that sound the same.

Chapter Review

I. Write *C* if the sentence is correct as it stands or *X* if it contains an error with possessives or contractions.

_______ 1. He'll never make it to the finals.

_______ 2. Its a hard rain that's going to fall.

_______ 3. The coachs' son is the star of the team.

_______ 4. That parrot is Marthas pride and joy.

_______ 5. Glenn's teacher is from India.

_______ 6. I saw it in my minds eye.

_______ 7. They'll be arriving any minute now.

_______ 8. We each danced with the other's wife.

_______ 9. Their never going to believe this!

_______ 10. Youll never guess whom I saw today.

II. Fill in the blank with a noun that shows possession.

1. It belongs to Sally; it is ______________________________
2. It belongs to Mr. Ross; it is______________________________
3. It belongs to Bill; it is______________________________
4. It belongs to my mother; it is ______________________________
5. It belongs to Aunt Betty; it is______________________________
6. It belongs to the company; it is ______________________________
7. It belongs to my son; it is ______________________________
8. It belongs to your friend; it is ______________________________
9. It belongs to the team; it is ______________________________
10. It belongs to Chris; it is______________________________

III. Fill in the blank with a possessive modifier or pronoun.

1. It belongs to Shirley; it is ____________________
2. It belongs to us; it is ____________________
3. It belongs to me; it is ____________________
4. It belongs to Sam; it is ____________________
5. It belongs to you; it is ____________________
6. It belongs to them; it is ____________________ property.
7. It belongs to me; it is ____________________ property.
8. It belongs to them; it is ____________________
9. It belongs to you; it is ____________________ property.
10. I don't know whom it belongs to; ____________________ is it?

IV. Circle the correct word given in the parentheses.

1. (Its, It's) a sin to tell a lie.
2. It is (their, they're) way of showing affection.
3. (Your, You're) the most beautiful woman I've ever seen.
4. I am the one (who's whose) paper you read.
5. The airplane is in trouble; (its, it's) wing has caught fire.
6. (Their, They're) never going to believe this back in Corner Brook.
7. He has been imitating (your, you're) style for some time.
8. Guess (whose, who's) coming to dinner.
9. It is the (captains, captain's) decision to make.
10. (Whose, Who's) going to clean it up?

V. Put apostrophes where necessary in the following sentences.

1. Womens wear is on the second floor.
2. Youre a very stylish dresser.
3. My sisters briefcase is overflowing.
4. That artists style is certainly unique.
5. Marcus friend is staying with him for the summer.

6. Those books are Bobbys and mine.
7. Youre such a good catcher that you could play on anyones team.
8. Lately I've grown close to Mikes wife.
9. My fathers business takes him to the Orient twice a year.
10. Did you heed the gurus advice?
11. Were learning the basic skills of writing.
12. The horse trotted to the winners circle.
13. The fireworks display was very exciting.
14. Your brothers van has a flat tire.
15. Lenins ideas do not appeal to everyone.
16. Those babies are twins!
17. The doctors office is closed today.
18. What is Brians idea of a good time?
19. Whos going to pay the cheque?
20. Lets go to the movies.

VI. All the following sentences contain errors in the use of possessives or contractions. Rewrite the sentences, correcting the errors, in the space provided.

1. It's your's, so do with it as you please.

   ____

2. I think its never going to stop raining.

   ____

3. She's minding someone elses shop today.

   ____

4. It was my employers idea to give me a raise.

   ____

5. Weve visited Marjories beach house twice before.

   ____

6. I met you're brother at the VIA Rail station.

   ____

7. Our familys motto is "Live and let live."

8. The musicians trumpet has been stolen.

9. The RCMPs the best police force in the world.

10. Those criminals records show they're history.

11. Lead me to the mens room, please.

12. I borrowed my parents car.

13. Wheres the beef?

14. Kasumis piano needs to be tuned.

15. The sisters husbands have lunch together every Monday.

16. Womens haircuts are generally quite attractive.

17. James new car has a CD player.

18. The employees lunchroom is located downstairs.

19. My aunts tapioca pudding is the best in the world.

20. Dont try telling me that you're way is better.

VII. Rewrite the following passages, correcting any errors in the use of possessives or contractions.

In Canada, our pets names are both unique and amusing. While we genuinely love our pet's, theyre likely called by names that we wouldnt name anyone else in the family. Whose going to deny that theyve had some rather unusual names for their pet's? Of course, theres the obvious Peter for a pet rabbit. Peters lucky to be named after a storybook character. Palmolives name fits a pet skunk, and all the Pooh's in the world are also likely skunks. Dogs and cats are also known by "pet" names, and even though our pet's are one of lifes great pleasures, we do tend to get carried away at times when we try to think up suitable names for them.

Ive never been one to keep New Years resolutions. Its always been easy enough for me to promise to give up mine bad habits, but I just dont seem to keep my promises. Once, the day after Id resolved never to smoke cigarettes again, my wife found a pack around and yelled, "Who's are these?" "Their mine," I answered sheepishly. Its a sure bet Ill resolve to quit again this year, but unless I get serious, Im sure my wifes advice "Your never serious about something until your serious about it" will once again prove true.

Summary of Points Covered

CHAPTER 1

Points

1. Identify the subject of the sentence by asking *who* or *what* is doing something (or being something). (p. 6)
2. A subject may be a *noun.* (p. 8)
3. A subject may be a *pronoun.* (p. 9)
4. A subject may be an *-ing* word. (p. 11)
5. A subject may consist of more than one word. (p. 12)
6. A subject may appear anywhere in the sentence. (p. 14)
7. The subject is never within a phrase that begins with such words as *on, in, of, before, behind, near.* (p.14)

CHAPTER 2

Points

1. A *verb* is a word (or group of words) used to express action. (p. 20)
2. The *tense* of a verb shows the time when the action happened—past, present, or future. Many verbs can be changed from the present tense to the past tense by adding *-d* or *-ed* to the end. (p. 21)
3. A *linking verb* is used to link the subject to a descriptive word in the sentence or to another noun. (p. 23)
4. Verbs ending in *-ing* require another verb (often some form of the verb *to be)* before them. (p. 24)
5. Some verbs are *irregular.* They do not follow a set pattern when they change tenses. (p. 26)
6. The *to* form of a verb is incomplete, and needs another verb before it. (p. 30)
7. Be sure to identify the *complete verb* in a sentence. (p. 31)
8. A sentence may contain two or more verbs. (p. 32)

CHAPTER 3

Points

1. Use singular verbs with singular subjects, and plural verbs with plural subjects. (p.41)
2. When it is used as a subject, a pronoun must agree with the verb. (p. 42)
3. When a subject is compound (includes two or more elements), make sure it agrees with the verb. (p. 43)
   a. Compound subjects joined by *and* take plural verbs. (p. 43)
   b. Compound subjects joined by *or* or *nor* take singular verbs when both subjects are singular. (p. 44)
   c. When a singular subject is joined to a plural subject by *or* or *nor*, the verb agrees with the subject closer to the verb. (p. 44)
4. Some indefinite pronouns are singular and take singular verbs. (p. 45)
5. Some indefinite pronouns are plural and take plural verbs. (p. 48)
6. Singular subjects followed by phrases that describe the subject take singular verbs; plural subjects take plural verbs. Subjects are sometimes followed by phrases beginning with *with, as well as, together with, including*, and so forth. (p. 49)
7. A collective noun (group word) takes a singular verb when the group is referred to as a single unit; it takes a plural verb when the members of the group are being considered as a set of individuals. (p. 51)
8. When the verb comes before the subject of the sentence, it is especially important to identify the subject and make the verb agree with it. (p. 52)
9. Words or names that are plural in form but singular in meaning take a singular verb. (p. 53)

CHAPTER 4

Points

1. Make sure every sentence has a subject and a verb. (p. 62)
2. Watch out for *-ing* words. No word ending in *-ing* can ever be the complete verb of a sentence. (p. 64)
3. A group of words containing a subject and a verb is called a *clause.* (p. 66)
4. When a dependent clause comes at the beginning of a sentence, it is followed by a *comma.* However, if the independent clause comes first, you may or may not need a comma. (p. 68)
5. Every sentence must have at least one independent clause. (p. 70)
6. Avoid other common types of fragments, such as the "list" type. (p. 72)
7. Command sentences do not contain obvious subjects, but they are still complete and correct. (p. 73)

CHAPTER 5

Points

1. Connect two independent clauses with a comma *plus* one of the connecting words: *and, but, for, or, nor, yet, so.* (p. 83)
2. Separate two independent clauses with a semicolon. In addition, connecting words such as *however, therefore, consequently, nevertheless, likewise, besides, also, then*, and *furthermore* may be used after the semicolon. (p. 84)
3. Make the two independent clauses into two sentences by using a period, a question mark, or an exclamation mark. (p.87)
4. Change one of the independent clauses into a dependent clause. (p. 89)

CHAPTER 6

Points

1. A *modifier* is a word (or group of words) that describes or explains another word (or group of words) in a sentence. (p. 101)
2. Place a modifier as close as possible to the word it modifies. (p. 102)
3. When dealing with modifiers, ask yourself, *what goes with what?* (p. 104)
4. Be sure that words such as *almost, even, hardly, just, merely, only, nearly,* and *scarcely* refer clearly to the words they modify. (p. 106)
5. Avoid placing a modifier between two words when its explanation can apply to either word. (p. 107)

CHAPTER 7

Points

1. A modifier is said to be *dangling* when there is no word in the sentence for it to modify. (p. 115)
2. When a sentence begins with a group of words introduced by an *-ing* word, the person or thing performing the action (the subject) should be identified right after the *-ing* phrase. (p. 116)
3. Put the modifier as close as possible to the word it explains. (p. 118)
4. Sometimes you can turn a dangling modifier into a dependent clause. (p. 120)
5. A group of words that has an *-ing* word somewhere in it must refer clearly to the subject of the sentence. (p. 122)
6. Modifiers beginning with a *to* form of a verb must refer clearly to the word they modify. (p. 123)

CHAPTER 8

Points

1. A pronoun may be used as the subject of a sentence. (p. 132)
2. A pronoun may be used as the *object* of a verb in a sentence. (p. 134)
3. Often a sentence contains both a noun and a pronoun that refers to the noun. To decide whether to use a subject pronoun or an object pronoun, look at the pronoun's relation to *its own verb.* (p. 136)
4. When a sentence contains two or more nouns, place the pronoun as close as possible to the noun it refers to, and make sure the reference is clear. (p. 138)
5. Be sure that pronouns refer to a single noun and not to a whole idea. (p. 140)
6. Be sure that a pronoun has a word, and not an unexpressed idea, to refer to. (p. 141)

CHAPTER 9

Points

1. When elements are parallel in thought, use parallel forms to express them. (p. 151)
2. Balance a noun with a noun, a verb with a verb, a modifier with a modifier, and so on. (p. 152)

3. Use parallel constructions for words joined by such connectors as *and, but, nor, or.* (p. 154)
4. Use parallel structure with such constructions as *either . . . or, neither . . . nor, not . . . but, not only . . . but also, both . . . and.* (p. 156)
5. Make sure that *parallel groups of words* in a sentence have parallel structure. (p. 157)

CHAPTER 10

Points

1. *Number* refers to the number of units referred to. In English grammar, there are only two numbers: singular and plural. (p. 168)
2. Be sure to keep number consistent throughout a sentence. (p. 169)
3. There are only three *persons* in English grammar. Each person may be either singular or plural. (p. 171)
4. Be sure to keep person consistent throughout a sentence. (p. 173)
5. Be sure to keep *tense* consistent throughout a sentence. (p. 174)

CHAPTER 11

Points

1. Use a *period* at the end of a sentence that makes a statement. (p. 187)
2. Use a period after an abbreviation. (p. 188)
3. Use a *question mark* after a direct question. (p. 189)
4. Use an *exclamation mark* after an expression or statement that show strong feeling. (p. 190)
5. Use *quotation marks* to enclose the exact words of a speaker or writer. (p. 191)
6. a. Periods and commas are always placed *inside* quotation marks. (p. 193)
   b. Question marks and exclamation marks are placed *outside* quotation marks except when the quotation itself is a direct question or an exclamation. (p. 193)
   c. Semicolons and colons are placed outside the closing quotation marks. (p. 193)
7. Use quotation marks to enclose the titles of short works such as a story, essay, short poem, song, or radio or television program. For longer works, such as novels, plays, movies, newspapers, full-length books, and magazines, use underlining instead of quotation marks. (p. 195)

CHAPTER 12

Points

1. Use a *semicolon* to separate two independent clauses. (p. 203)
2. Do not use a semicolon when two independent clauses are joined by such weak connecting words as *and, but, for, nor, or, so, yet.* However, if the clauses are joined by stronger connecting words such as *also, however, therefore, then, otherwise, nevertheless, moreover,* you should use a semicolon. (p. 204)
3. Use semicolons to separate items in a series when the items (a) have internal punctuation or (b) are long. (p. 206)
4. Use a *colon* to introduce a list following a noun that names the list. (p. 208)
5. Use a colon to set off a list or a statement that is introduced by the words *the following* or *as follows.* (p. 209)

CHAPTER 13

Points

1. Use *commas* to separate three or more items in a series. (p. 217)
2. Use a comma between two independent clauses if they are connected by such words as *and, but, for, or, nor, yet, so*. (p. 218)
3. Use a comma after a long introductory phrase or clause. Use a comma after a short introductory phrase if it is necessary to avoid unclear meaning. (p. 220)
4. Use commas on both sides of a word (or group of words) that interrupts the flow of the sentence. (p. 221)
5. Use commas to set off nonessential material. (p. 224)
6. Use a comma after every item in an address or date. (p. 226)

CHAPTER 14

Points

1. Capitalize the first, last, and important words in a title. (p. 237)
2. Capitalize the names of specific persons, places, languages, nations, and nationalities. (p. 238)
3. Capitalize names of days of the week, months, and holidays; do not capitalize names of the seasons. (p. 240)
4. Capitalize the first word of a direct quotation. (p. 241)
5. Capitalize words of family relationship when they are used as *names.* (p. 242)
6. Capitalize words such as *college, doctor, building,* when they are part of the names of specific people or things. (p. 243)
7. Capitalize events in history, movements, and periods. (p. 245)
8. Capitalize the names of specific school courses, but do not capitalize general words that refer to the courses. (p. 246)

CHAPTER 15

Points

1. Use *i* before *e*
   Except after *c*
   Or when sounded as *a*
   As in n*ei*ghbour or w*ei*gh. (p. 254)
2. In putting an additional ending on a word, drop a *final silent e* when the ending begins with a vowel; keep a final silent *e* when the ending begins with a consonant. (p. 255)
3. Change *y* to *i* when it is preceded by a consonant and followed by any letter other than *i*. Change *y* to *ie* when it is preceded by a consonant and followed by the ending *-s*. Do not change *y* when it is preceded by a vowel. (p. 257)
4. Add *-s* to form the plural of most nouns; add *-es* when the plural has an extra syllable, unless the singular ends in a silent *e*. (p. 258)
5. Double a *final single consonant* before an ending beginning with a vowel when *both* of the following occur: (a) a single vowel precedes the consonant, *and* (b) the accent is on the last syllable. (p. 261)

CHAPTER 16

Points

1. To determine ownership, ask, "Who owns what?" (p. 270)
2. Use -'s to form the possessive of most singular nouns. (p. 271)
3. Use only an apostrophe to form the possessive of nouns ending in *-s*. (p. 272)
4. Be sure to distinguish between plurals and possessives. (p. 275)
5. Do not use an apostrophe with possessive modifiers or pronouns. (p. 276)
6. A contraction (two words condensed into one) is formed by replacing a letter (or group of letters) with an apostrophe. (p. 278)
7. Do not confuse contractions with possessives. (p. 280)

Answers to Exercises

PRETEST, p. 1

I

1. V	6. C	11. V	16. C
2. V	7. V	12. C	17. V
3. S	8. S	13. S	18. V
4. C	9. C	14. C	19. C
5. S	10. V	15. S	20. C

II

1. <u>Jamie</u> is going out for the track team.
2. <u>The Expos and the Mets</u> play tonight.
3. <u>Correct grammar</u> is an important aspect of good writing.
4. In the cabana is <u>the rowboat.</u>
5. <u>Jazz</u> is my favourite kind of music.
6. <u>Hans and Lisa</u> bought that car.
7. <u>Organic food</u> is healthful but expensive.
8. <u>Exercising</u> is part of my morning routine.
9. Around the corner fled <u>the stray dog.</u>
10. <u>That hibachi near the garage</u> is broken.

III

1. My father <u>is retiring</u> from business.
2. We <u>have</u> never <u>been</u> to Europe.
3. She <u>grew</u> more and more tired.
4. I never <u>promised</u> you a rose garden.
5. You <u>should be</u> sure to check the oil.
6. Holding down a job <u>is</u> never easy for Luke.
7. I <u>have tried</u> my hardest to succeed.
8. Woodworking <u>requires</u> skill and patience.
9. We <u>spent</u> our paycheques yesterday.
10. 1 always <u>visit</u> my parents on the civic holiday.

CHAPTER 1

Exercise: Point 1, p. 6

1. plumber
2. Doug
3. tree
4. motorcycle
5. Lucy
6. family
7. speakers
8. sister
9. Fans
10. store

Another Exercise: Point 1, p. 7

1. S <u>Sally</u> ran after the bus.
2. S My <u>friend</u> built a new beach house.
3. P <u>Ducks</u> swim in that pond.
4. S The <u>airplane</u> needs to take on fuel at Mirabel.
5. S Our <u>daughter</u> gave us a surprise party.
6. S <u>Sam</u> writes extremely well.
7. P The <u>clouds</u> obscured the sun.
8. S <u>Jason</u> sings in the choir.
9. S <u>Ms. Peterson</u> bought a snowmobile.
10. S The <u>snowstorm</u> lasted for hours.

Exercise: Point 2, p. 8

1. Alberta joined Confederation in 1905.
2. Henry runs a mile every day.
3. Flowers grow best in sunlight.
4. Exercise strengthens the body.
5. The boy joined our club.
6. My watch comes from Japan.
7. The MPs voted on the bill.
8. Hata wrote a letter to her member of Parliament.
9. Starvation worries people all over the world.
10. Bills are a part of life.

Review Exercise: Points 1 and 2, p. 9

Answers to this exercise will vary. Check with your instructor if you need to.

1. Nova Scotia is a province in Atlantic Canada.
2. My mother taught me everything I know.
3. Computers are delicate instruments.
4. The jury deliberated for ten hours.
5. Cars are vehicles.
6. Carpentry takes a great deal of skill.
7. My brother appeared on television.
8. My uncle is my mother's brother.
9. White rats make good pets.
10. Ms. Kirkpatrick was my favourite teacher.

Exercise: Point 3, p. 10

1. He is a shrewd businessman.
2. She has just graduated from Mount Royal College.
3. It does not bother me.
4. We are going to write a song.
5. They make a lot of money.
6. She has visited Canada.
7. It takes time.
8. He surely knows how to water-ski.
9. They sent me birthday cards.
10. They understood each other.

Exercise: Point 4, p. 11

1. Singing is her chief talent.
2. Driving drives me crazy.
3. Jogging is good exercise.
4. I am losing my patience.
5. I don't like cleaning my apartment.
6. You are finding it difficult to concentrate.
7. Sewing was never her favourite activity.
8. Advertising is a good way to get votes.
9. They always go skiing in January.
10. Cooking is his favourite hobby.

Exercise: Point 5, p. 12

1. Collecting stamps is my hobby.
2. His sister is an expert pianist.
3. Looking for an apartment is hard work.
4. Herb and Everett are starting a dynamic new business.
5. Choosing a spouse can be confusing.
6. Using common sense is important.
7. Bowling on Wednesdays keeps me sane.
8. Clara's radio needs to be repaired.
9. Jack and Jill went up the hill.
10. A green light means that we may go.

Review Exercise: Points 1–5, p. 13

Answers to this exercise will vary. Check with your instructor if you need to.

1. Jogging is a good way to get exercise.
2. Cold beers go great with a barbeque.
3. Big cars use a lot of gasoline.
4. Bowling is more fun than watching television.
5. My sister is a great singer.
6. Sky-diving is exciting but dangerous.
7. Christmas comes once a year.
8. Baking biscuits makes me remember the good old days.
9. Those players always beat us in tennis.
10. Germany fought against the Allies.

Another Review Exercise: Points 1–5, p. 13

1. Practical jokes can get you into trouble.
2. Ms. Murphy is running for mayor.
3. Collecting coins is my hobby.

4. Robert and Richard are twin brothers.
5. Shopping for shoes can give you tired feet.

Exercise: Point 6, p. 14

1. Around the corner went the motorcycle.
2. In the box seats was the commissioner of the CFL.
3. There was a long line at the ticket booth.
4. Here is one way to solve the problem.
5. There is work to be done.
6. Down the ladder came a firefighter with a baby in his arms.
7. There was no way out.
8. Through the train walked the conductor.
9. In town this week is a great new show.
10. There was a sale in the department store today.

Exercise: Point 7, p. 15

1. program
2. woman
3. man
4. weeds
5. problem
6. dreaming
7. people
8. teachers
9. calm
10. beers

Review Exercise: Points 1–7, p. 16

1. Melvin wants to study law.
2. Obeying the speed limit helps conserve fuel.
3. He and I will do it together.
4. The switch in the glove compartment opens the trunk.
5. Eating low-calorie foods is one way to lose weight.
6. On the beach is a lighthouse.
7. The stores on Duckworth Street are closed today.
8. There must be something wrong with you.
9. The man in the bullpen will soon come in to pitch.
10. Around the corner is the new super mailbox.

Chapter Review, p. 16

I 1. X

2. S Listening to my stereo relaxes me in the evening.
3. S That dog with the floppy ears is mine.
4. X
5. S A collection of rare books is a real treasure.
6. S Ms. Strauss is coming to visit me.
7. X
8. S In the closet is a pillow.
9. S Leonard Cohen was a cultural hero of the 1960s.
10. S Spring cleaning is a necessary chore.

II 1. A fear of dogs is common to many people.

2. Phyllis travels to Japan with her husband.
3. Going on a picnic is a great way to spend an afternoon.
4. One part of my idea involves you.
5. Home repair might become a lost art.
6. Juggling required good eyesight and coordination.
7. There are three gas stations at that corner.
8. Of all my friends, Chris is the nicest.
9. Blowing my nose unclogs my ears.
10. That leak in the radiator should be fixed.
11. Choosing courses wisely is a student's responsibility.
12. She is the one for me.
13. The filter of an air conditioner should be cleaned regularly.
14. Going to the dentist was a painful experience for me.
15. We all believe his explanation.
16. Repaving the road takes time.
17. Who wrote the textbook?
18. Lost in space, the astronaut tried to radio Earth.
19. He got a job in the new shopping mall.
20. Over the river, the exploding fireworks shed light.

III Answers to this exercise will vary. Check with your instructor if you need to.

1. Her moped was parked illegally.
2. In the cupboard is a chocolate cake.
3. Insect repellent helps keep the bugs away.
4. The United States is the country just south of Canada.
5. Her grandparents are coming to see us.
6. My sister is learning how to play tennis.
7. The rearview mirror has to be adjusted.
8. Weightlifting is one way to stay in shape.

9. Rainy weather keeps people indoors.
10. Spareribs taste great when they are barbequed.
11. The windows were shattered during the storm.
12. Three young men were arrested for drunken driving.
13. Bats come out only at night.
14. Jean Chretien is prime minister of Canada.
15. In the sink was a huge stack of dirty dishes.
16. Politics can give me a headache.
17. I never want to see you again.
18. Trout fishing is my idea of fun.
19. Geraniums are beautiful house plants.
20. Through the city marched the high school band.

CHAPTER 2

Exercise: Point 1, p. 20

1. Paul mailed the letter.
2. The police officer directs the traffic.
3. I took that exam yesterday.
4. The dog chased the cat around the yard.
5. Arthur operated the ice cream maker.
6. The cow slept in the shade.
7. A good investment pays for itself.
8. A good fan cools a hot room.
9. The firefighter rescued the child from the burning
10. The spider crawled across my stomach.

Exercise: Point 2, p. 21

1. smiled	6. loved
2. laughed	7. exploded
3. agreed	8. adopted
4. fixed	9. rented
5. bounced	10. called

Review Exercise: Points 1 and 2, p. 22

1. Pr Russ smokes a pack of cigarettes a day.
2. Pa The poet imagined a better world.
3. Pa He confessed his part in the Riel Rebellion.
4. Pr The candle sheds a soft light.
5. Pr The neighbours play bridge every Thursday.
6. Pa I wandered through the public garden.
7. Pa I joined the fraternity as a sophomore.
8. Pr I cook her breakfast every morning.
9. Pa Carlos watered his bonsai.
10. Pr Our doctor treats his patients kindly.

Another Review Exercise: Points 1 and 2, p. 22

Answers to this exercise will vary. Check with your instructor if you need to.

1. Yesterday Normand called his mother on the telephone.
2. I voted for the candidate from the Yukon.
3. She doubted if he would ever return.
4. We go to the mall twice a week.
5. Theresa grows tomatoes in her garden.
6. To avoid an accident the driver swerved to one side.
7. I promised to send her a card on her birthday.
8. In a thunderstorm lightning often strikes a tree.
9. Peanuts and beer go well together.
10. The baby cried all night long.

Exercise: Point 3, p. 23

1. Wan is going.
2. You seem to read my mind.
3. This cigarette tastes stale.
4. The union members are ready to strike.
5. They were standing and applauding the famous athlete.
6. The actor appeared to have forgotten his lines.
7. She looked angry as she spoke.
8. The steak was rare and juicy.
9. The sky grew dark before the thunderstorm.
10. He sounded furious.

Exercise: Point 4, p. 24

1. Brian is washing his car.
2. The player began circling the bases.
3. Canadian soldiers were fighting at Vimy Ridge.
4. Kevin is weeding the garden.
5. I am preparing for the worst.
6. Mr. Potts is running for a post on the city council.
7. They keep trying to resolve their problems.
8. Canadians are choosing a new prime minister.
9. Lucy was singing in the nightclub.
10. We are attempting to improve our performance.

Another Exercise: Point 4, p. 25

1. We are going on a camping trip.
2. I was waiting for that bus for an hour.
3. You are trying too hard.
4. Janice was balancing her chequebook.

5. We were vacationing in the United States.
6. They are remodelling their basement.
7. The children were making all kinds of noise.
8. I am studying for an English exam.
9. Bobby is swatting flies.
10. The mayor was shaking everybody's hand.

Review Exercise: Points 1–4, p. 25

1. Ted was cleaning his room.
2. She seemed elated about the news.
3. He drives like a maniac.
4. I am vacuuming the carpet.
5. The baby grows more interesting every day.
6. Debra cut slices of her birthday cake.
7. We are developing new habits.
8. The day turned cold and bleak.
9. They started issuing free passes to Canada's Wonderland .
10. He remembered his father's advice.

Exercise: Point 5, p. 28

1. been
2. broken
3. lost
4. swum
5. grown
6. sunk
7. dealt
8. lain
9. laid
10. sung

Another Exercise: Point 5, p. 29

Answers to this exercise will vary. Check with your instructor if you need to.

Exercise: Point 6, p. 30

1. C The boys plan to come tomorrow.
2. I The boy to shake the apples from the tree.
3. C She meant to take a tour of Montreal.
4. C My younger sister is longing to have a horse of her own.
5. I The leaves to fall in September.
6. C They are hoping to go on a picnic tomorrow.
7. I My mother to go back to college next year.
8. I The lake to freeze if the temperature drops.
9. C Larry's brother tried to join the Royal Canadian Air Force.
10. C Do you expect to see Dolores on your vacation?

Exercise: Point 7, p. 31

1. She should have been elected class treasurer.
2. He has always wanted an outfit like that one.
3. They should never have lost that game.
4. Louise was appointed chairperson of the committee.
5. You should have learned from your mistakes.
6. Monica is learning to build cabinets.
7. He has just purchased a condominium in Sackville.
8. Gretchen had never experienced that before.
9. We had been hoping for better news.
10. It would not have alarmed me.

Review Exercise: Points 1–7, p. 32

1. Joe would have been the perfect candidate for the job.
2. Alice Munro and W.O. Mitchell are writing in Canada.
3. The pollution seems to be getting worse.
4. The caterpillars have eaten the leaves.
5. We are prepared to do anything necessary.
6. I am looking for true love.
7. The professor should not have assigned so much homework.
8. You will have to plug it in.
9. Joining the club will be good for you.
10. She was recalling her childhood.

Exercise: Point 8, p. 33

1. Randy washed the dishes and then dried them.
2. Tourists were swimming in the ocean and tanning themselves on the beach.
3. We stripped the wallpaper and painted the walls.
4. The fans were cheering and waving banners.
5. Renata took the course and learned to speak French .
6. He was moaning and groaning all night long.
7. In the summer, I sneeze a lot and get itchy eyes.
8. I called her and told her the news.
9. They were angry and did not hesitate to tell us so.
10. We have always worked hard, and now it is paying off.

Chapter Review, p. 33

I

1. I	6. C
2. C	7. I
3. C	8. C
4. I	9. I
5. I	10. C

II

1. I should never have brought that dog home.
2. Toni was talking with her professor.
3. I was raising the flag.
4. The bandits hid in the warehouse.
5. Raoul was spreading the good news.
6. Golf had never been so enjoyable.
7. We preserve our own vegetables every year.
8. The children want to play.
9. Herb has been named valedictorian.
10. We have always spent our summers in Summerside.
11. Pheobe had never before cooked spaghetti.
12. Alex is going to the dump tomorrow.
13. Mel appears to be making progress.
14. Shirley is worrying.
15. He was whining like a baby.
16. Margaret is an editor at a big publishing company.
17. He arrived late too often and lost his job.
18. She looked in the mirror and saw that her hair was turning gray.
19. The city lights look beautiful tonight.
20. We have begun saving money and planning for the future.

III Answers to this exercise will vary. Check with your instructor if you need to.

1. She was installing the storm windows.
2. I should have bought it when it was on sale.
3. Leslie looked lovely in that dress.
4. Yesterday, I read and had a great time.
5. We read and studied until class was over.
6. My mother screamed when I fell.
7. I like that magazine and buy it every month.
8. She is working until midnight tonight.
9. You should sweep and vacuum whenever you get the chance.
10. I am ready, willing, and able.
11. The job sounds interesting, but I have decided not to take it.
12. I would have taken you there if you had asked me.
13. Aniffa is directing and appearing in the drama.
14. Stuart works hard, but he is failing the course.
15. The teacher spent the entire class session explaining the poem "The Lonely Land."
16. We strolled around, looking for a theatre.
17. The fireworks display was a sight to behold.
18. I have chosen the best possible job.
19. Marija is practicing scales on the piano.
20. You are never going to get away with this.

MASTERY TEST p. 35

I

1. V	6. V	11. C	16. C
2. S	7. S	12. S	17. V
3. V	8. C	13. C	18. C
4. C	9. V	14. C	19. S
5. S	10. S	15. V	20. C

II

1. With the aid of a telescope, the class saw Jupiter.
2. Jasna and her friend arrived late.
3. Many detergents get clothes clean.
4. The piano and the drums are my specialties.
5. Into the stratosphere shot the Anik satellite.
6. The murmur of the ocean is music to my ears.
7. By changing your mind, you ruined our plans.
8. My dog is better than your dog.
9. A volcano is a mountain that expels ashes and lava.
10. Every sentence must have a subject.

III

1. Our plans include a trip to Niagara Falls.
2. I might have known better than to trust him.
3. Citronella candles keep the bugs away.
4. Last night they told us of their plans.
5. You are home!
6. This case smells of foul play.
7. He went out and had a great time.
8. Sculpture has always been my hobby.
9. We have been wondering where you were.
10. I have just spent my week's salary.

CHAPTER 3

Exercise: Point 1, p. 42

Answers to this exercise will vary. Check with your instructor if you need to.

1. S The detective solves the case.
2. P Trees are masterpieces of nature.
3. S The professor is a genius.
4. S A book falls off the shelf.
5. P Children visit the Metro Toronto Zoo.
6. P Motorcycles speed down the highway.
7. S My nephew loves his new chemistry set.
8. P Accidents happen to careless people.
9. S Karen is playing with her puppy.
10. P The apartments have been rented.

Exercise: Point 2, p. 43

Answers to this exercise will vary. Check with your instructor if you need to.

1. (Mr. Chan) He is a businessman.
2. (My sister) She has a new bicycle.
3. (All of us) We need to borrow a car.
4. (Cats) They are chasing a ball.
5. (The desk) It has a broken leg.
6. (Jacques and I) We wave to our friends.
7. (The police officer) He arrests the suspect.
8. (Jogging) It is good exercise.
9. (Windsor) It is on the American border.
10. (The two women) They are riding horseback.

Exercise: Point 3, p. 44

Answers to this exercise will vary. Check with your instructor if you need to.

1. The players and coaches sign autographs before the game.
2. My father or his friends are picking us up.
3. Iva and Lu applied for an auto loan.
4. A gentleman and a scholar are having an argument.
5. Either my aunt or my uncle is going to tuck in the children.
6. Cars, boats, and trains carry passengers.
7. Spring and summer are my favourite seasons.
8. Salary and benefits depend on your qualifications for the job.
9. The owner and manager is Mr. James.
10. Pieces of wood and glue are used in constructing models.

Review Exercise: Points 1–3, p. 45

Answers to this exercise will vary. Check with your instructor if you need to.

1. CP Jim and I are best friends.
2. S Professor Bukari is my teacher.
3. CP Neither my dog nor my cats behave very well.
4. P Traffic jams frustrate most motorists.
5. CP Rudi and his gerbil understand each other.
6. CP Either staples or paper clips satisfy the need for a fastener.
7. CP Violins and cellos echoed through the concert hall .
8. CS The owner and captain sailed the boat himself.
9. P Millionaires contribute to political campaigns.
10. CP Stu, Nicola, and I went to the beach.

Exercise: Point 4, p. 46

Answers to this exercise will vary. Check with your instructor if you need to.

1. One of them carries a large suitcase.
2. Anyone gets angry once in awhile.
3. Everyone here belongs to the club.
4. Nothing is meaningful according to some philosophers.
5. Anybody wants to be best in the class.
6. Everything counts on your final record.
7. Somebody is whistling in the next room.
8. Nobody wants to take the blame.
9. No one knows who the stranger is.
10. Neither of them is here.

Another Exercise: Point 4, p. 46

1. Neither of us cares to attend.
2. Either of you gets the starring role.
3. Anything serves the purpose.
4. Neither one of them deserves the award.
5. Neither pair of pants fits correctly.
6. Either flavour tastes delicious.
7. Either seat is fine with me.
8. Each of the tools works.
9. Neither of those candles has a wick.
10. No one does the work properly.

Review Exercise: Points 1–4, p. 47

1. The green car races through the street.
2. Neither of my friends calls me anymore.
3. No one bothers me anymore.
4. Neither of those batteries works.

5. Sears is a big mail-order house.
6. Sunbathers and children are on the beach.
7. Phil and Margaret buy A-Plus lottery tickets every month.
8. One of you dies!
9. Never again will they hitchhike.
10. The boxer and his manager know their business.

Another Review Exercise: Points 1–4, p. 47

Answers to this exercise will vary. Check with your instructor if you need to.

1. S Anyone is welcome in my house.
2. S Fishing is my favourite sport.
3. S Everyone who is anyone is here.
4. CP Buildings and grounds need a great deal of maintenance.
5. CP You and I have a lot in common.
6. S Either of those recipes produces a great cake.
7. S Somebody is parking a green car.
8. S Neither of those responses satisfies me.
9. P They cannot make it tonight.
10. CP Anne, Susan, and I love one another.

Exercise: Point 5, p. 48

1. Both of us are packed and ready to go.
2. Many of us need a vacation.
3. Several phones are ringing.
4. Each of the canisters is empty.
5. Each of the citizens votes once.
6. Few people wish upon stars.
7. Others want to change jobs.
8. Both of them visit often.
9. Each of us minds his own business.
10. Both Alex and Marty work for Bell Canada.

Exercise: Point 6, p. 49

1. The bus as well as the car was damaged in the accident.
2. The presentation of the trophies follows the game.
3. The books of Farley Mowat are interesting.
4. John, along with thirty friends, was in attendance.
5. The moon as well as some stars is visible tonight.
6. The children together with their father watch the movie.
7. The seasons of the year are all distinct in Canada.
8. The street singer with a crowd around him performs beautifully.
9. A pile of rocks has to be moved.
10. Sadie, in addition to her friends, is protesting the school board's decision.

Review Exercise: Points 5 and 6, p. 50

Answers to this exercise will vary. Check with your instructor if you need to.

1. Both food and drink are necessities of life.
2. Each time is better than the time before.
3. Both notebooks and rulers are sold at this counter.
4. Both coaches as well as their teams are nervous about the playoffs.
5. The ballerina, along with other dancers, dances for the National Ballet of Canada.
6. Everyone I care about is coming.
7. Both shoes and sneakers need laces.
8. Each member of the band has a special talent.
9. Part I together with Part II contains a review section.
10. The musicians, including the drummer, are on strike.

Review Exercise: Points 1–6, p. 50

1. Both you and I together with Ahmed want ice cream.
2. Neither of the sandwiches has onions.
3. Rakes and mowers are used by gardeners.
4. Each of the boys needs a haircut.
5. I will be glad to see anyone who wishes to come.
6. Neither of the boys was allowed to enter the race at Mosport.
7. Chris, Gina, and all their children visit us weekly.
8. Those cars, including the white Ford, are parked illegally.
9. Both women were hired.
10. A wild and woolly dog runs around our apartment.

Another Review Exercise: Points 1–6, p. 51

Answers to this exercise will vary. Check with your instructor if you need to.

1. Neither of the appointments was convenient for me.
2. Coffee, as well as tea, upsets my stomach.
3. Both coffee and tea contain caffeine.
4. Either one of the movies appeals to me.
5. You and I have exams on the same day.
6. Each daughter of mine is beautiful.
7. Nobody who is anybody will miss the event.
8. Strolling through the park is a good way to relax.
9. My girlfriend calls me twice an hour.
10. The area including First and Second Streets has badly deteriorated.

Exercise: Point 7, p. 51

1. A lot were trying out for the team.
2. My family is the most important thing in the world to me.
3. The band was louder than we expected.

4. A lot was accomplished at the last meeting.
5. The audience was booing and throwing tomatoes.
6. A number of items are missing.
7. A class is cancelled almost every week.
8. One team is Monique and Andra.
9. Today our committee reaches a decision.
10. A dozen are prepared to strike.

Exercise: Point 8, p. 52

1. There is a way to stop the leaking tap.
2. There are veterans of the war here tonight.
3. Inside the shack is a stray dog.
4. Over there is the premier of our province.
5. Behind that door waits danger.
6. There is more than one way to skin a cat.
7. Under the rock are over a hundred ants.
8. In our system, there is one lieutenant governor for each province.
9. Right behind me is everyone who supports me.
10. Beside the table was a high chair.

Exercise: Point 9, p. 53

Answers to this exercise will vary. Check with your instructor if you need to.

1. P The Oilers lead the league.
2. S The *Daily News* is our largest newspaper.
3. P Animals are my best friends.
4. S Shakespeare's Hamlet was a good book.
5. P The five senses are not equally important to existence.
6. S Mathematics is the study of number theory.
7. P Shouts echoed through the halls.
8. P Games build competitive spirit.
9. S Economics is not my favourite subject.
10. S Business tends to ignore the rights of the consumer.

Review Exercise: Points 7–9, p. 54

Answers to this exercise will vary. Check with your instructor if you need to.

1. There are twenty students in this class.
2. The *London Times* is an excellent newspaper.
3. Up the hill ran Jack and Jill.
4. There is danger involved in that plan.
5. Have you any spare change?
6. L.M. Montgomery has written many children's books.
7. Yesterday there was a terrible snowstorm.
8. *The Pickwick Papers* is a novel by Charles Dickens.
9. The Expos are a baseball team.
10. There is a good audience tonight.

Another Review Exercise: Points 7–9, p. 54

Answers to this exercise will vary. Check with your instructer if you need to.

1. The House of Commons is part of the government.
2. My family prefers not to eat in fast-food restaurants.
3. Many of us were astonished.
4. There is no one here who can help us.
5. Here are my ideas for the project.
6. Liberal arts is the cornerstone of education.
7. Beside the field are the lost sheep.
8. Our English class is going to present a debate.
9. The members of our class are all about the same age.
10. A heap of trash was left after the parade.

Chapter Review, p. 55

I
1. Almost everybody has some difficulty with writing.
2. Neither the chipmunk nor the squirrels are bothering us.
3. Both of us are voting in the next election.
4. Milo, Aharon, and I were offering our help.
5. Neither of you jumps to conclusions.
6. Some say the Native people been treated unfairly.
7. There were only two choices on the menu.
8. Rudy as well as his cat likes milk.
9. She is my boss and friend.
10. Sunbathing is my favourite form of exercise.
11. Either of us has to pay the fine.
12. The twins and their parents travel together.
13. Nobody believes your alibi.
14. The United States and Canada are neighbours.
15. "Safe" and "out" are two calls in baseball.
16. Neither of them dances to rock music.
17. Each serves a different purpose.
18. The hammer as well as the saw makes work easier.
19. Jacques was working for his uncle last year.
20. Our team plays hard every night.
21. Neither of the boys has to shave.
22. The Johnsons, including their son Mike, ski.
23. The Seven Wonders of the World are extraordinary.
24. Mount Royal and Olympic Stadium are in Montreal.
25. Time flies when you're enjoying yourself.
26. Either Cathy or the Chans cook dinner on Fridays.

27. Each of the brothers has been on television.
28. My husband and I were late for the movie.
29. There was no way out of the tunnel.
30. You are nobody until somebody loves you.

II Answers to this exercise will vary. Check with your instructor if you need to.

1. The enemy was captured late last night.
2. I suppose the workers are safe now.
3. Nothing excites those two.
4. It stands as testimony to a great person.
5. One of us always guesses the right answer.
6. The Dhimans live in the next apartment.
7. Violins and cellos are musical instruments.
8. Someone has to take me to the station.
9. I was disappointed with their performance.
10. They were the best of times.

III Answers to this exercise will vary. Check with your instructor if you need to.

1. The furnace is not working today.
2. Paul and Paula are expecting their first child.
3. Most of us signed up for the marathon.
4. Neither of us cares much for caviar.
5. Thunderstorms and hurricanes are examples of foul weather.
6. Jamie and Dave, together with Mr. Buryta, are going sailing.
7. Mark, Bonnie, and Nancy want more food.
8. My parents went shopping for a used car.
9. There are never enough hours in the day.
10. Fishing is a good way to pass the time.

IV

1. X Sylvie as well as Amy does not wish to register.
2. X Alex Colville is a famous Canadian painter.
3. X One of you has to sit on my lap.
4. X Babies are innocent and adults are not.
5. X Neither of us is in the mood.
6. X Weddings are fun.
7. X Alfonso buys records and listens to them in his room.
8. X Both of them wish they were going.
9. X Grammar and spelling are being tested.
10. X Anyone who winks at me embarrasses me.

V Answers to this exercise will vary. Check with your instructor if you need to.

1. Each of the teams in the CFL plays half of its games at home.
2. Either of those latex paints covers beautifully.
3. Swimming in salt water does wonders for your hairstyle.
4. The National Arts Centre is in Ottawa.
5. There are six kittens in the litter.
6. Here is the man I've been talking about.
7. Rain and sleet are road hazards.
8. The group, including fifty women, had many interests in common.
9. The skater is graceful.
10. Frederico and Luis attend the same school.

VI Answers to this exercise will vary. Check with your instructor if you need to.

Carpenters use many different tools in their work. When they are faced with jobs that are particularly difficult, they have to use their patience as well as their skills. Without patience, hammers, saws, or screwdrivers will do carpenters no good. They have to be able to understand their problems, and find the best ways to solve them. Sometimes, the quickest solutions are not the best ones. Their customers, or clients, have to be pleased with their work, or they lose their chances to be hired for other jobs. There are great pressures on carpenters to succeed. By no means are their jobs easy ones.

VII Answers to this exercise will vary. Check with your instructor if you need to.

People who grow up in the tropics get used to warm weather. There is never a major snowstorm there, although hurricanes are not unusual. A Canadian, on the other hand, has to learn to live with harsh weather for several months of each year. People who travel from one continent to another are almost always surprised at the change of climate. Although a person from the tropics thinks that warm weather is nice all year round, a Canadian may enjoy the change of seasons.

VIII Answers to this exercise will vary. Check with your instructor if you need to.

In Margaret Laurence's novel *The Stone Angel*, the main character is Hagar Shipley, a ninety-two-year-old woman who reflects upon her past. She remembers her life as a young girl in a bleak prairie town, her marriage to a farmer, and her relationship with her two sons, Marvin and John. Her widowhood and years alone have made her a short-tempered complainer, but her humour, pride, and self-reliance show the virtues of pioneer life that she learned as a young girl, qualities that make her, in the eyes of Laurence's readers, a believable and lovable human being.

CHAPTER 4

Exercise: Point 1, p. 62

1. Heating costs are on the upswing.
2. Robert W. Service wrote poems about the Klondike.
3. There is a pickle in the refrigerator.
4. Many people read best-selling novels during the summer.
5. That train is late as always.
6. Babies require a great deal of attention.
7. A good meal improves my disposition.
8. You are a sight for sore eyes.
9. Gardening is therapeutic for some.
10. These are the best years of your life.

Another Exercise: Point 1, p. 63

Answers to this exercise will vary. Check with your instructor if you need to.

1. C
2. F We live near the centre of town.
3. F We ate at a famous restaurant.
4. C
5. C
6. F We will dine at my grandparents' house.
7. C
8. F I can't buy a record with only fifty cents.
9. F Susie attends the University of New Brunswick.
10. C

Exercise: Point 2, p. 64

Answers to this exercise will vary. Check with your instructor if you need to.

1. The customer was asking a question.
2. I hear the birds singing in the trees.
3. The man was trying to escape.
4. My neighbour is always working on her house.
5. The woman is beginning a new career.
6. I am practising the piano.
7. The attendant was checking the tire pressure.
8. The convict was trying to evade the Ontario Provincial Police.
9. She was smiling at me from across the room.
10. Heng was making his career plans.

Review Exercise: Points 1 and 2, p. 65

Answers to this exercise will vary. Check with your instructor if you need to.

1. F The motorcyclist was racing wildly through the park.
2. F She was falling in love.
3. C
4. F The businessmen are all millionaires.
5. F The old man rarely displayed any emotion.
6. F The hail was dropping like stones from the sky.
7. C
8. F He received the punishment that he deserved.
9. C
10. F I am choosing a new major.

Exercise: Point 3, p. 67

1. D	6. D
2. D	7. D
3. I	8. D
4. D	9. D
5. D	10. I

Another Exercise: Point 3, p. 67

Answers to this exercise will vary. Check with your instructor if you need to.

1. I We went to the movies.
2. D Let's sing while we are waiting.
3. I Abby and I are married.
4. D We got both kinds because some people prefer Labatts.
5. D I can't make it although I promised otherwise.
6. D Listen to the sound effects before the song begins.
7. D I am willing to go there if it is a good place to shop.
8. I The Rockies are magnificent.
9. D I will quit unless you give me a raise.
10. D He had to drop out of the Canadian Open after he sprained his ankle.

Exercise: Point 4, p. 68

1. Because it is raining, we cannot go outside.
2. While you wait, you may read a magazine.
3. Stephen Leacock, the Canadian humourist, died in 1944.
4. If you want to go, you will have to buy a ticket.
5. If you go swimming, wear a swimcap.
6. Unless you change your ways, you will lose your job.
7. When he left, the room was dark.
8. After this inning, the game will be over.
9. I want to try even if it is difficult.
10. After I swept the floor, I dusted.

Review Exercise: Points 1–4, p. 69

Answers to this exercise will vary. Check with your instructor if you need to.

1. He hopes to go tonight even though he is tired.
2. I have been so happy since I fell for you.

3. You will be amazed if I decide to go along with your wishes.
4. Although he has been teaching for twenty years, he is boring.
5. Until they discover a cure for the common cold, I guess I'll just have to keep sneezing.
6. He met her while he was standing at the meat counter in the supermarket.
7. She will leave him unless he changes his vile ways.
8. We will go inside after the sun goes down.
9. As the world turns, I get dizzy.
10. We checked to be sure we had everything before we packed the car.

Exercise: Point 5, p. 70

1. Even though there is enough time, I feel rushed.
2. Unless you work harder, you will receive a poor grade.
3. As long as you use suntan lotion, you will not get burned.
4. The show begins when the curtain rises.
5. My paper was better after I revised it.
6. If I am nominated, I will not run.
7. I didn't like olives until I had them on pizza.
8. I am happy when I am reading.
9. As soon as the match ends, the winner will be crowned.
10. Lock the door before you leave.

Another Exercise: Point 5, p. 71

Answers to this exercise will vary. Check with your instructor if you need to.

1. Since we painted the house, we've gotten lots of compliments.
2. I'll call you back as soon as I finish the assignment.
3. He leafed quickly through the gift book before calling to say thank you.
4. Let's wait until the tide comes in.
5. You can count on me whenever you need a friend.
6. Even though we have known each other for years, there are still surprises in our relationship.
7. While working the night shift, I dozed off.
8. I will do it because there is no other choice.
9. Although there was little hope for recovery, we prayed for his health.
10. Whenever I'm feeling depressed, I take the dog out for a run.

Review Exercise: Points 1–6, p. 72

Answers to this exercise will vary. Check with your instructor if you need to.

1. Several people, including my friend Sonya, are going.
2. We can leave as soon as the mail arrives.
3. John wants to attempt to break the world record.
4. I like sports; for example, hockey and football.
5. Even though we used to be friends, now we can't stand each other.
6. After she finished the manuscript, she mailed it to the editor.
7. Everyone celebrated, including my parents and me.
8. Reference books such as the dictionary and the thesaurus are valuable.
9. It started to rain while I was weeding the garden.
10. The dog tried to find his way home.

Exercise: Point 7, p. 73

1. C	6. C
2. C	7. C
3. C	8. F
4. F	9. F
5. C	10. C

Chapter Review, p. 74

I
1. F
2. C They lost the battle.
3. F
4. F
5. C Come over for dinner.
6. C Never say die.
7. F
8. F
9. F
10. F

II
1. F
2. F
3. C Sports cars are fun.
4. F
5. F
6. C I was amazed at the performance.
7. F
8. C Bring it tomorrow.
9. F
10. F

III
1. We played lacrosse until it grew too dark.
2. Even though it was foggy, we made a smooth landing at Gander.
3. Because he hurt himself, he could not play.
4. I should quit smoking because it's unhealthy.

5. Although she has a quick temper, Huda kept calm.
6. While I'm here, I should call my aunt.
7. After you run, take a shower.
8. We bought his album after we saw him in concert.
9. I brought my guitar since I knew you would be here.
10. When you come to the third stop light, turn left.

IV Answers to this exercise will vary. Check with your instructor if you need to.

1. Because I want to know you better, I will encourage your honesty.
2. Even though I am broke, I can find a way to amuse myself.
3. Unless you change your mind, we're going.
4. When the time comes, I will have completed the project.
5. As long as you are away, I might as well visit some friends.
6. We will eat after we go for a swim.
7. I will peel the carrots while you chop the omons.
8. I'll send you a road map so that you can find your way.
9. I always get a wonderful dinner whenever I visit my grandparents.
10. He became an actor, although he was shy.

V
1. C Call me if you need me.
2. F
3. F
4. F
5. F
6. F
7. F
8. C I know.
9. C It's okay with me.
10. F

VI Answers to this exercise will vary. Check with your instructor if you need to.

1. C The traffic was heavy.
2. F Everyone loves a gorgeous autumn afternoon.
3. F I am trying to make the dean's list.
4. F We need to find a bigger apartment.
5. F I was exhausted after chasing my dog around the block.
6. F It was very crowded, with all the noise and confusion of a busy airport.
7. F She arrived at the last possible moment.
8. F She was laughing and crying at the same time.
9. F Let's go now before I change my mind.
10. F I enjoy soft drinks like root beer and ginger ale.

VII
1. As long as you're not lazy, I won't complain.
2. We're celebrating tonight because I gave up cigarettes.
3. If you want to play, change your clothes.
4. Having moved to the country, he leads a quieter life.
5. After all, we have known each other for a year.
6. We hated summer until we bought an air conditioner.
7. Since you left me, I am so lonely.
8. You have to fix the leak before you can go sailing.
9. As soon as we arrived in Cavendish, we ran out to the beach.
10. We are raising a family because we love children.

VIII Answers to this exercise will vary. Check with your instructor if you need to.

1. I worked hard so that I could get a promotion.
2. Although she enjoys painting, she doesn't take art courses.
3. We went to the circus, where we saw lions and clowns.
4. Tell me the truth if you know it.
5. There have been many improvements since he was elected mayor.
6. I love facing danger wherever I can find it.
7. I am too tired to go for a walk.
8. He was arrested because he was drinking and driving.
9. You will find the underwear in the drawer where I keep my socks.
10. Judging the distance and holding her breath, she jumped.

IX Answers to this exercise will vary. Check with your instructor if you need to.

Today, more and more people are becoming interested in discovering their roots. After the beginning of the American Revolution, many people loyal to the British cause fled to Canada and settled in various parts of the country, especially Ontario and the Maritimes. Some of the larger settlements were at places such as the Niagara Peninsula, Cornwall, Kingston, the Fredericton area, Halifax, and Charlottetown. If a person finds that his or her relatives were United Empire Loyalists, that person may be able to use the initials UE after his or her name. For this reason, many Canadians are interested in tracing their ancestries.

Ten years ago there were not as many shopping malls as there are today. In a mall, many stores are gathered together under one roof. Shoppers appreciate the convenience a mall can offer, because they can make one stop and accomplish all their shopping in one place. On Saturday, malls are usually very crowded, with people walking, talking, eating, and buying all over the place. Malls are air-conditioned so that shoppers can browse comfortably. You can buy a birthday card, a mattress, a baseball mitt, or a pizza, all under one roof. Shopping malls offer a great way to shop.

When we moved from an apartment to a house, we discovered that we had more belongings than we thought. So much stuff had to be packed, so we used boxes, suitcases, and even large garbage bags. We rented a truck from the local gas station so we could avoid spending the extra money to hire a mover. We certainly put in a full day's work that day. Although the process was long and hard, it was worth it.

CHAPTER 5

Exercise: Recognition, p. 81

1. I like rock music | I don't like jazz.
2. The invitation was beautifull | it was hand-lettered.
3. The tide is high | it is a good time to swim.
4. Marcel is a trucker | he is from Saskatchewan.
5. I often take your advice | you are usually right.
6. Babies are cute | they cry a lot.
7. He is my friend | he understands me.
8. The trip was postponed | we had no sleeping bags.
9. The firefighters were called | they handled the blaze.
10. I raked the beach | there is no seaweed left.

Another Exercise: Recognition, p. 82

1. RO
2. RO
3. RO
4. C
5. RO
6. C
7. RO
8. RO
9. RO
10. RO

Third Exercise: Recognition, p. 82

1. RO
2. RO
3. C
4. C
5. RO
6. RO
7. RO
8. RO
9. RO
10. RO

Exercise: Point 1, p. 83

Answers to this exercise will vary. Check with your instructor if you need to.

1. It was my mother's birthday, so I called her on the phone.
2. Going out to dinner is fun, but it is expensive.
3. I won't do it, and you can't make me.
4. We can usually see for miles, but today it is too cloudy.
5. I want that job, but I don't think I have enough experience.
6. We found some shells on the beach, and they were beautiful.
7. The temperature reached 45°C in Saskatchewan in 1947.
8. Tell me your problem, so I can help you.
9. Our daughter is in the third grade, and she is very bright.
10. I've never tried blueberry ice cream, but I bet I will like it.

Another Exercise: Point 1, p. 84

One way to correct a run-on sentence is to connect two independent clauses with a comma *plus* one of these connecting words: *and, but, for, or, nor, yet, so.*

Exercise: Point 2, p. 85

1. I received the most votes; therefore, I was elected.
2. The ship sails from Argentia; it leaves at 2:00 p.m.
3. We lost; however, we still lead the league.
4. The play was a tragedy; we left the theatre weeping.
5. You want your freedom; nevertheless, you will have to get a job.
6. I am running for office; furthermore, I intend to win.
7. She must be out of town; otherwise, she would be here.
8. First buy your ticket; then get in line.
9. Those shoes are comfortable; I'll take two pairs.
10. There was no heat; consequently, we froze all night.

Review Exercise: Points 1 and 2, p. 86

Answers to this exercise will vary. Check with your instructor if you need to.

1. We rented a floor buffer, but it did not work.
2. Joe ran all the way home; consequently, he was tired.
3. I cooked a hamburger for dinner, but I forgot to buy a roll.
4. The horse I bet on came in second; nevertheless, I lost money.
5. The window was shattered, so we had to get a new one.

6. The candle burned for hours; therefore, we did not have to use the lamp.
7. Apple pie is delicious; however, it is fattening.
8. The show came on too late; besides, she wasn't really interested in seeing it.
9. Summers are hot and humid, but winters are cold and dry.
10. He was wealthy, so he could buy anything he wanted.

Another Review Exercise: Points 1 and 2, p. 86

1. Connect two independent clauses with a comma *plus* one of these connecting words: *and, but, for, or, nor, yet, so.*
2. Separate two independent clauses with a semicolon.

Exercise: Point 3, p. 87

1. She asked for a raise. She got it.
2. That is a new hall. The acoustics are fantastic.
3. He is a good father. He pays attention to his children.
4. The birds are chirping. They sound so happy.
5. The parade is beginning. Let's get a good spot.
6. Your paper is late. Therefore, it will lose a grade.
7. He failed the test. Consequently, he will have to take it again.
8. Why did you go partying? You were tired.
9. That suit fits. You should buy it.
10. Bowling is fun for the whole family. It is good exercise.

Review Exercise: Points 1–3, p. 88

Answers to this exercise will vary. Check with your instructor if you need to.

1. The sun went down, and the mosquitoes came out.
   The sun went down; the mosquitoes came out.
   The sun went down. The mosquitoes came out.
2. Ben ran a good race, and he came in second.
   Ben ran a good race; he came in second.
   Ben ran a good race. He came in second.
3. We applauded the actress, so she came out for a second bow.
   We applauded the actress; therefore, she came out for a second bow.
   We applauded the actress. Therefore, she came out for a second bow.
4. I like Chaucer, but I like Shakespeare even better.
   I like Chaucer; however, I like Shakespeare even better.
   I like Chaucer. I like Shakespeare even better.
5. I am happy to be here, and I'm glad you are with me.
   I am happy to be here; I'm glad you are with me.
   I am happy to be here. I'm glad you are with me.
6. Turn right here, and park where you can.
   Turn right here; park where you can.
   Turn right here. Park where you can.
7. I quit smoking, so I feel much better.
   I quit smoking; consequently, I feel much better.
   I quit smoking. I feel much better.
8. I love visiting you, for you treat me so well.
   I love visiting you; you treat me so well.
   I love visiting you. You treat me so well.
9. I have hay fever, and I take allergy pills.
   I have hay fever; therefore, I take allergy pills.
   I have hay fever. I take allergy pills.
10. I'm in my second childhood, and I feel young again.
    I'm in my second childhood; I feel young again.
    I'm in my second childhood. I feel young again.

Exercise: Point 4, p. 90

Answers to this exercise will vary. Check with your instructor if you need to.

1. While we went to the museum, Bob went to the ball game.
2. Because you are my friend, I trust you.
3. Although I don't like crowds, I enjoy going to the beach.
4. The temperature dropped as soon as it started to rain.
5. When I answered the phone, the caller hung up.
6. The kids are building sand castles while the adults have a conversation.
7. Let's find our seats before the show begins.
8. Even though I locked the door, they still broke in.
9. Since you were fired, the place has not been the same.
10. While you were gone, the plumber came.

Review Exercise: Points 3 and 4, p. 90

Answers to this exercise will vary. Check with your instructor if you need to.

1. We moved here. We have been very happy.
   Since we moved here, we have been very happy.
2. Trash is collected on Mondays. It is taken to the dump.
   After trash is collected on Mondays, it is taken to the dump.
3. There is no easy remedy. We must research the matter further.
   Since there is no easy remedy, we must research the matter further.
4. I started taking violin lessons. I improved my style.
   Since I started taking violin lessons, I improved my style.
5. That type of defence will never work. The other team is too good.
   That type of defence will never work because the other team is too good.

6. We go swimming every night during the summer. The pond is nearby.
We go swimming every night during the summer, since the pond is nearby.
7. We drove cross-country. We had no idea how beautiful Canada is.
Until we drove cross-country, we had no idea how beautiful Canada is.
8. You don't look well. Lie down for a while.
Since you don't look well, you should lie down for a while.
9. The professor raised his voice. He was very angry.
Whenever the professor raised his voice, he was very angry.
10. He looks grubby. He has not shaved for weeks.
He looks grubby because he has not shaved for weeks.

Chapter Review, p. 92

I

1 RO Shirts sometimes come with cardboard in them | it protects them from wrinkling.
2. C You need matches to start a fire.
3. RO Fred wears madras shirts | they have gone out of style.
4. C Before you paint, you have to strip the surface.
5. C She was hired because she was the best one for the job.
6. RO There is a late show tonight | what time does it start?
7. RO Al called last night | he is getting married.
8. RO Rest is important | vitamins will help.
9. RO It is your turn | roll the dice.
10. RO Max takes flying lessons | he is getting a licence.

II Answers to this exercise will vary. Check with your instructor if you need to.

1. RO Guns are dangerous; they can cause a lot of trouble.
2. C
3. RO Lilacs are fragrant, so we should grow some.
4. RO Construction workers wear hard hats because they need protection.
5. RO Come outside if you want to see the stars.
6. RO Poker is a great game, because it takes skill as well as luck.
7. RO I read a great novel; you can borrow it.
8. C
9. RO I chose a button-down shirt because I like that style.
10. RO I wrote a letter to the editor, and it was printed.

III

1. We want to buy a new car, but it is too expensive.
2. She is a teacher; therefore, she has her summers off.
3. I wrote my member of Parliament. He replied with a form letter.
4. He started slowly. Then he speeded up and won the race.
5. Al went to the ball game; he ate peanuts and drank beer.
6. Italy is a lovely country, and so is Spain.
7. We had a picnic, and Marie played the guitar.
8. Although we got lost, we arrived on time.
9. Young people are often energetic; furthermore, they have great ambition.
10. Since we bought the fan, it has been much cooler in here.

IV Answers to this exercise will vary. Check with your instructor if you need to.

1. Bring me my slippers, and see if you can find my pipe.
2. I've never been there, and I don't want to go.
3. I would like to get a bird's-eye view of things, but I can't fly.
4. You must do your homework, or you'll get a poor grade.
5. I don't usually read that magazine, but I did see that article.
6. The movie was hilarious, and I saw it twice.
7. I like playing tennis, but I'm not very good at it.
8. I take lessons, and I practise every day.
9. She wears army boots, and she rides a motorcycle.
10. I have hay fever, but it only bothers me in August.

V Answers to this exercise will vary. Check with your instructor if you need to.

1. Farming is hard work, but it is satisfying.
2. We listened to oldies on the radio; it was an evening of memories.
3. Although some people say horse races are fixed, they are fun to watch.
4. Avoid poison ivy. It can irritate your skin.
5. A fireplace is romantic. Besides, it can keep you warm.
6. My teacher was close to me. She was almost my best friend.
7. I arrived late, so I missed the interview.
8. Although I can balance my chequebook, I cannot complete my income tax forms.
9. I ate three donuts today; however, I am still hungry.
10. Writing is an important skill, but it takes time to develop.

VI Connect two independent clauses with a comma *plus* one of these connecting words: *and, but, for, or, nor, yet, so.*

VII 1. Ming loves golf, so he plays a round every day.
Ming loves golf; he plays a round every day.
Ming loves golf. He plays a round every day.
Because Ming loves golf, he plays a round every day.

2. I built a desk, and I keep it in my bedroom.
I built a desk; I keep it in my bedroom.
I built a desk. I keep it in my bedroom.
Since I built a desk, I keep it in my bedroom.

3. We travelled to Europe, and we saw the Eiffel Tower.
We travelled to Europe; we saw the Eiffel Tower.
We travelled to Europe. We saw the Eiffel Tower.
When we travelled to Europe, we saw the Eiffel Tower.

4. English is my favourite subject, so I get good grades.
English is my favourite subject; therefore, I get good grades.
English is my favourite subject. I get good grades .
Because English is my favourite subject, I get good grades.

5. I mixed the ingredients, and I put the batter in the oven.
I mixed the ingredients; then I put the batter in the oven.
I mixed the ingredients. Then I put the batter in the oven.
After I mixed the ingredients, I put the batter in the oven.

6. I love summer, but I don't like the humidity.
I love summer; I don't like the humidity.
I love summer. I don't like the humidity.
I love summer although I don't like the humidity.

7. The mail arrives late here, for the letter carrier walks a long route.
The mail arrives late here; the letter carrier walks a long route.
The mail arrives late here. The letter carrier walks a long route.
The mail arrives late here because the letter carrier walks a long route.

8. I enjoyed the dinner, but I feel a bit bloated now.
I enjoyed the dinner; however, I feel a bit bloated now.
I enjoyed the dinner. However, I feel a bit bloated now.
Although I enjoyed the dinner, I feel a bit bloated now.

9. I see moisture in the basement, so there must be a leak somewhere.
I see moisture in the basement; there must be a leak somewhere.
I see moisture in the basement. There must be a leak somewhere.
If I see moisture in the basement, there must be a leak somewhere.

10. The wine is imported from France, and it is very good.
The wine is imported from France; it is very good.
The wine is imported from France. It is very good.
Because the wine is imported from France, it is very good.

VIII Answers to this exercise will vary. Check with your instructor if you need to.

1. Ofra is a whiz at photography, whereas Sally is an excellent painter.
2. Because the sprinter won the world championship, he is a great athlete.
3. Hamburgers are delicious, and cheeseburgers are absolutely scrumptious.
4. Tom is lazy, although he knows how important exercise is.
5. Tansu wants to be a registered nurse, so he is going to school to get his degree.

IX Answers to this exercise will vary. Check with your instructor if you need to.

1. A summer breeze is lovely; it cools the body and the mind.
2. That dog is very smart; sometimes it seems he can communicate with us.
3. When she bought a Volkswagen, she traded in her Ford.
4. Backpacking is a great way to spend the day, but it requires a lot of stamina.
5. He is my best friend, but he has moved to Swift Current.

X Answers to this exercise will vary. Check with your instructor if you need to.

The cost of fossil fuels affects us all. As the price of home-heating fuel keeps rising, it gets too expensive to stay warm. One way to solve the problem is to buy a wood-burning stove, which, in some cases, can heat a whole house. Wood is also costly unless you have access to a supply. Since it comes in many different styles, a stove can be a beautiful addition to a house or apartment. Each kind of stove suits a different purpose.

Cats make great pets, but you have to be affectionate with them. As they are rather independent animals, they do not always come when you call them. Many people prefer dogs, because you can train them to come, or sit, or fetch a bone. With cats, on the other hand, you have to be willing to let them live their own lives. If you attempt to train them, you may become discouraged. If you put two cats in the same room, you are in for quite a treat. They chase each other, usually all in fun. When one catches the other, the real show begins. Oftentimes they will cuddle and clean each other, but sometimes they will fight. The wise pet owner will know when to break up a fight and when to let it go, since it is only play for the cats. They can be great company if you understand them.

Tennis is a sport that has gained great popularity over the last ten years. Both men and women enjoy it. Tennis courts are being built all over; they can be found in cities, in the country, and in the suburbs. People of all ages can play. In fact, some of the greatest players in the world are in their teens or early twenties. The most important and prestigious tournament is held every summer at Wimbledon, a suburb of London. However, Canada's most important tournaments are the Canadian Open Men's Championships, and the Canadian Open Woman's Championships. One does not have to be a star athlete to enjoy tennis. It is great fun even for those who just want some fresh air and exercise.

CHAPTER 6

Exercise: Point 1, p. 102

1. sunken
2. silently through the room
3. picket
4. with all her strength
5. with some reluctance; away from her family
6. home-made
7. is the largest island
8. lovingly with his niece
9. with three red stripes
10. handsome

Exercise: Point 2, p. 103

1. A man in a sharkskin coat sold us a lottery ticket.
2. We strolled along the boardwalk until the sun set.
3. The crowd cheered excitedly when Lindros came onto the ice.
4. The banana comes in its own natural yellow wrapper.
5. I saw my grandmother climbing the steps in her house.
6. As usual, he spoke only about himself.
7. We watched the horses approaching the finish line.
8. Sergio smiled happily when he heard the news.
9. She warned me in a whisper never to do that again.
10. The elastic man in the circus is a sideshow attraction.

Review Exercise: Points 1 and 2, p. 104

1. MM Amazingly, Rick got an A on the test.
2. MM The ugly monster waited in the cave.
3. C
4. MM The quarterback instantaneously made the decision to run.
5. MM We watched the motorcyclist heading for a crash.
6. MM The city council voted unanimously to fund the project.
7. MM Wearing only his underwear, Max was chasing the dog.
8. MM The panhandler without a cent to his name approached the millionaire.
9. MM The furnace exploded with a crash, but no one was hurt.
10. MM My father, who is bald, bought a toupee.

Exercise: Point 3, p. 105

1. of the fifteenth century
2. riding her bicycle
3. dressed in many colours
4. in the basement
5. with the floppy ears
6. loudly
7. promising better times for all
8. for fifty dollars
9. with the creamy complexion
10. barking at the fire hydrant

Exercise: Point 4, p. 106

Answers to this exercise will vary. Check with your instructor if you need to.

1. After almost an hour, he was ready to go.
2. She does not even know his name.
3. You are hardly the one I need for this job.
4. She had just finished painting when I touched the doorknob.
5. There are just three eggs left in the refrigerator.
6. I received the only passing grade on the exam.

7. I put on a last burst of speed and nearly won the race.
8. The host had provided scarcely enough food for all the guests.
9. The police officer merely informed us of our rights.
10. This time we nearly made it.

Review Exercise: Points 1–4, p. 107

Answers to this exercise will vary. Check with your instructor if you need to.

1. The birds in the trees are singing their songs of love.
2. I heard on the radio about the big music festival.
3. I almost fell over from laughing so hard.
4. She sighed happily when the good news came.
5. Nearly everyone loves a barbeque.
6. Pete turned away bashfully when he saw the girl of his dreams.
7. He sat on the roof watching his neighbours below.
8. We badly needed someone to work overtime.
9. I am talking on the telephone and relaxing.
10. You are the only one for me.

Exercise: Point 5, p. 108

Answers to this exercise will vary. Check with your instructor if you need to.

1. Every day she told him to change his socks.
   She told him to change his socks every day.
2. Clara said she felt better after her operation.
   After her operation, Clara said she felt better.
3. He always told me to be practical.
   He told me to be practical always.
4. At midnight, we were told the show would begin.
   We were told the show would begin at midnight.
5. On her way out, Ruth promised to close the door.
   Ruth promised to close the door on her way out.

Chapter Review p. 108

I
1. MM The man in the blue sweater was stopped for speeding.
2. MM I saw almost the whole movie, but I fell asleep around midnight.
3. MM Nguyen left the door hanging on one hinge.
4. MM The initials carved on the tree were those of the lovers.
5. C
6. MM The doctor told him to take a pill every four hours.
7. C
8. MM The woman with the high heels walked into the elevator.
9. MM The jet with 200 passengers landed at the airport.
10. C

II. Answers to this exercise will vary. Check with your instructor if you need to.
1. MM With admiration, I watched the mechanic fix the car.
2. MM He barely made it in time.
3. C
4. MM We borrowed a mower that was broken from a neighbour.
5. MM We saw a squirrel climbing up the telephone pole.
6. C
7. MM The cat was rescued by a firefighter after the building had been set on fire.
8. MM We've found almost all the pieces to the puzzle.
9. MM Vandals stole the sign from the corner.
10. MM I badly need food.

III Answers to this exercise will vary. Check with your instructor if you need to.
1. C
2. MM I've seen hardly any of those films.
3. C
4. MM I read a new book by my favourite author.
5. C
6. MM The boy with a crewcut waved to the Queen.
7. C
8. MM She was happy, she said in an interview.
9. MM We flew through a terrible storm in a plane with a faulty engine.
10. MM Midori was skiing down the slope when she broke her ankle.

IV
1. After the game, the coach treated the team to beers.
2. We saw a cowboy wearing a ten-gallon hat in the street.
3. The crowd cheered vigorously when the speaker stood.
4. We buy vegetables in the supermarket five kilometres from here.
5. The principal stopped the students running down the hall.
6. She gave the baby in the crib a bottle.
7. I bought a red shirt to go with my yellow slacks.
8. We bought a picture that had been painted by an artist from British Columbia.
9. She used a shampoo which she bought yesterday and then her usual conditioner.
10. They promised to visit her when they reach town.

V
1. The criminal almost laughed when he was arrested.
2. He bought a suit with brass buttons and treated himself to a fancy dinner.

3. Hamed loves to ride around town in his scooter.
4. The cat barely escaped before the blaze spread.
5. We put insulation down in the attic, and now we are cool.
6. There is a friendly teller in that bank.
7. There is a noisy dog in our neighborhood.
8. He occasionally surprised his wife with a rose.
9. She bought a bookend made of brass for her husband.
10. We are just about ready to leave.

VI 1. Sam fixed the pocket which had a hole in it with a needle and thread.
2. I said I would tell you about my trip when I got home.
3. The tire with the puncture went flat.
4. The hunter barely escaped from the bear's claws.
5. The buyers watched the models in the latest designer fashions parade on stage.
6. Robin brought her dog with an injured tail to the veterinarian.
7. On his wedding day, he vowed to love, honour, and cherish.
8. My father-in-law snores loudly when he sleeps.
9. She bought a ring that was made of gold and enamel from the jeweller.
10. We first baked a cake in the new oven for our friends.
11. I ran barefooted into the street.
12. We sent invitations in blue envelopes to all our friends.
13. He left the clothing store with a new pair of socks and bought a newspaper.
14. That salesperson with a bow tie sold me a Pontiac.
15. From the car, I watched my sister jumping rope.
16. Chakriya said, "I will be a millionaire before I am twenty."
17. I would like a banana in my sundae and a glass of water.
18. The suit with the brass buttons is at the cleaners.
19. The hospital where I was born has been torn down.
20. I banged up a car that did not belong to me in an accident.

VII Answers to this exercise will vary. Check with your instructor if you need to.

I nearly forgot to send holiday greetings this year. All my relatives in different parts of the country would have been disappointed. It really is not that much of a strain since I need to send only ten cards. It is as easy as writing, "Hi, how are you?" on a note, putting it in an envelope, and mailing it. I usually work from a list of my friends' and relatives' names, which I keep in my desk. Luckily, I remembered the cards three days before the holiday; I just hope that I did not mail them too late.

Raising a family is really an easy task. Everyone thinks he knows the best way; scarcely anyone does it perfectly. Many people read Dr. Spock's book, which presents clearly one accepted method. Nearly everyone has heard of that book at least.

No matter what method they follow, parents constantly are advised to be kind and affectionate toward their children. After the baby is born, some parents say their lives are changed completely for the better. They don't even mind if the baby cries. Pacing the floor, they rock the baby back to sleep. They calmly accept the trouble, knowing the baby will soon outgrow that stage. If they have prepared themselves as early and completely as they could for the new arrival, they are almost never really upset by the little problems that come up.

These days, many people in all parts of the country are trying health foods. The "back to nature" movement has affected nearly everyone in one way or another. Producers of health foods use no preservatives, which they claim are bad for the system, in their products. Cereals such as granola, a totally natural food, are especially popular. People are also eating unstarched rice, which is supposed to be particularly good for the digestive system. Even ice cream comes in new, natural flavours such as banana, which is made with fresh bananas, and coconut. Certainly, health food companies are trying hard to attract customers interested in better nutrition.

CHAPTER 7

Exercise: Point 1, p. 116

1. Driving in heavy traffic
2. Seasoning meat
3. Crossing the border
4. Choosing a career
5. preparing my costume
6. Mowing the lawn
7. Examining philosophy
8. Thinking aloud
9. Getting a tan
10. Practising the piano

Exercise: Point 2 p. 117

1. C Billy
2. DM
3. C cat
4. C I
5. DM
6. C Patty
7. DM
8. DM
9. C audience
10. C pitcher

Review Exercise: Points 1 and 2, p. 117

Answers to this exercise will vary. Check with your instructor if you need to.

1. Preparing to land, the pilot radioed the tower.
2. Making a decision, she pulled over to the curb and stopped.
3. Training for the marathon, Oliver ate no sweets.
4. Staring out the window, she recalled her past.
5. Adjusting her rear-view mirror, my mother checked her hairstyle.
6. Checking my shoe size, the salesperson noted that one foot was larger than the other.
7. Following close behind, I never lost sight of my friend's car.
8. Growing prematurely bald, Steve began wearing a hat.
9. Crying in the crib, the baby let everyone know she was hungry.
10. Finally breaking through the clouds, the sun warmed our bodies and spirits.

Another Review Exercise: Points 1 and 2, p. 118

Answers to this exercise will vary. Check with your instructor if you need to.

1. When ready, the dinner will be served.
2. Although a stranger, he seemed very nice.
3. At my high school graduation, I bade farewell to my old friends.
4. While shopping for a home computer, Peter tested over twenty models.
5. From under the table, the dog watched his master's guest.
6. In her younger days, she was a well-known singer.
7. By the way you dress, I can tell you like the latest fashions.
8. On my stereo television, I can enjoy the latest videos.
9. If damaged in shipment, this appliance should be returned.
10. When used properly, the attachments make sewing a lot easier.

Exercise: Point 3, p. 119

Answers to this exercise will vary. Check with your instructor if you need to.

1. Reaching the finals, <u>the Tigers</u> won the game.
2. Playing skillfully, <u>the home team</u> made a touchdown.
3. Shouting, <u>Joe</u> offered his opinion.
4. Painting the ceiling, <u>she</u> got white paint on her hair.
5. Speaking for the community, <u>Mrs</u>. Santos raised the issue.
6. Losing his temper, <u>his father</u> shouted.
7. Running frantically, <u>the ball carrier</u> tripped on a loose shoelace.
8. Being fond of romance, Julie liked late-night movies.
9. Endorsing the cheque and handing it to the teller, <u>Alex</u> received twenty dollars.
10. Lighting the candle, I got hot wax all over myself.

Exercise: Point 4, p. 120

Answers to this exercise will vary. Check with your instructor if you need to.

1. While we were fooling around, the lamps got broken.
2. As they were dashing through the snow, a stone upset the sleigh.
3. As I pedalled fiercely, my bicycle moved faster.
4. While we were eating dinner, the dishes got dirty.
5. As the crowd was leaving the stadium, a section of the bleachers collapsed.
6. As my brother was taking out the garbage, snow started to fall.
7. When I called her on the phone for the first time, my throat was dry.
8. As she was watching a horror movie, her palms started to sweat.
9. When I was going into the sixth grade, my father's company transferred him to a different town.
10. Because she was spending a lot of time partying, her grades slipped.

Review Exercise: Points 1–4, p. 121

Answers to this exercise will vary. Check with your instructor if you need to.

1. Scoring in the final seconds, our team won the game.
2. Going to the grocery store, he bought food for dinner.
3. Travelling alone, Ashoona took Air Canada from Fredericton to Halifax.
4. Running for mayor, Ms. Lee shook hands with everyone.
5. His biceps bulged when he flexed his muscles.
6. After escaping from prison, the convict was captured by the warden.
7. She was smiling broadly as her hair blew in the wind.

8. As she recalled the past, a memory of her friend came to mind.
9. Crying and kicking, the child was sent to his room.
10. Because he was smoking a cigar, the room started to stink.

Exercise: Point 5, p. 123

Answers to this exercise will vary. Check with your instructor if you need to.

1. Since moving to Manitoba, I have learned to appreciate open land.
2. Before selecting a business partner, you should interview several candidates.
3. While waiting for the service technician, she tried the machine again.
4. After getting a credit card, she went on a spending spree.
5. By having the oil filter changed, we saved money.
6. On hearing about your divorce, I was really distressed.
7. While installing a skylight in my house, I discovered my talent for building.
8. While riding my bicycle, I passed a group of people in strange costumes.
9. Since moving to the country, we have come to appreciate peace and quiet.
10. By choosing to live in Dawson Creek, he decided to enjoy the cold weather.

Exercise: Point 6, p. 124

Answers to this exercise will vary. Check with your instructor if you need to.

1. To appreciate the music, you should turn up the volume.
2. To clean the roof gutters, you will need a ladder and a pair of gloves.
3. To be a good friend, we should always be sincere.
4. To stay healthy, eat well and exercise daily.
5. To understand poetry, you need to read it closely.
6. To find the secret of life, look within yourself.
7. To avoid trouble, mind your own business.
8. To play professional baseball, you need skill and luck.
9. To prepare lasagna, he always bought high-quality ingredients.
10. To finish a cabinet, you should use a good stain.

Review Exercise: Points 1–6, p. 124

Answers to this exercise will vary. Check with your instructor if you need to.

1. While he was skating on the frozen pond, his ankles buckled.
2. To run for public office, a person must meet certain requirements
3. After I put up a scarecrow, the birds tore it apart.
4. While Carl was marching in the parade, the drum he was playing broke.
5. Jumping rope, Andrea sprained her ankle.
6. To make a decision, you should first have firm convictions.
7. To go camping, you need a tent and a flashlight.
8. When I was reading the book, the character reminded me of you.
9. Driving in Winnipeg, Mr. Al-Raschid hit a cat.
10. To pass this course, you need to write one paper each week.

Chapter Review, p. 125

I

1. (Making a pizza,) the chef ^ flipped the dough into the air.
2. (To learn to play the violin,) a fellow ^ must have patience and neighbours who really like him.
3. (To work up a sweat,) Reynaldo ^ jogs four kilometres.
4. (Since starting college,) Su Mei ^ has learned the meaning of hard work.
5. (While filling the gas tank,) the attendant ^ told us about the new show in town.
6. (Barking furiously,) the puppy ^ chased the cat.
7. (Pretending to be asleep,) she ^ listened to the transistor radio.
8. (Before finding a parking space,) they ^ had driven around the block three times.
9. (Not paying attention,) the students ^ dozed off.
10. (To relax,) you ^ can put your feet up ^ and read a good book.

II Answers to this exercise will vary. Check with your instructor if you need to.

1. Barking and wagging his tail, the collie showed his affection for his master.
2. Swerving to the left, the truck hit a lamppost.
3. To be a movie star, you need good looks and talent.
4. When lost in a strange city, I always use my CB to get directions.
5. In northern Saskatchewan, the winter is generally very cold, and there is always a lot of snow.
6. Playing his role, the actor persuaded the audience that he really was Hamlet.
7. After dialling the wrong number, my friend asked the operator for assistance.
8. When scrambled with cheese and onions, eggs are absolutely delicious.
9. At the age of sixty, Dr. Katz retired from her job.
10. Using his professional knowledge, the plumber repaired our leaky tap.

III Answers to this exercise will vary. Check with your instructor if you need to.

1. By sending her children to camp, Mrs. Mullins made her whole family very happy.
2. To make a Spanish omelet, use tomatoes, peppers, onions, and eggs.
3. After realizing he had made the wrong turn, Alex turned around.
4. When Kitty voices her opinion, people pay close attention.
5. When feeling depressed, listen to some music.
6. Thinking of you, I always get a chill up my spine.
7. On being appointed president of the club, Joan delivered an eloquent speech.
8. While working in that restaurant, I made a lot of money in tips.
9. To cancel your appointment, simply call twenty-four hours in advance.
10. During her career as a newscaster, Jane visited nine foreign countries.
11. Ordering everyone around, the bully quickly made enemies.
12. Scrubbing the kitchen floor, Gene gets down on his hands and knees.
13. To lend me a hand in this job, you can pass me the tools when I need them.
14. After vacationing in Canada, we decided that we enjoyed vacationing in our native land.
15. At the age of twelve, Andrea had already read the complete works of Earle Birney.
16. Expecting to see her boyfriend, Ellen put on her sexiest dress.
17. To change engine oil, you will need a pan to catch the old stuff.
18. When looking up a word in the dictionary, one should always check the part of speech.
19. Seeing his arch rival, he ducked around the corner.
20. To show me that you love me, tell me that you love me five times a day.

IV

1. D the captain	6. (D)
2. D him	7. (D)
3. C	8. C
4. D winner	9. C
5. (D)	10. D chicken

V Answers to this exercise will vary. Check with your instructor if you need to.

1. Because he had forgotten his meal ticket, the student could not get lunch.
2. Before pruning the trees, I had to sharpen the blades.
3. To get the student rate, you must meet certain requirements.
4. When playing the guitar, many people use finger picks.
5. His vision was impaired when he drove at night.
6. The blender broke while I was making the frappe.
7. When I was six, I fractured my finger.
8. While she was sailing on the lake, her hat blew away.
9. To lose weight, you must follow a diet.
10. To play golf, you need a set of clubs.
11. Before hitting the jackpot, he performed a good-luck dance.
12. While I was in a cast, the nurse told me to take it easy.
13. Since I fired Ben, business has improved.
14. By considering the options, we made a decision.
15. Being a pirate, he covered his right eye with a patch.
16. The dogcatcher chased the rabid dog, which was foaming at the mouth.
17. The crowd watched the fireworks exploding in brilliant colours on Canada Day.
18. You have to use the stick shift to put the car in reverse.
19. When a person is tired and hungry, a ham and cheese sandwich really hits the spot.
20. In setting a table, you must place forks, knives, and spoons correctly.

VI Answers to this exercise will vary. Check with your instructor if you need to.

On arriving in Canada, Pierre was amazed by the sights and sounds. Since he had travelled alone, the sight of so many people hurrying around and shouting came as a jolt to him. Coming from a small village in the south of France, the young traveller had never before witnessed so much commotion. He was only eight years old and a bit nervous, and his luggage seemed to be his only companion. On this trip, his cousins in Quebec City would be his hosts. Looking for them at the gate, he was not able to find them. Then an attendant took him to the information booth and paged his cousins over the loudspeaker. To locate them, the attendant had to make the announcement twice. Then Pierre recognized his relatives running through the terminal, from the other end of the building. Feeling relieved, Pierre ran to them and escaped the crazy crowds of Canada.

To throw a successful party, you must take several factors into consideration. When making up a list of people to invite, you should be sure they are compatible. After deciding on the guests, you must decide the amount of food and drink. If you are preparing a fruit punch, a large bowl and a ladle are necessary. If you want to save money, a fruit punch is often better than serving everyone individual cocktails. Preparing the food in advance is also a good idea. When you are planning the meal, you must, of course, consider the number of guests. By cooking ahead of time, you may avoid a lot of bother. I suggest making lasagna, which is always a favourite. When a host serves punch and lasagna, you can be almost certain that the party will be a success.

As a way of fighting the high cost of travel and of conserving fuel, more people are buying smaller automobiles. Both on the highway and in the city, a small car saves gas and gets better mileage. A driver should bring his small car in for a tuneup after he has driven about 15 000 kilometres. After receiving the proper care, the vehicle is ready for continued efficient use. When you think about it, the day of the big car is gone.

CHAPTER 8

Exercise: Point 1, p. 133

1. They are going on a vacation.
2. We will haul this stuff to the dump.
3. She is learning how to water-ski.
4. It has been snapped in half.
5. They are planning a strike.
6. He served in Holland with the Canadian army.
7. They are celebrating an anniversary.
8. We spent the day at the Glenbow Museum.
9. She is going for her Ph.D. at Dalhousie University.
10. It gives Fritz great pleasure.

Exercise: Point 2, p. 135

1. She hit him with it.
2. I wrote it about her.
3. They starred in it.
4. She bought it.
5. He paid for it.
6. He told them to move it right away.
7. They called us.
8. We called them.
9. Do you smoke it?
10. It is important to them.

Review Exercise: Points 1 and 2, p. 136

1. We them
2. She him
3. It her
4. They it
5. He them
6. They it
7. She it him
8. It them
9. He it them
10. We it

Exercise: Point 3, p. 137

1. boat (S) it (O)
2. dress (O) it (S)
3. Martha and I (S) us (O)
4. Tom and his friend (S) they (S)
5. she (S) Dolores (S)
6. skateboarding (O) it (O)
7. Willie (S) him (O) he (S)
8. Sandra (S) flat tire (O) She (S) it (O) her (O)
9. test (O) it (O)
10. a notebook and some pens (O) them (O)

Exercise: Point 4, p. 138

Answers to this exercise will vary. Check with your instructor if you need to.

1. Stan told Barbara, "You will be elected class president. "
2. He added pepper, salt, and then, more pepper.
3. The Blue Bombers won when they played the Lions.
4. Marie lived in an orphanage before Ms. Rae adopted her.
5. Bill felt great when he finally approached his father.
6. The car was damaged when it hit the telephone pole.
7. My mother was quite upset when she scolded my little sister.
8. Paul told his nephew, "You will be a great Canadian some day."
9. The doctor told her patient, "You will have to take some time off."
10. The boys were embarrassed when they asked the girls to dance.

Review Exercise: Points 1–4, p. 139

1. O him one of the boys
2. S she Lee
3. O it The traffic
4. S he The premier
   O it bill
5. O me Eddie
   S you Ivan
6. O it The vase
7. O him Craig
8. S you Dave and Sandy
9. S she Carol
10. O it The carton

Exercise: Point 5, p. 140

1. F which The class show was a great success
2. F which He hadn't heard about the change in plans
3. C
4. F This People continue to drive after drinking.
5. F This Every Canadian has the chance to be whatever he or she chooses.
6. F It Buses never seem to keep to the schedules anymore.
7. F that I miss my family,
8. F which She takes a ballet lesson every Thursday,
9. F this my mother always bugged me about keeping my room clean.
10. F which He always carries a calculator with him,

Exercise: Point 6, p. 142

1. his nervousness
2. fish
3. a redhead
4. members of the fraternity
5. a home run
6. the students' laziness
7. Revenue Canada *or* the government
8. the musicians
9. the fact that her sandwich was stale
10. the trip

Review Exercise: Points 1–6, p. 142

Answers to this exercise will vary. Check with your instructor if you need to.

1. (5, 1) Everyone who worked on the class show was pleased that it was a great success.
2. (5, 2) Because he hadn't heard about the change in plans, he was late.
3. (5, 3) Correct.
4. (5, 4) It is ridiculous that people continue to drive after drinking.
5. (5, 5) One of the basic concepts of Canadian democracy is that every person has the chance to be whatever he or she chooses.
6. (5, 6) Buses never seem to keep to the schedules anymore. The problem is really getting out of hand.
7. (5, 7) I go home for the holidays every year, because I miss my family.
8. (V, 8) To help strengthen her leg muscles, she takes a ballet lesson every Thursday.
9. (5, 9) When I was younger, my mother always bugged me about keeping my room clean. But she stopped doing it as I grew older and more mature.
10. (5, 10) He always carries a calculator with him. Having it makes his work a lot easier.
11. (6, 1) Joseph is nervous about the upcoming exam, but his nervousness doesn't show.
12. (6, 2) Whenever I swim in Lake Huron, the fish always nip at my feet.
13. (6, 3) Paula bought some red dye for her hair so she could become a redhead.
14. (6, 4) He joined the fraternity at Western because its members enjoy the same things he does.
15. (6, 5) Although he made a home run, he was intimidated by all the home-run hitters in the lineup.
16. (6, 6) Some teachers feel that their students are lazy, and that the laziness is a result of too many hours spent watching television.
17. (6, 7) To avoid getting penalized for a late return, you have to send Revenue Canada your income tax forms by April 30.
18. (6, 8) The concert was sold out, so we will have to see the group some other time.
19. (6, 9) Her sandwich was stale, because she had not wrapped it properly.
20. (6, 10) When we flew to Europe, I was surprised at how quickly the trip went.

Chapter Review, p. 144

I

1.	I	11.	we us
2.	She me	12.	her
3.	him	13.	They
4.	her	14.	him her
5.	him	15.	He I
6.	us them	16.	she I he
7.	They us	17.	We us
8.	them	18.	she
9.	him me	19.	He
10.	us	20.	we they

II Answers to this exercise will vary. Check with your instructor if you need to.

1.	she	6.	he
2.	it	7.	we
3.	they	8.	you
4.	them	9.	her
5.	her	10.	it

III

1.	F	6.	C	11.	C	16.	F
2.	F	7.	F	12.	F	17.	F
3.	F	8.	F	13.	F	18.	C
4.	F	9.	F	14.	F	19.	F
5.	F	10.	C	15.	F	20.	C

IV Answers to this exercise will vary. Check with your instructor if you need to.

1. My wife was pleased that I changed my mind about buying a motorcycle.
2. The saw fell down when he put it on the shelf.
3. Betty said, "Jenny, you are the best cook in the world."
4. I bought a new pair of sneakers, but I always wear my old ones, which are still pretty good.
5. We were late because we could not find a parking space.
6. Gene moved there because he loves nature.
7. She told her sister, "I have found true love."
8. Because I did not know how to fix it, I brought the broken tool to the hardware store.
9. There is plenty of snow in Moosonee.
10. As soon as I pumped up the tires, I went for a ride on my bike.
11. She made her debut in a play at the Stratford Festival .
12. My wife went crazy when I used her coupon.
13. Vincent told Stephen, "You have been awarded a medal of honour."
14. Rudy said that he had heard I was moving to Nova Scotia. I am not.
15. He is a good father because he pays a great deal of attention to his children.

16. Although his happiness never shows, Oscar is happiest when he is working.
17. I got the job because I knew the president of the company.
18. Sally said that her mother's plans were outrageous.
19. When I went to the supermarket, I was happy to see that pork chops had gone down in price.
20. It is an elementary fact in mathematics that two plus two equals four.

V Answers to this exercise will vary. Check with your instructor if you need to.

Learning to drive a car was a harrowing experience. I took ten weeks of very helpful lessons at a driving school. But it was not until I was preparing for my road test that I found out how inexperienced I really was. Inexperience was really the problem.

In my last trial run, I backed the car out of my driveway and hit a lamppost, but the car was not badly damaged. That incident was only the beginning. I finally got the car moving smoothly, and was nervous about running into something else, but I didn't let my nervousness show. I was cruising along at 40 kilometres per hour with the radio playing, since the radio always helped to calm me down. A police officer who was patrolling the neighbourhood must have thought I was going too slowly and pulled me over. We talked for a few minutes, and the conversation turned out to be rather helpful: he suggested I use the headlights while driving at night.

I was excited when I heard about the rally. As soon as I heard about the demonstration, I got my shoes ready. They had shiny leather tops, brand-new laces, and thick rubber soles. Just looking at them put me into the right frame of mind for walking. I looked forward to the march because I really believed in the cause. Although I never let my weariness show, sometimes I get tired during a long walk. Besides, this was a truly important demonstration! This time when I slid into my shoes, my feet did not ache at all.

The nine-to-five workday, which millions of Canadians experience five times a week, may be slowly dying out. Many people would be very happy if it did vanish. Employers are saying that their employees could use some extra time to themselves. A four-day work week may be with us shortly, and people are pleased to have the chance to spend more time with their families. Fathers and mothers will be able to take up new hobbies and pursue new interests, and the increase in free time will serve to improve the health of many people. Both physical and mental health will be improved. Working fewer hours would make millions of people very happy, but there would also have to be a promise of no drop in income. There are still some problems in setting up the shortened working schedule, but its promoters are confident that as the need for it becomes more apparent, it will come about.

CHAPTER 9

Exercise: Point 1, p. 152

1. dancing, singing, laughing
2. to blend, to mix, to stir
3. pushed, pulled, shoved
4. have written, have stamped, have sent
5. fed, swallowed, digested
6. building, painting, whitewashing
7. rose, sank, reappeared
8. to love, to honour, to obey
9. drove, parked, paid
10. living, laughing, loving

Exercise: Point 2, p. 153

Answers to this exercise will vary. Check with your instructor if you need to.

1. hungry, thirsty, tired
2. proud, brave, patriotic
3. brunette, brown-eyed, dark-complexioned
4. weaving, crocheting, sewing
5. bought, traded, sold
6. to replace, to repair, to restore
7. playing baseball, playing football, playing soccer
8. exciting, fantastic, thrilling
9. planting, reaping, storing
10. dreamed, desired, wished

Exercise: Point 3, p. 154

Answers to this exercise will vary. Check with your instructor if you need to.

1. Eduardo has always enjoyed fishing and hunting.
2. You can see the moon and stars in the sky tonight.
3. As an accountant, Phyllis adds and multiplies figures all day long.
4. I will probably be washing the dishes or mopping the floor when you arrive.
5. He is old but alert.
6. Filling the gas tank and checking the oil are two of the responsibilities of a gas station attendant.

7. A teacher expects his students to do their <u>homework, to attend classes regularly,</u> and to pay attention to lectures.
8. Before she left, <u>she combed her hair, polished her fingernails,</u> and applied her makeup.
9. When customers are not satisfied, they <u>return the merchandise</u> or make a complaint.
10. The day is <u>sunny, hot,</u> and humid.

Review Exercise: Points 1–3, p. 155

Answers to this exercise will vary. Check with your instructor if you need to.

1. Put the cheese between two slices of bread and fry it.
2. He was a good lecturer, a kind man, and a hard worker.
3. A lifeguard supervises the beach, flirts with girls, and rescues swimmers who are having difficulty.
4. Lynn is preparing her résumé, reading the want ads, and going on interviews.
5. A good friend is thoughtful, truthful, and supportive.
6. I enjoy seeing shows, reading good books, and going to the movies.
7. To be a doctor, one must have ambition, persistence, and willingess to work long hours.
8. The cat purred, meowed, and cleaned itself.
9. He was forced to pawn his watch, sell his radio, and try to find a new job.
10. To be or not to be; that is the question.

Exercise: Point 4, p. 156

1. P	6. P
2. X	7. P
3 P	8. P
4. X	9. X
5. P	10. P

Exercise: Point 5, p. 157

Answers to this exercise will vary. Check with your instructor if you need to.

1. Our house is located near the bus station, the laundromat, and the supermarket.
2. By taking lessons and practising daily, Andrea has become a fine violinist.
3. My dream is to have a good job, a family, and a house in the country.
4. Washing my car, removing the rust, and getting a good finish takes time.
5. He said that he would stop by our house, deliver the package, and eat dinner with us.
6. I bought a car with whitewall tires, leather seats, and an AM-FM radio.
7. She asked me where I went to school and what degree I earned.
8. Waiting for the bus and becoming a bit nervous, Hal started biting his nails.
9. I promise to dress properly and to arrive on time.
10. Doris wants to be a violinist, a music teacher, or a conductor.

Review Exercise: Points 1–5, p. 158

Answers to this exercise will vary. Check with your instructor if you need to.

1. He accepted the money, promised to spend it wisely, and went for a ride in his car.
2. Not only was she intelligent, but her sense of humour was also good.
3. They went to the Okanagan Valley on their vacation to camp and to have fun.
4. This book is boring and long.
5. Her coat has six brass buttons, flared sleeves, and a detachable hood.
6. Eating breakfast, eating lunch, and eating dinner are my three favourite activities of the day.
7. Therese was either angry or irritable.
8. The fullback is strong, big, and fast.
9. We went to the concert with Fred, Jane, and Zelda.
10. They were interested in buying the air conditioner, but were not willing to spend so much money.

Chapter Review, p. 159

I
1. achieving a sense of satisfaction
2. escaping in the green Ford
3. having good luck
4. to comb his hair
5. his ability to keep cool
6. the piano player sang
7. by herself
8. charging at us
9. to do arithmetic
10. kind

II

1. to cash a cheque	6. to get undressed
2. looking out for bears	7. mowing the lawn
3. with pimples	8. sturdy
4. looking outside	9. on the sofa
5. riding	10. to meet the neighbours

III Answers to this exercise will vary. Check with your instructor if you need to.

1. It is my ambition <u>to be successful</u> and to be popular.
2. Franz can speak both <u>English</u> and French.

3. She said that she would be on either the 7:00 bus or the 9:15 bus.
4. The brown puppy was wagging its tail and licking my hand.
5. The cabinet she built is made of pine and is painted blue.
6. We strolled under the boardwalk and along the beach.
7. He wants to move to Brandon and to live there permanently.
8. Judy kept a rabbit's foot, a four-leaf clover, and a horseshoe in her drawer.
9. When we visited Toronto, we rode the streetcars, went to Ontario Place and attended the ballet at the O'Keefe Centre.
10. When left alone, he gets sad, lonely, and depressed.

IV Answers to this exercise will vary. Check with your instructor if you need to.

1. He admitted that he had committed the crime and that he deserved to get caught.
2. We were disappointed with our grades, but we understood them.
3. Batting, throwing, and fielding are important skills in baseball.
4. The dog dug up the bone and found it to his liking.
5. Ramon knows that he should work on his writing and should improve his spelling.
6. His lunch included soup, a roast beef sandwich, a peach, and dessert.
7. I respected his intelligence, his strength, and his humour.
8. It would make my day complete to see you, to go to a movie, and to have dinner with you.
9. That cigarette tastes harsh and is probably stale.
10. Marianne spends her day attending classes, studying, and listening to music.
11. The day was sunny, bright, and dry.
12. The dean told the teacher that classes were suspended and that the students could go home.
13. She could read on a bus, in an elevator, or in line at the bank.
14. The camper learned how to tie a knot, how to start a fire, and how to ride horseback.
15. That car with four-wheel drive can get out of mud, snow, and deep potholes.
16. There were news items about the rising price of coffee, the increasing crime rate, and the growing energy shortage.
17. The grass needed water and turned brown.
18. Going for a walk in the evening and meeting a friend on the street are both pleasant.
19. I wish I knew more about croquet and badminton.
20. Stupid questions make me angry and make me lose my temper.

V Answers to this exercise will vary. Check with your instructor if you need to.

1. I was watching the ball game and eating hot dogs.
2. We learned that we had won Loto 649 and also that we had become instant millionaires.
3. She was running, jumping, and trying to catch a butterfly.
4. We cooked our dinner, and then we cleaned the dishes.
5. I want to save money so I will be able to buy presents.
6. I enjoy going to a dance, choosing a partner, and dancing with her.
7. I like putting my feet up, listening to the radio, and relaxing.
8. He was sure that he could stand no more and that he would lose his temper.
9. That skirt is thin and flimsy.
10. Keeping good notes and using a tape recorder are valuable aids to study.
11. I went to Commonwealth Stadium with my buddies.
12. The first steps to finding work are applying for a job and scheduling an interview.
13. The face of the cliff was steep, dangerous, and slippery.
14. We have a family reunion on Mother's Day, on Father's Day, and on Canada Day.
15. When I am happy, I laugh.
16. You will find mothballs around the corner in aisle three.
17. If I got the job, when would I start working?
18. I enjoy building a fire and roasting marshmallows.
19. She told me that I was her best friend and that she wanted me to read her poetry.
20. I want both to have friends and to be free.

VI Answers to this exercise will vary. Check with your instructor if you need to.

A library is a good place to spend an afternoon and to relax. You can read the newspaper from any major city, look for a good novel, or listen to a record. Librarians can tell you where to find a particular book and can suggest a quiet place where you can read it.

Many libraries have display halls where you can observe artwork or just stroll around.

People find many different things to do in the library. There is usually someone studying or writing a research paper; there are those who read periodicals and those who just chat with friends. All things considered, the library is an excellent place for meeting people, reading, or relaxing.

When we heard that we had won the lottery, we wanted to jump for joy, scream our lungs out, and pat each other on the back. We immediately made plans for renting a car, dining, and dancing. We went wild, spending the evening eating the best food we had ever tasted, drinking only the finest wines, and riding to the top of the CN Tower to get a dramatic view of Toronto. Finally at around 3:00 a.m. we decided that we were pooped, that we had to go home, and that climbing into bed seemed just right.

Sir Frederick Banting was one of Canada's most famous doctors. Not only was he a war hero, but he also was the co-discoverer of insulin. Insulin is used to treat diabetes.

In 1920, he wrote down an idea aimed at isolating the secretion from the pancreas. He received support from Dr. J. MacLeod and Dr. Charles Best. In the winter of 1921–22, they discovered insulin. Banting was the principal discoverer because he began the research, was prominent in its early use, and fought for recognition. Banting won the Nobel Prize in 1923, and was knighted in 1934.

Banting's discovery gave diabetes victims a new chance at life. During his lifetime, he was this country's most famous living Canadian.

CHAPTER 10

Exercise: Point 1, p. 169

1. S	6. S
2. S	7. P
3. P	8. S
4. S	9. P
5. P	10. P

Exercise: Point 2, p. 170

1. A reporter should always write his stories objectively.
2. If a driver is careful, he will avoid accidents.
3. A model should always look his best when he is being photographed.
4. Breakfast cereals are tasty, and they supply vitamins and minerals.
5. The headmaster works in his office.
6. A disc jockey plays records; also, he reads commercials.
7. A teacher should be familiar with his material; moreover, he should be able to present it in a clear manner.
8. Our boss is vacationing in her trailer.
9. My grandmother is making her special soup.
10. The fans are waiting in line for their turn.

Review Exercise: Points 1 and 2, p. 171

Answers to this exercise will vary. Check with your in structor if you need to.

1. A successful comedian tries to get a sense of his audience.
2. A person should try to understand his limitations.
3. I was looking for my hat, but I could not find it.
4. You have two chances, so use them wisely.
5. Teachers grade papers, and sometimes they also write comments.
6. A lawyer advises his clients, but his fees are often excessive
7. Athletes often get their backs massaged.
8. The radio is broken, but it can be repaired.
9. Ms. Kanter is cooking her special pot roast.
10. A party can be a lot of fun, but it must be well planned.

Exercise: Point 3, p. 172

1. 3	6. 2
2. 1	7. 3
3. 3	8. 1
4. 3	9. 3
5. 3	10. 3

Exercise: Point 4, p. 173

1. A person can run for public office if he meets certain requirements.
2. If he were really my friend, he wouldn't have made that remark.
3. If one is running for office, he should always tell the truth.
4. One could ask her a question and he would never get a answer.
5. Anyone can quit smoking if he really puts his mind to it.
6. She sat in the sun for three hours, and one can't do that without getting a severe burn.

7. You can do it if you put your mind to it.
8. The bowler scored seven strikes in a row; one has to be skillful to do that.
9. After we left, we felt that we wanted to visit again.
10. A lawyer should advise his clients carefully.

Review Exercise: Points 1–4, p. 174

Answers to this exercise will vary. Check with your instructor if you need to.

1. A good businessman is always helpful to his clients.
2. Students who study hard are sure to find satisfaction for themselves.
3. Roller coasters are exciting to ride, but some think they are dangerous.
4. She likes to watch television, but one should spend some of one's time reading.
5. A person should brush his teeth after every meal.
6. A son may sometimes try to take after his father.
7. Sherry always keeps her chequebook balanced.
8. A butcher must be careful not to back into his meat slicer, or he may get a little behind in his work.
9. Mt. Logan in the Yukon is Canada's highest mountain.
10. Wise people look ahead to the future; they do not get themselves forever tied up in the past.

Exercise: Point 5, p. 175

1. She <u>gave</u> him good advice, but he ignored her.
2. I <u>lost</u> my library card, so I got a new one.
3. I <u>could not find</u> my way, so I asked for help.
4. It <u>was</u> one of the weirdest experiences I ever had.
5. The police officer <u>stopped</u> him because he was jaywalking.
6. I <u>miss</u> you and want you.
7. When I <u>tell</u> her that I love her, she is happy.
8. She <u>asked,</u> "Are you coming?" and I said, "No."
9. We <u>stayed</u> for the entire show and then went out for ice cream.
10. The road <u>was</u> rocky, but because he was driving carefully, we arrived safely.

Review Exercise: Points 1–5, p. 175

Answers to this exercise will vary. Check with your instructor if you need to.

1. We bought an air conditioner, so we stayed cool all last summer.
2. He was a man who always put his best foot forward.
3. A teacher must prepare his lesson plans every night.
4. She berates her brother and hits him, too.
5. A great chef will never tell you his secret recipes.
6. Everyone who was at the Queen's Plate had his fanciest clothes on.
7. I saw her at a distance, and then I ran to her.
8. A politician must know how to address his constituency.
9. If one intends to get an A in the course, he will have to work hard.
10. Explorers founded Montreal before they discovered the prairies.

Chapter Review, p. 176

I

1. A fashion designer has his work cut out for him.
2. When you know the answer, raise your hand.
3. She was hired yesterday and celebrated last evening.
4. Whenever he sneezes, he causes quite a ruckus.
5. Children should respect their parents.
6. The golfer measured the putt and tapped his ball in for a par.
7. A car should be serviced regularly or it will not run well.
8. We went skiing at Lake Louise, had drinks before a fireplace, and got to know each other better.
9. When a baby cries, it often means that he wants his dinner.
10. Some people never get their car tuned.
11. Man's best friend is his dog.
12. Don't lose your cool!
13. We go for a ride, have a picnic, and then come home and have another party.
14. I came, I saw, I conquered.
15. A computer is useful to its owner.
16. The rock group wrote most of its songs.
17. Food is very expensive today; also, heating costs are higher.
18. She ran out of the room and said, "I am leaving. "
19. As Canadians, we are supposed to have the opportunity to improve our future.
20. The singer signalled for her musicians to pick up the tempo.

II Answers to this exercise will vary. Check with your instructor if you need to.

1. A person may get his hair cut, or he may get it styled.
2. A doctor should be sympathetic with his patients.
3. We ate and drank until we were full.
4. A dog is man's best friend; it always comes when one calls.
5. I missed the bus, so I waited for another.
6. Children should respect their parents.
7. If you cross the street in the middle of the block, you have to be very careful.

8. A public official should heed the opinions of his constituents.
9. The building inspector expressed her opinion that the old house should be torn down.
10. The dog chased the man and bit his leg.
11. One should exercise his right to vote.
12. A student should try to hand in his papers on time.
13. The principal called the teachers in for a meeting and addressed them on methods of discipline.
14. The car swerved and hit a telephone pole.
15. A person should try to make his dreams come true.
16. People should try to make their dreams come true.
17. You are my best friend, for you always listen when I have problems.
18. The bus driver wanted the exact change, but we did not have it.
19. She wanted her boss to give her a raise.
20. Go tell Aunt Rodie that the old gray goose is dead.

III
1. they are
   their <u>number</u>
2. decide <u>tense</u>
3. you present
   your <u>person</u>
4. your <u>person</u>
5. got <u>tense</u>
6. his <u>number</u>
7. your <u>person</u>
8. your <u>person</u>
9. they are <u>number</u>
10. use <u>tense</u>

IV Answers to this exercise will vary. Check with your instructor if you need to.

1. First he read the novel, then he wrote the paper.
2. Sportscasters should be objective, but they always seem to root for the home team.
3. If a student studies regularly, he will not have to cram the night before a test.
4. She enjoys reading, but she dislikes writing.
5. One must participate in class discussion, or his grade will suffer.
6. Anyone can learn home repair if he concentrates.
7. Hansel and Gretel finally found their way home.
8. She counted to ten before she lost her temper.
9. Pilots always try to make their passengers feel at ease.
10. A person can educate himself if he puts his mind to it.
11. King Arthur ate with all of his knights at the Round Table.
12. Every morning she washes her face, brushes her teeth, and combs her hair.
13. I am sentimental whenever I hear old favourite melodies.
14. Almost anyone can learn to play the recorder if he takes lessons.
15. He whines whenever he does not get his way.
16. Many taxpayers need an accountant to figure out their returns.
17. I don't enjoy shopping for clothes because I have to spend so much time in dressing rooms.
18. If one intends to quit his job, he should give two weeks' notice.
19. Pediatricians must like children, because they deal with them every day.
20. I went to the Royal Winnipeg Ballet and saw some beautiful costumes.

V Answers to this exercise will vary. Check with your instructor if you need to.

If one intends to be a writer, he must first learn the great task of self-discipline. Most novelists, or poets, or dramatists do not work in an office; they often work at home. If they are unable to rid themselves of distractions, they will probably find that they do very little work. There are always plenty of reasons or excuses not to write, but if the writer is able to set his mind to his work, they will not bother him. Some writers make schedules for themselves; others choose to work when they are inspired. Whatever the case, the point remains the same: if one wants to write, he writes; if one does not, he doesn't.

Today, news programs and magazines are quite the rage. Everywhere you look, you can see news of this strike or that tax increase thrown at you. A newspaper should be objective, but its writers always seem to inject their own opinion into the stories. Because of the subjective nature of the news, more and more magazines find their way onto the newsstands. Moreover, these magazines often produce more in-depth accounts of the news. I suppose every form of the news media has its place.

I work in a bank in Surrey, and when one has that type of job, he has to be willing to wake up at a very early hour. Each morning, I drive to work, park my car, and walk a block to work. I get a lunch break every day at noon, and I love to eat at the delicatessen around the corner. I worked at the bank for over a year, and decided that I had had enough. After looking around for a new job, I found one where I had to be at work by 6:00 a.m. This job was in a restaurant where I had to stand up all day, and after six months, I decided to go back to the bank. The manager was very nice to me and said, "You can have your old job back if you promise to stay at least two years." I took the job, and I enjoy an extra hour of sleep every morning.

CHAPTER 11

Exercise: Point 1, p. 188

1. S They promised to arrive on time.
2. S The humidity bothers me.
3. X
4. S The repairman asked whether we had fooled around with the plug.
5. X
6. S Prince Edward Island is Canada's smallest province.
7. S I bought a new needle for my record player.
8. S Let's build a bonfire tonight.
9. S They danced the tango.
10. X

Review Exercise: Points 1 and 2, p. 189

1. Dr. Mitchell cancelled my appointment.
2. *Ms.* magazine is very popular reading these days.
3. A Ph.D is an advanced degree.
4. Combine 57 g butter with 114 g sugar.
5. Now I get it.
6. Mrs. Ames raised an objection.
7. I have been instructed to report on Sept. 30.
8. Gen. Burns was a great man.
9. There are never enough hours in the day.
10. The room measured 5 m^2.

Exercise: Point 3, p. 190

1. C
2. X
3. X
4. C
5. X
6. X
7. X
8. X
9. X
10. X

Exercise: Point 4, p. 191

Answers to this exercise will vary. Check with your instructor if you need to.

The alarm clock was shrieking. I woke up with a start. When I looked at the clock, it said 8:30. Oh, no! I had meant to set it for 7:30. Now I'd never get to the bus stop on time! I jumped out of bed, yanked on my clothes, and grabbed a couple of doughnuts from last night's party. They would have to do for breakfast; I couldn't even take time to make coffee. With the doughnuts in one hand and my coat in the other, I dashed out the door and ran down the street. The bus was coming. I would never make it. Then, at the last minute, the traffic light turned red. The bus had to wait. I put on a last burst of speed and made it to the bus stop just as the bus rolled up. As I scrambled aboard, panting, the driver grinned. "I saw you coming," he said. "I would have waited for you." I ought to have thanked him, but the way he grinned made me want to hit him instead. I collapsed into the nearest seat, puffing like an overweight elephant. It didn't matter—I had caught the bus!

Review Exercise: Points 1–4, p. 191

1. Working by candlelight can be inspiring.
2. Has the mail arrived yet?
3. She asked him if he would like to go out for dinner.
4. We do not take credit cards here.
5. I would like a corned beef sandwich.
6. Are you still taking violin lessons?
7. Good grief, he's having a heart attack!
8. Is there any reason to continue?
9. You had better comb your hair and straighten your tie.
10. I hope I don't have any cavities.

Exercise: Point 5, p. 192

1. The teller said, "I'm sorry, but your cheque has bounced."
2. "I'll never lie again," he said. "I promise."
3. "This assignment is due Tuesday," the teacher announced.
4. I warned him to drive slowly on the icy roads.
5. "Do you know the answer?" the teacher asked.
6. The doctor said, "Take two aspirins and go to sleep. "
7. Carol asked me if she could have a ride home.
8. "You can't get there from here," said the tour guide.
9. "I am telling the truth," he said. Then he added, "I know you won't believe me."
10. "Why don't you and Jane come for dinner?" she asked.

Exercise: Point 6, p. 194

1. X Joyce said, "I think I have a cold."
2. X "Do you love me?" he asked.
3. X "Mend your ways!" I screamed.
4. X Billy asked, "Why is it always me?"
5. X I can't believe you actually said, "Fishing is for the birds"; you have a weird sense of humour.
6. X "Does this car need oil?" the attendant inquired.
7. X "Out, damn Spot!" she screamed, throwing her dog out the door.
8. C
9. X Did you shout, "Bargains galore"?
10. X Cries of "Help!" echoed through the building.

Exercise: Point 7, p. 195

1. Last night we saw "The Diviners" on television.

2. Before my vacation I read Europe on Ten Dollars a Day.
3. "Grammar Review" is the first part of Trouble-shooting.
4. I read an article entitled "In Praise of Canadian Heroes.
5. My essay was titled "The Decline of Canadian Culture."
6. *Surfacing* is one of Atwood's most enjoyable novels.
7. "O Canada" is Canada's national anthem.
8. The Canadian edition of *Time* magazine contains many interesting articles.
9. Dorothy Livesay wrote a poem entitled "The Three Emilys."
10. Alannis Morisette's first hit CD was "Jagged Little Pill."

Review Exercise: Points 5–7 p. 196

1. Annie asked, "Are you going to sing that song again?"
2. I plan to read *The Diviners* this summer.
3. "Are you my friend or aren't you?" she asked.
4. "The time is right," he said, "for us to move on."
5. One of Oscar Peterson's earliest compositions was "Canadiana Suite."
6. She said that she would be studying all night.
7. Ahmed said, "Come visit us next weekend."
8. "Before I go," she said, "let me ask you one question."
9. "Do you read *Maclean's?"* she asked.
10. "Get that car out of my driveway!" the man hollered.

Chapter Review, p. 197

I
1. X
2. X
3. X
4. X
5. C
6. C
7. X
8. C
9. X
10. X

II
1. I am spending more time in the library these days.
2. Have you ever eaten smelts?
3. Don't try any funny business with me!
4. I wonder why they say blondes have more fun.
5. The show is on channel 5.
6. He has a lighter with his initials on it.
7. Did you say that you were driving to Cape Breton this summer?
8. The bellboy asked whether we needed any help with our bags.
9. Dr. McCarthy is the new chairman.
10. Mira is working toward her Ph.D.
11. What kind of fool am I?
12. Get lost, Buster!
13. Where were you on the night of June 3?
14. Should I wait for her?
15. Let's go, Tiger Cats!
16. She asked whether she could expect a raise.
17. Have you heard about Shollet and Luis?
18. A rolling stone gathers no moss.
19. Sgt. Anderson is an excellent detective.
20. Should we call you Ms. Burns or Mrs. Burns?

III
1. "I'm thinking. Give me some time!" Enrico snapped.
2. Suzanne asked, 'Will there be an essay question on the test?"
3. "We're late," she cried, "hurry up!"
4. The move Ben Hur is considered a classic.
5. The short story "The Window" is from *Mrs. Golightly and other Stories*.
6. "The metric system is too confusing," he complained.
7. "Don't you get the joke?" she asked.
8. "Block that kick!" the crowd chanted rhythmically.
9. His mother pleaded, "Finish your vegetables. There are people starving in India."
10. "Why don't you come up and see me some time?" she sang.
11. "Get lost!" we screamed at the hoodlums.
12. The lyrics are, "Chestnuts roasting on an open fire, Jack Frost nipping at your nose."
13. The doctor asked, "Are you feeling better?"
14. "This won't hurt a bit, " the nurse said as he stuck the needle into my arm.
15. "What is your hurry?" asked the oldtimer.
16. Paul Anka wrote the song "My Way" for Frank Sinatra.
17. I heard her say, "This is the worst party I've ever been to!"
18. "Hold it right there!" the police officer shouted.
19. "I hate peas!" wailed the child.
20. "Run a mile a day," she advised, "and you're sure to feel better."

IV Answers to this exercise will vary. Check with your instructor if you need to.

1. Sunita asked, "Can I lend a hand?"
2. The little boy cried when he hurt his leg.
3. Inez asked her brother, "Did Mom say when she'd be back?"
4. She wondered if he would ever ask her out.
5. As I always say, "If you can't lick them, join them!"

6. Ms. Yee said, "The job is yours."
7. He responded by saying, "Sorry, lady. It's too risky."
8. Do you know that song called "The Homecoming"?
9. My favourite movie is still *The Homecoming.*
10. The doctor warned us not to let him get up right away.

V 1. "I love scary movies," my sister informed us.
2. Dr. Gomez is an M.D.
3. "Where do you think you're going?" my mother asked.
4. "I wonder," he said, "if the economy will ever improve. "
5. My sister said that she was going to run off to the Orient.
6. "Why must you always complain?" I asked her.
7. "The End of the World" is a short story by Mavis Gallant.
8. "Full speed ahead!" shouted the captain.
9. "What's the deal?" he whispered.
10. Was it you who said, "I'm definitely not hungry"?
11. "I'm working as a file clerk this summer," he said.
12. Was it you who asked that stupid question?
13. "There's no green cheese up here," said the astronaut.
14. "There's a Hippo in my Tub" was a very popular children's song.
15. "Get out of my life!" she cried. "I've had enough!"
16. "While I'm away," he said, "please water my plants."
17. "Why are you so good to me?" she sighed.
18. "You fool!" screamed the man whose car I had just hit.
19. "Will I ever be able to learn programming?" Thomas asked.
20. "You will be a great writer," his teacher told him.

VI "This is the third paper of the semester that you have turned in late," said Professor Martin, "and you are simply going to have to change your work habits."

"I know," said Bruce, "and I promise to change my ways. "

Mr. Martin said, "Don't tell me your dog chewed up the paper. What happened?"

"I don't have a dog," replied Bruce, "but I do have a little brother."

"And he tore it up?" Mr. Martin asked.

"No," said Bruce, "but he wrote it for me, and since his spelling was so bad, it took me two whole days to correct it."

Three men were stationed in the farthest reaches of the Yukon, and their supply of whiskey was running low. Two of the men felt that they could take advantage of the third, so they told him to go out into the blizzard and buy some more whiskey in the nearest town. The third man said, "I will go only if you promise to save the last drop of this remaining whiskey for me."

"Don't worry," the others said, "we promise."

"I will definitely not go if you drink that last drop," the third man said.

"We promise, we promise," the others assured him.

With that, the third man left. A day went by. Two days went by. A week and then two weeks went by. The two men figured that the third must have died in the blizzard and decided to drink the last bit of whiskey. They took the bottle down from the shelf, said, "Cheers," and were about to indulge when the third man flung the door open.

"I told you," he announced, "I wasn't going to go if you drank that last drop!"

CHAPTER 12

Exercise: Point 1, p. 203

1. My family vacationed in Alberta; we visited Lake Louise and Banff.
2. The baseball game was exciting; it went into extra innings.
3. We always see the latest horror films; we like being scared.
4. Mary lost her I.D. card; she couldn't get the student rate.
5. The lawn was overgrown; Dave volunteered to mow it.
6. Firefighters have to be brave; they risk their lives almost every day.
7. We got the mortgage; we bought the house.
8. I will use a road map; I will not lose my way.
9. The Mariposa Folk Festival was given outdoors; it was at the end of June.
10. He talks to his house plants; they just don't want to grow.

Exercise: Point 2, p. 205

I. X	6. C
2. C	7. C
3. C	8. X
4. X	9. C
5. X	10. X

Review Exercise: Points 1 and 2, p. 205

1. The weather was miserable; it rained all day.
2. The cabinet is handcrafted; it is made of oak.
3. Mr. Ryan got a new job; however, he is not very happy in it.
4. We went skiing in the Gatineaus last weekend; the snow was perfectly packed.
5. I witnessed the accident; therefore, I will testify in court.
6. Alice missed a week of class; nevertheless, she passed the exam.
7. I enjoy reading novels of the occult; however, I find the movies boring.
8. Reporters have strict deadlines; they work under great pressure.
9. Raking leaves is spiritually rewarding; it is also exhausting.
10. I have planted a garden; I expect tomatoes by the end of the summer.

Exercise: Point 3, p. 207

1. I read in the newspaper about the premier's efforts to lower automobile insurance rates; the latest troubles in the Middle East; and a new program for providing hot meals for the elderly on holidays.
2. In my refrigerator are the remains of a bacon, lettuce, and tomato sandwich, which I made two weeks ago; some cheddar cheese, which could probably be used for penicillin; a fried egg; and two bottles of beer, which I should probably drink to forget about the sad state of my refrigerator.
3. Nancy has lived at three different addresses: 86 Hutcherson Square, Buckingham, Quebec; 21 Renfield Crescent, Dorval, Quebec; and 714 Welland Avenue, Brooks, Alberta.
4. Our neighbourhood council has resolved that street lights will be turned on every evening at 7:30; that parents should keep a close watch on their children to see that vandalism declines; and that a recycling dropoff point will be established at the corner of Northend and Pleasant Streets.
5. The terms of the contract stated that the work must be finished by August 15; that payment would be made in two installments, one by September 30, the other by December 30; and that all work must be presented in a manner judged acceptable by the employer.

Exercise: Point 4, p. 208

1. C CDs
2. X
3. C talents
4. X
5. X
6. C uses
7. C vices
8. X
9. X
10. C types

Review Exercise: Points 4 and 5, p. 209

1. X Every morning I eat cereal, eggs, and toast.
2. X She has promised to love, to honour, and to cherish.
3. C
4. X I am learning to drive, to swim, and to type.
5. X Important English skills include grammar, spelling, and punctuation.
6. X Equipment necessary for tennis is sneakers, tennis balls, and a racquet.
7. X Directions are north, east, south, west.
8. X Line up two by two, and in order of height.
9. X Steps in cooking spaghetti include boiling the water, adding the spaghetti, cooking for ten minutes, and draining.
10. C

Chapter Review, p. 210

I

1. X
2. X
3. X
4. C
5. C
6. C
7. X
8. X
9. C
10. X

II

1. The car has a flat tire; there is a spare in the trunk.
2. I didn't finish the assignment; I was too busy.
3. That dress comes in three colours: red, blue, and yellow.
4. We've never travelled so much; it's fun.
5. He told me the following: that he was fed up with the city and that he was moving to the country.
6. I'm exhausted; moreover, I still have more to study.
7. Carl has only two desires: to be rich and to be famous.
8. Linda had two jobs before this one: waitress and grounds keeper.
9. Russian dressing is good; nevertheless, I prefer Italian.
10. We were late for the concert; the usher made us wait until the first number had been completed.
11. John Donne once wrote, "Ask not for whom the bell tolls; it tolls for thee."
12. They drove through three provinces: Alberta, Manitoba, and Saskatchewan.
13. You cook with love; therefore, your dinners are wonderful.
14. We went horseback riding in the afternoon; then we settled down to an evening of food and good talk.

15. Human needs: food, clothing, and shelter.
16. I don't enjoy flying; nevertheless, we flew to Europe last summer.
17. Norm used to smoke cigarettes; now he smokes a pipe.
18. Intramural sports are great; they give you a chance to exercise without high-pressure competition.
19. Ingredients for a salad: lettuce, tomatoes, carrots, and peppers.
20. You have been given three wishes; make them carefully.

III 1. We bought tickets well in advance; therefore, we got good seats.
2. I would love to go; however, I am too tired.
3. Choose one essay question; answer it in 500 words or less.
4. I keep losing my ball-point pens; I should get one with a clip.
5. Our team won the championship; we were awarded a trophy.
6. You must learn to control your temper; it can get you into trouble.
7. My favourite actress starred in the movie; she gave a great performance.
8. A calendar watch can be a great convenience; however, it has to be reset once a month.
9. A sense of humour is important; try to develop one.
10. I get hay fever attacks every August; however, they do not bother me much with my new allergy pills.

IV 1. I have two reasons to be depressed: my girlfriend left me, and I'm developing dandruff.
2. Shakespeare wrote plays in different styles: comedy, tragedy, and history.
3. We had a great dinner: veal, spaghetti, green beans, and wine.
4. Aspects of a novel: plot, character, setting, theme, and tone.
5. Our teacher stressed two points: that we should attend class regularly and that we should hand assignments in on time.
6. Janos has two pairs of sneakers: one for tennis and one for basketball.
7. You will receive the following: a demonstration lesson and a free career brochure.
8. We went to two stores today; Wal-Mart and Zellers.
9. I have written three parts of my essay already; the first word, the second word, and the third word.
10. Choose one main dish: chicken chow mein or chop suey.

V Answers to this exercise will vary. Check with your instructor if you need to.

VI Answers to this exercise will vary. Check with your instructor if you need to.

1. Janet works in the Library of Parliament; she is a page.
2. You don't understand; I apologize for my thoughtlessness.
3. That store sells jeans, jeans, and more jeans.
4. I have been to that part of town once, but I will never go back.
5. He was arrested on the following charges: assault and battery and armed robbery.
6. Beatrice exercises daily, and it shows in her fine physique.
7. Call me anytime; I'm here when you need me.
8. Birds fly, fish swim, and snakes crawl.
9. He sang as follows: off-key and very loud.
10. The cast rehearsed for weeks; still, they were nervous on opening night.
11. There's no business like show business; I should know.
12. She appeared calm; on the inside, though, she was scared.
13. It was Pierre's fault; he is such a klutz.
14. Tomorrow is her birthday; she'll be twenty-five.
15. We watch the news and the business report every night.
16. He is responsible for the following: tending the garden, painting the house, and washing the car.
17. The jury announced its verdict as follows: guilty of first-degree murder.
18. First the leaves turn colours; then they fall.
19. I want bigger muscles; therefore, I lift weights.
20. Omer doesn't take care of his teeth; consequently, he gets at least six cavities a year.

VII Answers to this exercise will vary. Check with your instructor if you need to.

The team was in trouble; it had dropped from first place to last in three weeks. The manager called a meeting of the players at which the following issues were discussed: the importance of developing a winning attitude, whereby the players would place the goals of the team over their individual achievements; the imposition of a strict curfew so that the players would be well rested for the games; the problem of teammates competing among themselves for higher salaries and greater coverage in the newspapers; and last but not least, the general lack of hustle and determination on the part of the team's stars.

My friends and I recently spent a day driving around the Maritimes trying to hit as many hamburger joints as we could in 16 hours. Our travels took us to the following places: Halifax, Nova Scotia, where we prepared our stomachs with thick shakes and French fries; Truro, Nova Scotia, where we indulged in double cheeseburgers; Amherst, Nova Scotia, where we settled for soft drinks; Borden, Prince Edward Island, where we each downed a filet of fish; and finally to Charlottetown, P.E.I., where we celebrated with chicken sandwiches. We ate dessert at the quick lunch bar at Holland College in Charlottetown.

CHAPTER 13

Exercise: Point 1, p. 217

1. She was lonely, depressed, and nostalgic.
2. Kathy planted tulips, daffodils, and roses.
3. It is hot and muggy today.
4. He stormed out of the house, went for a walk, and came back the next morning.
5. I've been to South America, Central America, and Europe.
6. Bend me, shake me, break me; do anything you want.
7. The letter was signed, sealed, and delivered.
8. We strolled along the beach and gathered shells.
9. This library has books, books, and more books.
10. For lunch we had soup, salad, and a sandwich.

Exercise: Point 2, p. 219

1. He thinks he should be a star, but he really isn't very talented.
2. I can type very fast, but I make a lot of mistakes.
3. That's the way it goes, and you will have to accept it.
4. Brenda tries to rush me, yet I always take my time.
5. She had a cold, so she stayed in bed all day.
6. I'm taking flying lessons, but I can't seem to get the hang of making turns.
7. Randy will graduate from Capilano College this year, and he hopes to get a job in the clothing industry.
8. Friendship is simple yet complex.
9. Be truthful with me, or I will leave you.
10. He is very bright but can't seem to get his head together.

Review Exercise: Points 1 and 2, p. 219

1. Joe, Sue, and Anne were invited to the party.
2. We hoped the humidity would end, but it didn't.
3. There were cows and horses roaming around the field.
4. 1 ate pizza, and she ate a salad.
5. We spoke seriously yet insincerely.
6. She used parsley, garlic, and tarragon in the sauce.
7. She is superstitious, and her husband is a nervous wreck.
8. We got to the concert on time, but we left at the intermission.
9. Reading, writing, and arithmetic are the basics of education.
10. We sang, laughed, and danced all night long.

Exercise: Point 3, p. 221

1. After the party ended, we cleaned the apartment.
2. Yes, we have no bananas.
3. As I said before, the lecture is cancelled.
4. Not wanting to go, I said I wasn't feeling well.
5. Since you wanted popsicles, I bought some.
6. By the way, you have been promoted.
7. Whenever I hear that CD, I feel better.
8. As I feared, the end is near.
9. Thinking about the past, I always get melancholy.
10. Unfortunately, your plan will never work.

Another Exercise: Point 3, p. 221

Answers to this exercise will vary. Check with your instructor if you need to.

Exercise: Point 4, p. 222

1. I told you once, Margie, and I will not tell you again.
2. Bliss Carman, for example, wrote beautiful poems.
3. I think, therefore, that we should adjourn immediately.
4. My grandmother, strangely enough, bought a motorcycle.
5. Watch out, Hubert!
6. I believe, on the other hand, that there is too much violence on television.
7. Her illness, of course, is the reason for her absence.
8. Jogging, as it turns out, has helped me lose weight.
9. Your theory, I am certain, is worthy of more consideration.

10. A car, if it is not tuned regularly, is likely to break down.

Review Exercise: Points 1–4, p. 222

1. At the barbeque we had hamburgers, hot dogs, and chicken.
2. We saw the game at the Pacific Coliseum, and we watched the highlights on television.
3. After we finished eating, Harry and Gail went for a walk.
4. I am asking you, Mr. Maxwell, to give me a direct answer.
5. A bagel with cream cheese makes a great snack.
6. The manager, however, refused to listen to the demands of the employees.
7. During her road test, Trudy had to parallel park, back up, make a U-turn, and park the car on a hill.
8. He made copies of the article and circulated them among the students.
9. Without taking much time, Pat answered all the questions on the test.
10. A parent, if he wants his child to do well in school, should encourage him to work his hardest.

Another Review Exercise: Points 1–4, p. 223

1. The poet spoke to the audience and answered questions.
2. Before making up her mind, Linda asked her counsellor for advice.
3. We cast our votes, as usual, just before the polls closed.
4. By the way, Mom, Happy Mother's Day.
5. Reading *The Hockey News* is my favourite way to relax.
6. In addition to mastering the use of commas, you have improved your vocabulary.
7. I am, have always been, and always will be your best friend.
8. Those wind chimes are lovely, but they are too expensive.
9. Never before in my life have I met such a man.
10. That puppy with the floppy ears is mine.

Exercise: Point 5, p. 224

1. His car, which had been repaired at Moe's Garage, broke down again.
2. My sister, an Aquarian, was born in January.
3. Mr. Thomas, the coach of our football team, called practice off for today.
4. Her suggestion that we feed the cats was reinforced by a chorus of meows.
5. This cottage, which was built in 1901, is our favourite vacation spot.
6. The tea kettle that I bought at the bazaar is an antique.
7. Tomorrow, June 20, is our wedding anniversary.
8. Joey, smiling like a fool, looked ridiculous.
9. The kerosene lamp, which we always use in an emergency, came in very handy.
10. The job that you applied for has been filled.

Another Exercise: Point 5, p. 225

Answers to this exercise will vary. Check with your instructor if you need to.

Review Exercise: Points 1–5, p. 225

1. A fool and his money are soon parted.
2. It is, I think, the best way to solve the problem.
3. Chicken soup, which some people believe can cure diseases, is delicious.
4. He can play the flute, the clarinet, the oboe, and the trumpet.
5. After a while, even the most exciting entertainment can become boring.
6. That, in fact, is exactly the reason I am here.
7. As sure as I'm breathing, you're a double for my brother.
8. Backgammon, a game which involves gambling, is very popular.
9. A nuclear plant, which some people feel is destructive to the environment, is being built in Pickering, Ontario.
10. We browsed in the bookstore for an hour.

Exercise: Point 6, p. 226

Answers to the last question in this exercise will vary. Check with your instructor if you need to.

1. Paul was born on September 3, 1953.
2. Renee works at Mohawk College, Fennel and West 5th St., Hamilton, Ontario.
3. The paper is due on Monday, May 15.
4. The play opened on September 1, 1985, at the Arts and Culture Centre, Prince Phillip Drive, St. John's, Newfoundland.
5. We celebrated our anniversary July 19 in Yellowknife, North West Territories.

Review Exercise: Points 1–6, p. 227

1. There were no runs, two hits, and two men left on base.
2. That guy in the blue suede shoes is really wild.
3. After deliberating for two hours, the jury reached a verdict.
4. Toby, Al, and Dave have moved to Thunder Bay, Ontario.
5. Biology, the study of living things, is my favourite subject.
6. I have, after much thought, reached a decision.
7. We walked and talked all night long.
8. I'm afraid it will rain, although I hope it doesn't.

9. I have, up until now, handed in my assignments on time.
10. Are you sure, pal, that you want to come along?

Chapter Review, p. 228

I

I. X	6. X
2. C	7. C
3. X	8. X
4. X	9. C
5. C	10. X

II
1. This section, therefore, will be closed.
2. Hey, wait!
3. While waiting for the bus, we told each other jokes.
4. Why, Mr. Carl, must you be so rude?
5. The television set, which was stolen last week, was found in the basement of a warehouse.
6. The store is located at 520 Elm Street, Chatham, New Brunswick.
7. We must, if we are ever to change our ways, begin today.
8. I'd love to go to The Citadel, but she won't let me .
9. Sometimes, when I am feeling blue, a good record can lift my spirits.
10. You know, of course, that our television is broken.
11. In a sense, you are right.
12. We plan, if the weather is good, to go swimmmg tomorrow.
13. He had always wanted to participate in the Olympics, but he had never trained properly for the trials.
14. The recipe directs you to mix the batter with one egg, add the premeasured packet of chocolate chips, and bake the mixture for forty-five minutes in an oven set at 120° C.
15. Time, as it always does, has a way of changing things.
16. While showering, I sing to myself.
17. The novel, which, by the way, I have never read, is supposed to be excellent.
18. A sandwich, if made with whole wheat bread, is delicious and healthful.
19. There has never been, as far as I can remember, such a destructive storm.
20. Well, how do you like that!

III

1. (4)	6. (4)	11. (2)	16. (3)
2. (4)	7. (3)	12. (4)	17. (4)
3, (1)	8. (4)	13. (4)	18. (4)
4. (2)	9. (4)	14. (1)	19. (4)
5, (3)	10. (1)	15. (4)	20. (1)

IV Answers to this exercise will vary. Check with your instructor if you need to.

V
1. Waving her wand, the princess performed some magic.
2. Never, never will you get away with that.
3. I had a bacon, lettuce, and tomato sandwich for lunch.
4. Who, in your opinion, is the world's greatest athlete?
5. Her latest poem is superb.
6. As of next week, the prisoner will be a free man.
7. His answer, which was wrong, made the class laugh.
8. That dog barking at the tree is mine.
9. We were wed on April 17, 1977.
10. When our guests arrived, we greeted them at the door.
11. Once upon a time, there was a dog who could fly.
12. We met, as usual, at the corner of Yonge and Bloor.
13. I waited for nearly a month for your letter.
14. It is my choice, however, to travel alone.
15. For once, try studying.
16. You are mine, and I am yours.
17. Write to me at 65 Market Street, Banff, Alberta.
18. You are all prepared, I'm sure, for the test.
19. Ice cream, if it is made at home, is very good.
20. As long as I live, I will love to dance.

VI When we spent the day at my grandmother's cottage on the beach, we had a great time. My wife and I, together with two friends, drove about sixty kilometres from our home to the small two-room beach house, which had been built over a hundred years ago. We stopped at a small market to pick up some food for sandwiches and ate as soon as we arrived at the cottage. We spent the rest of the day eating, drinking, sunning ourselves, going for walks, and swimming. By the time the sun went down, we were thoroughly exhausted. Isn't it strange, I ask you, that doing nothing can make someone so tired?

Liberal arts, contrary to what some people think, provides a good basis for an education. It is important, I believe, for every student to be well grounded in such subjects as art, history, science, politics, and English. These subjects give students a good idea of what has been accomplished in the history of the world, and of what is yet to be accomplished. By the time one completes a full program in liberal arts, he or she will be ready to live with vigour and vitality.

CHAPTER 14

Exercise: Point 1, p. 238

1. Have you ever been to The Art Gallery of Ontario?
2. I read an article entitled " Offra Harnoy: World-Class Cellist."
3. One of Freud's most important books is called *The Interpretation of Dreams*.
4. We saw the Shaw Festival's production of *Peter Pan*.
5. I have a book called *How to Grow Beautiful House Plants*.

Another Exercise: Point 1, p. 238

Answers to this exercise will vary. Check with your instructor if you need to.

Exercise: Point 2, p. 239

1. The Fowlers always spend their vacation in Victoria.
2. Mel gave up his United States citizenship when he moved to Canada.
3. Joe Perry has moved to Red Deer, Alberta.
4. Does Lori know how to speak German?
5. Venezuela, Argentina, Mexico, and most of Latin America have been free countries since they rebelled against Spain.
6. Lou takes great pride in his Italian-Canadian heritage.
7. The school is going to ofter a course in Native Canadian history next semester.

Another Exercise: Point 2, p. 239

Answers to this exercise will vary. Check with your instructor if you need to.

Exercise: Point 3, p. 240

1. September 21 is the first day of autumn.
2. I am on the road on Monday and Thursday.
3. Canada Day falls on July 1.
4. We visit my family on the first Sunday of every month.
5. September and October are the loveliest months of the year.

Another Exercise: Point 3, p. 240

Answers to this exercise will vary. Check with your instructor if you need to.

Review Exercise: Points 1–3, p. 240

1. I read *The Progress of Love* last spring.
2. Barry Smith works in Edmonton, but he lives in St. Albert.
3. On Monday we will discuss Shakespeare's play *King Lear*.
4. I travel to the mountains every autumn.
5. Lina was born in the United States, but she lives in Manitoba and considers herself a Canadian.
6. The police found the stolen car in Norfolk County.
7. Have you read the article "In Search of the Canadian Identity."?
8. Be careful on April Fool's Day.
9. She is reading a book about Canada's First Nations peoples.
10. Last summer we visited Nova Scotia, New Brunswick, and Newfoundland.

Exercise: Point 4, p. 242

1. John asked Lucy, "Will you come to the dance with me?"
2. The pharmacist said, "Here is your prescription."
3. "When will we get our tests back?" I asked.
4. "You are all invited to the victory party," the candidate announced.
5. "Please pick up some tomatoes," she said.

Another Exercise: Point 4, p. 242

Answers to this exercise will vary. Check with your instructor if you need to.

Exercise: Point 5, p. 243

1. Happy birthday, Sister.
2. I'm not eating these lima beans, Mom.
3. My aunt is a champion at poker.
4. Have you heard from Uncle Ebenezer?
5. My brother is also my best friend.
6. I heard that Ed's father used to play professional baseball.
7. My grandmother married a man half her age.
8. Is it true that Father knows best?
9. I visited Grandpa Mac in his office.
10. Abby's cousin Lisa is very pretty.

Exercise: Point 6, p. 244

1. We took a boat ride on the Fraser River.
2. The ice cream shop is located on Franklin Drive.
3. She teaches literature at Acadia University.
4. He has been our MPP for twelve years.
5. Mr. Ramlall is our professor.
6. He expects us to call him Professor Ramlall.
7. She was the architect for the Wilson County Courthouse.
8. Have you ever visited Stanley Park in Vancouver?
9. They went swimming in Lake of the Woods.
10. They went swimming in Great Bear Lake.

Review Exercise: Points 1–6, p. 244

1. Dr. Meyer's office is on Queen Street.
2. On the first night of Chanukah, we visited Grandma and Grandpa.
3. We went to Nathan Phillips Square on New Year's Eve.

4. Our teacher is from the Iberian Peninsula.
5. "When will you hand in that paper?" the professor asked.
6. I answered, "I will hand it in next Tuesday."
7. I read an article in *Byte* magazine.
8. Next winter we will ski in the French Alps.
9. Does your brother still work at the plant?
10. In the fall we will go camping at Long Point Provincial Park.

Another Review Exercise: Points 1–6, p. 245

Answers to this exercise will vary. Check with your instructor if you need to.

Exercise: Point 7, p. 246

1. The Constitution Act was signed in 1982.
2. Life was exciting in the Frontier Age.
3. The raid on Dieppe was thought by many to be a tragedy .
4. Leonardo da Vinci was an important figure during the Renaissance.
5. The Throne Speech was delivered by the Governor General.

Another Exercise: Point 7, p. 246

Answers to this exercise will vary. Check with yout instructor if you need to.

Exercise: Point 8, p. 246

1. She is studying English with Professor Ross.
2. Do you expect to take German 101 next semester?
3. Esther plans to major in anthropology.
4. I wanted to take English 2a, but my advisor suggested I take Basic Composition.
5. He got an A on his physics final.

Another Exercise: Point 8, p. 247

Answers to this exercise will vary. Check with your instructor if you need to.

Review Exercise: Points 1–8, p. 247

1. The Hotel Frontenac in Quebec City is more than one hunded years old.
2. Aunt Tilly is preparing her annual holiday dinner.
3. Next winter we will ski in the Laurentians.
4. "Why didn't you fill that prescription?" Dr. Cohen asked.
5. Do you refer to Niagara Falls, Canada, or to Niagara Falls, New York?
6. Anett got a B in Biology 2a last term.
7. So, Mom, do you think I should buy a Ford or a Chevy?
8. Canada entered World War II after Germany attacked Poland.
9. Can we try that new French restaurant?
10. Were you whale watching near Trinity Bay, Newfoundland?

Chapter Review, p. 248

I

1.	X	6.	X
2.	X	7.	X
3.	X	8.	X
4.	C	9.	X
5.	X	10.	X

II

1. He is my uncle from Brandon.
2. The professor asked, "Who knows the answer to this question?"
3. I always buy *La Presse* on Sunday.
4. Victoria is the capital of British Columbia.
5. The boutique is located on Willis Avenue.
6. Don't capitalize every letter you see!
7. I just finished reading *The Lark in the Clear Air.*
8. Did you see the football game on Labour Day?
9. When, Dad, will you ever understand me?
10. Zelda lives a zesty life in Zanzibar.
11. Mr. Allesandrino, our biology teacher, is also coach of the basketball team.
12. The Vancouver Grizzlies is a new NBA franchise.
13. You can find the book you want at the Kelowna Public Library.
14. For the second time, I flunked Economics 101.
15. "I live near the Bow River," he said.
16. Rajesh plans to join the RCMP.
17. In October the leaves begin to fall.
18. When we were in Ottawa, we visited the Parliament Buildings.
19. She teaches Spanish at Lethbridge High School.
20. He was born in North Bay and he lives in Selkirk,

III Answers to this exercise will vary. Check with your instructor if you need to.

IV

1.	summer	11.	Metis, prairies
2.	father	12.	weekending
3.	volleyball, high school	13.	do
4.	Why	14.	time
5.	Doctor	15.	bagpipes
6.	Latin	16.	Winter
7.	aunt	17.	Ages
8.	teacher	18.	sister, school
9.	Flames	19.	Greek
10.	River	20.	whether

V

1. "Lucy in the Sky with Diamonds" is a Beatles song.
2. He was born in Wasaga Beach, and he has lived there all his life.
3. I would like to drive a Rolls Royce.
4. I'm only asking you, Dad, to give me another chance.

5. The babysitter pleaded, "Behave yourself."
6. My grandfather will be ninety years old next month.
7. The Ottawa Senators are in the National Hockey League.
8. Let's see the fireworks on Victoria Day!
9. Albert's Aunt Alberta has arrived!
10. We ate dinner in the restaurant at the top of the building.
11. Is there a doctor in the house?
12. When you are in Winnipeg, visit the Centennial Arts Centre.
13. Come on, Horatio, you're holding us up.
14. I asked Dr. Aresta if I could change my appointment.
15. Mario is the manager of a big department store.
16. Mail the form to John Doe, Anytown, Canada.
17. I read the bestseller called *Borderline.*
18. Everyone wants to know when the stock market will improve.
19. My brother exclaimed, "So this is your apartment!"
20. John Polyani won the Nobel Prize for Chemistry.

VI Many people think of hockey as the great Canadian game. And why not? Fans get to sit in beautiful arenas such as the Calgary Saddledome, eat hot dogs, watch an exciting event, and yell their lungs out. All the fun and excitement typifies the spirit of Canada. A Canadian author, Scott Young, has examined the international ice hockey game in his book titled *War on Ice.* It makes great reading for the serious and even the not-so-serious fan.

If you need someone to fix something in your apartment or house, don't call me! I have read *The Book of Home Repair,* and still cannot manage to hang a picture or fix a leaky faucet. Whenever something goes wrong in my home, I always call my uncle, who is a whiz at such things. Last fall – I believe it was around Thanksgiving – our garbage disposal overflowed. As usual, I called my uncle, who said, "This is getting a bit out of hand. You can't expect me to drive all the way from Yarmouth to fix your garbage disposal!" Seeing as we lived in Digby, he was right. I called a plumber instead, who charged me a hundred dollars for the job; the lake on the kitchen floor vanished, but I vowed I would either learn something about home repair or move to Yarmouth.

CHAPTER 15

Exercise: Point 1, p. 255

1. priest
2. C
3. receipt
4. weight
5. retrieve
6. C
7. piece
8. feign
9. sleigh
10. C

Exercise: Point 2, p. 256

1. entirely
2. coming
3. improvement
4. guidance
5. loveless
6. smoked
7. safety
8. likable
9. useful
10. completion

Review Exercise: Points 1 and 2, p. 256

1. Fernando weighs 94 kilograms.
2. You will need a stepladder to paint that ceiling.
3. Your pleasure is my pleasure.
4. Nghia a great oneness to her mother.
5. We expressed our condolences at the funeral.
6. The hobo scrambled aboard the freight train.
7. She always speaks sincerely about the most delicate of issues.
8. This is one weird party!
9. I was truly amazed at the endurance of marathon swimmers.
10. One pays a price for being famous.

Exercise: Point 3, p. 258

1. gullies
2. worried
3. happiness
4. repaying
5. attorneys
6. strayed
7. frying
8. necessarily
9. applied
10. loneliest

Exercise: Point 4, p. 259

1. girls
2. typewriters
3. churches
4. traces
5. cigars
6. apartments
7. porches
8. buses
9. aches
10. taxes

Review Exercise: Points 1–4, p. 260

1. Norman was cursing his fate.
2. I have already applied to three graduate schools.
3. I'm looking for a piece of the action.
4. His whole apartment is lighted by gas lamps.
5. There are three different styles of couches to choose from.
6. That is a great weight off my shoulders.
7. We are looking ahead hopefully to the next election.
8. Richard is pursuing a new career.
9. Honey, you are my shining star.
10. This sandwich is just awful.

Exercise: Point 5, p. 261

1. controlled
2. admitting
6. developed
7. suffering

3. beginning
4. smallest
5. screaming
8. fishing
9. puffed
10. stirring

Review Exercise: Points 1–5, p. 262

1. This is a chapter about spelling.
2. I am admitting no fault whatsoever.
3. We visited Ripley's Believe It or Not Museum.
4. Tomorrow we will go horseback riding.
5. I have resisted greater temptations in the past.
6. Those bananas are rotting!
7. Come to this office immediately!
8. This corner is the busiest one in Estevan.
9. Everyone benefited by his generosity.
10. All waiters should report to the dining room.

Chapter Review, p. 264

I
1. radios
2. arranging
3. C
4. fortieth
5. C
6. C
7. developed
8. receive
9. C
10. bushes
11. paying
12. grief
13. eightieth
14. lively
15. C
16. despairing
17. ladders
18. association
19. leisure
20. C

II
1. getting
2. guiding
3. satisfied
4. spies
5. running
6. seizure
7. partying
8. relieved
9. likeness
10. hopeless
11. praying
12. timed
13. spiteful
14. toying
15. guidance
16. managed
17. married
18. pitted
19. chopped
20. pitiable

III
1. goats
2. babies
3. guitars
4. envelopes
5. woes
6. trees
7. histories
8. tacos
9. churches
10. glasses

IV
1. criticism
2. embarrassed
3. careless
4. pays
5. friendly
6. uncontrollable
7. privilege
8. seized
9. sophomore
10. employed

V
1. Ken slipped on the ice and broke his ankle.
2. My girlfriend spends too much time studying.
3. The lamp broke into hundreds of pieces.
4. Forget it; it is neither my business nor yours.
5. I'll be flying high if I get good news.
6. The administration has adopted a new policy on energy.
7. Camping in New Brunswick was such a pleasure.
8. She is the fairest and loveliest child I know.
9. The criminal was sentenced to ninety years in prison.
10. You have embarrassed me with your remark.
11. Church and state must be separated.
12. "Describe the man you saw," said the detective.
13. This is your third absence from class this week.
14. I admitted my secret passion.
15. Welcome to the neighbourhood!
16. The weather around here is so changeable.
17. We have gone to four parties already this week. 18. I can't stand shopping for shoes.
19. The strings are broken and have to be replaced.
20. I am a very happily married man.

VI Late summer is truly a lovely time of the year. After being fried by the heat and drenched by the humidity, many people feel that it is a great relief to experience the cool evenings that promise the coming of autumn. As the cool weather returns, people seem to regain much of the energy that they had lost during the hot and sticky months of July and August. There are all kinds of outdoor activities: baseball games, barbeques, campfires. It is as if the cool breezes bring with them a fresh and new feeling for life.

There is probably no greater thrill or privilege than watching the birth of your own child. Many of my friends have accepted the responsibility of taking part in the process, particularly by acting as an assistant to the doctor. These husbands have helped their wives with breathing and relaxation techniques. Above all, they get the definite pleasure of witnessing what is surely the most amazing act of all.

CHAPTER 16

Exercise: Point 1, p. 271

1. I own the house.
2. The police officer owns the whistle.
3. The dancer owns the leotard.
4. The car has the headlights.
5. My father owns the newspaper.
6. My mother has the credit card.
7. My wife owns the ring.
8. The engine has the power.
9. My baby sister owns the dolls.
10. Aretha owns the fountain pen.

Exercise: Point 2, p. 272

1. my mother's idea.
2. Judy's plants
3. the library's copy machine.
4. the people's choice
5. the detective's job
6. the camper's mail
7. Sam's pants
8. the bookie's money
9. the baby's rattle
10. the boy's paper route

Exercise: Point 3, p. 273

1. the babies' crying
2. my cousins' home town
3. the barbers' chairs
4. the rooftops' slant
5. the cigars' smell
6. the exhibits' duration
7. the professors' offices
8. the men's running shoes
9. the players' salaries
10. the tables' legs

Review Exercise: Points 1–3, p. 274

1. John's mother belongs to the Professional Women's Club .
2. Have you read Mark's essay on sexual freedom?
3. The women's marathon is the next event.
4. Is this Carlos' raincoat?
5. Have you ever been to a world's fair?
6. The publishers wanted to buy Martha's manuscript.
7. One of Toronto's popular meeting places is Yorkville.
8. Mr. Dickens' daughter will be married next week.
9. The manager's lineup card was taped to the dugout wall.
10. The Canadians' home arena is The Forum.

Exercise: Point 4, p. 275

1. animals
2. professors'
3. titles
4. courses'
5. trees
6. parents'
7. bugs'
8. candles
9. stars
10. show's

Exercise: Point 5, p. 277

Answers to this exercise will vary. Check with your instructor if you need to.

1. It is his decision to make.
2. We will have to change our approach.
3. That sewing machine is hers.
4. The storm had taken its toll.
5. Whose beautiful garden is this?
6. What can I do to make you change your mind?
7. They are taking their children to the Royal Winnipeg Ballet.
8. I bought it, so it is mine.
9. I must be losing my mind.
10. 1 am sorry, sir, but that coat is not yours; it is his.

Review Exercise: Points 1–5, p. 277

1. The children's play group meets once a week.
2. Mr. Jones's car needs to be washed.
3. Great writers' messages are sometimes misunderstood.
4. That seat is not yours, it is mine.
5. The superintendent's apartment was vandalized last night.
6. Now it is someone else's game to win or lose.
7. Whose ten-speed bicycle are you using?
8. The teachers' union supported the strike.
9. Do you understand the reasons for my decision?
10. The Athabaska River overflowed its banks.

Exercise: Points 6, p. 279

1. He's never been to summer camp before.
2. I'll buy the chips if you'll make the dip.
3. They'd have arrived on time if they didn't have a balky car.
4. I'm sorry, but this time it's not my fault.
5. She'll never know what hit her.
6. I'd have chosen a different colour.
7. Let's work together for a change.
8. He wouldn't mind if you combed his hair with a rake.
9. I haven't been to the dentist in three years.
10. Patti doesn't plan to be an Avon lady all her life.

Exercise: Point 7, p. 280

1. It's a beautiful day for a drive in the country.
2. Whose bright idea was that?
3. This is your problem, not mine.
4. Do you approve of the way they raise their children?
5. My soda has lost its fizz.
6. Who's the leader of the New Democratic Party?
7. You're good man, Charlie Brown.
8. They're never going to be able to straighten out their finances.
9. It's a sure bet!
10. Who's going to pay for all this damage?

Review Exercise: Points 1–7, p. 281

1. We're hoping that she'll pass her English exam.
2. It's Russ's car, and he'll be angry if you drive it.
3. The day's work isn't done yet.
4. The Regina Symphony's performance was outstanding.

5. Is the responsibility yours or Tim's?
6. Lately we've been keeping a hawk's eye on our diets.
7. That actress's lines should be rewritten.
8. That's Ernie's problem, not mine.
9. Cheryl's motorcycle isn't running smoothly these days.
10. It's never too late to say you're sorry.

Chapter Review, p. 282

I

1. C	6. X
2. X	7. C
3. X	8. C
4. X	9. X
5. C	10. X

II

1. Sally's	6. the company's
2. Mr. Ross's	7. my son's
3. Bill's	8. your friend's
4. my mother's	9. the team's
5. Aunt Betty's	10. Chris's

III

1. hers	6. their
2. ours	7. my
3. mine	8. theirs
4. his	9. your
5. yours	10. whose

IV
1. It's a sin to tell a lie.
2. It is their way of showing affection.
3. You're the most beautiful woman I've ever seen.
4. I am the one whose paper you read.
5. The airplane is in trouble; its wing has caught fire.
6. They're never going to believe this back in Corner Brook.
7. He has been imitating your style for some time.
8. Guess who's coming to dinner.
9. It is the captain's decision to make.
10. Who's going to clean it up?

V
1. Womens' wear is on the second floor.
2. You're a very stylish dresser.
3. My sister's briefcase is overflowing.
4. That artist's style is certainly unique.
5. Marcus' friend is staying with him for the summer.
6. Those books are Bobby's and mine.
7. You're such a good catcher that you could play on anyone's team.
8. Lately I've grown close to Mike's wife.
9. My father's business takes him to the Orient twice a year.
10. Did you heed the guru's advice?
11. We're learning the basic skills of writing.
12. The horse trotted to the winner's circle.
13. The fireworks display was very exciting.
14. Your brother's van has a flat tire.
15. Lenin's ideas do not appeal to everyone.
16. Those babies are twins!
17. The doctor's office is closed today.
18. What is Brian's idea of a good time?
19. Who's going to pay the check?
20. Let's go to the movies.

VI
1. It's yours, so do with it as you please.
2. I think it's never going to stop raining.
3. She's minding someone else's shop today.
4. It was my employer's idea to give me a raise.
5. We've visited Majorie's beach house twice before.
6. I met your brother at the VIA Rail Station.
7. Our family's motto is "Live and let live."
8. The musician's trumpet has been stolen.
9. The RCMP's the best police force in the world.
10. Those criminals' records show their history.
11. Lead me to the men's room, please.
12. I borrowed my parents' car.
13. Where's the beef?
14. Kasumi's piano needs to be tuned.
15. The sisters' husbands have lunch together every Monday.
16. Womens' haircuts are generally quite attractive.
17. James's new car has a CD player.
18. The employees' lunchroom is located downstairs.
19. My aunt's tapioca pudding is the best in the world.
20. Don't try telling me that your way is better.

VII In Canada, our pet's names are both unique and amusing. While we genuinely love our pets, they're likely called by names that we wouldn't name anyone else in the family. Who's going to deny that they've had some rather unusual names for their pets? Of course, there's the obvious Peter for a pet rabbit. Peter's lucky to be named after a storybook character. Palmolive's name fits a pet skunk, and all the Poohs in the world are also likely skunks. Dogs and cats are also known by "pet" names, and even though our pets are one of life's great pleasures, we do tend to get carried away at times when we try to think up suitable names for them.

I've never been one to keep New Year's resolutions. It's always been easy enough for me to promise to give up my bad habits, but I just don't seem to keep my promises. Once, the day after I'd resolved never to smoke cigarettes again, my wife found a pack around and yelled, "Whose are these?" "They're mine," I answered sheepishly. It's a sure bet I'll resolve to quit again this year, but unless I get serious, I'm sure my wife's advice, "You're never serious about something until you're serious about it" will once again prove true.

Index

STUDENT QUESTIONNAIRE

In preparing the next edition of TROUBLESHOOTING, we would appreciate your evaluation of the present edition. Your suggestions will definitely affect the contents of the next edition, so please return this questionnaire to us. Once you've made your comments, simply detach this page, fold it in half, tape it shut, and mail (the address is on the other side).

Name ____________________ Date ____________________

School ____________________ Course title ____________________

Instructor ____________________

1. Did you find this book ❑ too easy? ❑ too difficult? ❑ about right?
2. Which chapters did you find most helpful? Which chapters did you find least helpful?

    ____

	Helpful	Not Helpful
Grammar Review		
Subjects	____	____
Verbs	____	____
Writing Better Sentences		
Subject-Verb Agreement	____	____
Fragments	____	____
Run-ons	____	____
Misplaced Modifiers	____	____
Dangling Modifiers	____	____
Pronouns and Faulty Pronoun Reference	____	____
Faulty Parallelism	____	____
Shifts in Number, Person, and Tense	____	____
Punctuation		
Period, Question Mark, Exclamation Mark, Quotation Marks	____	____
Semicolon and Colon	____	____
Comma	____	____
Mechanics		
Capital Letters	____	____
Spelling	____	____
Possessives and Contractions	____	____

3. Did this book help you to write better? ❑ Yes ❑ No
4. Do you intend to keep this book? ❑ Yes ❑ No
5. What changes should we make in the next edition?

    ____

    ____

    ____

(fold here and tape shut)

Canada Post Corporation / Société canadienne des postes

Postage paid | **Port payé**
If mailed in Canada | si posté au Canada

Business Reply | **Réponse d'affaires**

0116870399 **01**

0116870399-M8Z4X6-BR01

Heather McWhinney
Director of Product Development
HARCOURT BRACE & COMPANY, CANADA
55 HORNER AVENUE
TORONTO, ONTARIO
M8Z 9Z9